A Mission to the Heart of Young People

CATHOLIC CURRICULUM

Jim and Therese D'Orsa

THE BROKEN BAY INSTITUTE
MISSION AND EDUCATION SERIES

Published in Australia by
Vaughan Publishing
32 Glenvale Crescent
Mulgrave VIC 3170

Vaughan Publishing
A joint imprint of Broken Bay Institute and Garratt Publishing

© 2012 Copyright James D'Orsa and Therese D'Orsa
All rights reserved. Except as provided by Australian copyright law, no part of this publication may be reproduced in any manner without prior permission in writing from the publisher.

Edited by Geraldine Corridon
Designed by Cristina Neri, Canary Graphic Design
Cover image – Thinkstock.com

Printed in Australia by Advent Print Management

Nihil Obstat: Reverend Gerard Diamond MA (Oxon), LSS, D. Theol
        Diocesan Censor

Imprimatur: Most Reverend Les Tomlinson DD
        Titular Bishop of Siniti
        Vicar General

Date: 7 December 2011

The Nihil Obstat and Imprimatur are official declarations that a book or pamphlet is free of doctrinal or moral error. No implication is contained therein that those who have granted the Nihil Obstat and Imprimatur agree with the contents, opinions or statements expressed. They do not necessarily signify that the work is approved as a basic text for catechetical instruction.

National Library of Australia Cataloguing-in-Publication entry

    Author: D'Orsa, James.

    Title: Catholic curriculum : a mission to the heart of young people / Jim and Therese D'Orsa

    ISBN: 9780987306005 (pbk.)

    Subjects: Catholic schools--Australia--Curricula.
           Catholic universities and colleges--Australia--Curricula.
           Religious education--Australia--Curricula.

    Dewey Number: 371.071294

Acknowledgments
Standing Council on School Education and Early Childhood (SCSEEC)
Figure 9.3 Reprinted by permission from Hermeneutics and Education by Shaun Gallagher, the State University of New Your Press © 1992, State University of New York.
All rights reserved.

DEDICATION

This book is dedicated to the memory of Fr Dan Conquest (1910–2006). Fr Conquest was Director of Catholic Education in the Archdiocese of Melbourne from 1940–1954.

Fr Conquest and his team were pioneers in responding to the challenge of ensuring that the total curriculum was both a reflection of a Catholic worldview and a vehicle for student growth in faithful living of the Gospel.

ACKNOWLEDGEMENTS

The financial support for the Mission and Education series by the following educational authorities is gratefully acknowledged:

Queensland – The Catholic Education Offices of Brisbane, Toowoomba, Rockhampton, Townsville, and Cairns.

New South Wales The Catholic Education Offices of Sydney, Parramatta, Broken Bay, Wagga, Wollongong, Newcastle, and Armidale.

Victoria The Catholic Education Offices of Ballarat and Sale.

South Australia The South Australian Catholic Education Commission (Archdiocese of Adelaide and Diocese of Port Pirie).

Tasmania The Catholic Education Office of Hobart.

Religious Orders Good Samaritan Sisters and Marist Brothers (Sydney Province).

While the authors of this study have a longstanding interest and involvement in the Catholicity of the entire curriculum of Catholic schools, the immediate stimulus for this volume was a conference, *Prophets of a Future Not Our Own,* sponsored by the Queensland Catholic Education Commission on the theme of Catholic curriculum. The interest and encouragement of the Executive Director of Catholic Education in the Archdiocese of Brisbane, Mr David Hutton, who chaired the conference planning committee, has been significant in enabling this work **Catholic Curriculum: A Mission to the Heart of Young People** – to be brought to completion.

Catholic Curriculum: A Mission to the Heart of Young People

RECOMMENDATIONS

If Catholic schools and colleges are to preserve their true mission and their religious integrity in the face of secularism and the colonising power of 'national economic requirements', then they must possess a distinctive cultural heart which is an authentic Catholic Curriculum. Drawing upon the wisdom of theology, missiology, sociology, history, philosophy and anthropology, the authors of this impressive text have produced a major educational resource to show Catholic educators how this could be achieved.

This is a landmark publication, of great value, not only to educators in Australia, but also internationally.

    Professor Gerald Grace,
    Director Centre for Research and Development
    in Catholic Education (CRDCE)
    University of London

A learned and thoroughly researched study, this book should fruitfully enlighten and encourage discussion of curriculum in Catholic schools.

    Professor Gerald O'Collins S.J.
    Emeritus Dean of Theology
    The Pontifical Gregorian University Rome.

An excellent book that combines intricate knowledge and understanding of updated curriculum thinking with piercing insight into the challenges implied by such thinking for Catholic schools. The book challenges a range of facile approaches to being a Catholic school in a public setting, including that the Catholic school can ignore its wider public context or that being Catholic means simply adding a layer of RE to an essentially public enterprise. The book goes to the heart of the justification of Catholic schooling by illustrating a range of differences that might be notable in a distinctively Catholic Curriculum. In a day and age of much talk about Catholicity and Catholic Identity, the D'Orsas make it plain that there is no simple formula, nor can it ever be viable that there is only one way of being Catholic. 'Catholic Curriculum' is a complex term that can only be meaningfully applied in the real context of a multitude of societal influences and educational stakeholders. The book's stated task is to reframe the conversation around Catholic Curriculum, a goal well achieved in my view.

    Professor Terence Lovat
    Professor Emeritus
    The University of Newcastle.

THE BROKEN BAY INSTITUTE MISSION AND EDUCATION SERIES

The purpose of the Mission and Education Series is to explore aspects of contemporary Catholic education in the light of the Church's official teaching on mission, and of the experience of those who attempt to embrace this mission in their personal and professional lives.

The richness of the resources now at the disposal of those who seek to explore education theologically can come as a surprise. Because the faith held by the Catholic community is a living faith, Catholic Church teaching on mission has developed, and continues to develop, in the light of contemporary societal and cultural changes. Similarly, Scripture continues to yield its treasures. Only now, for example, is the Bible being widely recognised as a witness to God's purpose, that is to God's mission in the created universe, and as an account of human response to the unfolding of that mission.

We live in a period of rapid cultural development driven at the local level by global dynamics. This has its impact on how we understand what knowledge is, how it is acquired, and how schools are best led and organised so as to maximise student learning and the economic and social benefits that are presumed to flow from sound educational policies. Very often the emphasis in such developments shifts from 'the learning student' to the more abstract concept of 'student learning'. Such a development sits uneasily with the concept of a Catholic education.

The consequence of rapid societal change is that in our time new areas of mission present themselves with real urgency. It is now clearly necessary to include both the processes of knowledge construction and meaning making, and the modes of Christian participation in the new public space created by both globalisation and the communications media. These new areas of mission take their place alongside those fields already familiar to the faith community.

The Mission and Education Series seeks to bring together, in the one conversation, the light that culture, faith and human experience throw on particular topics now central to the future development of Catholic education. It also seeks to honour the significant efforts that Catholic educators make, on behalf of young people, to address the mission agendas within the total process of education. It provides a forum designed to stimulate further conversation about the 'what' and the 'how' of Catholic Education as a work of the Gospel in our complex society and culture.

It is the hope of the Mission and Education Editorial Board that Catholic educators, both in Australia and beyond, will view the series as an invitation to contribute their own creativity to this vital conversation.

Therese D'Orsa
Commissioning Editor
Mission and Education Series
Broken Bay Institute

Also in this series

Explorers, Guides and Meaning makers:
Mission Theology for Catholic Educators

CONTENTS

Introduction: Reframing the conversation — 1
A conversation in context — 1
Resolving the curriculum
leadership dilemma — 2
The target audience — 3
Towards a working definition of
a Catholic curriculum — 3
Developing an interpretive map — 4
    Public worldviews as sources of meaning — 4
    Having confidence in tested and living traditions — 6
Structure of the book — 6
Methodology — 8
How do we know whether our school's curriculum is Catholic? — 9

PART A
CATHOLIC CURRICULUM: SITUATING THE CONVERSATION — 11

1 Catholic curriculum: The challenge in context — 13
Curriculum in the Australian context — 14
    National policy on education — 15
    A Discipline-Based National Curriculum — 18
    Providing an education that is holistic — 18
Core concepts in exploring the Catholic curriculum — 19
    Worldview — 20
    Worldview of the age — 20
    Worldview of culture — 21
    The Worldview of faith — 21
The national curriculum – Opportunity or 'business as usual'? — 22
PRINCIPLE 1: *The Pivot Principle* — 23
PRINCIPLE 2: *The Public Curriculum Principle* — 23

2	**Catholic curriculum: Scope of the conversation**	**24**
	Opening up lines of enquiry	24
	Current perspectives on	
	'Catholic curriculum'	25
	1 Religious Education as intellectual discipline	25
	2 Values-integration approach	25
	3 Teachable moment approach	25
	4 Colonial perspective	26
	5 Agnostic perspective	26
	'Catholic curriculum' as curriculum	26
	Scholar academic perspective	27
	Social efficiency perspective	27
	Learner-centred approach	27
	Social reconstruction approach	28
	Curriculum in the perspective of critical theory	28
	Curriculum and worldviews	30
	Empirical approach to curriculum	31
	Catholic curriculum as 'Catholic'	32
	Utilising a received wisdom	32
	The Kingdom dimension	34
	PRINCIPLE 3: *The mission principle*	36
3	**Catholic curriculum: A working definition**	**37**
	'A Catholic curriculum assists young people to engage constructively…'	37
	'…with the wisdom and faith of the community…'	38
	'…in a way that is meaningful to them…'	39
	'…living in a cultural and historical context…'	40
	'…within the life-chances this offers and the constraints it imposes…'	41
	'…in establishing their identity as individuals and as members of the community.'	43

PART B
CATHOLIC CURRICULUM HAS A HUMAN FACE   46

4	**Educating in an era of deep change**	**48**
	The lived experience of teachers	48
	The experience of deep change	49
	The main drivers of deep change	50

Globalisation's many faces	50
Modern pluralism: Loosening a grip on the foundations of certainty	53
Secularisation: Friend or foe?	55
Limits to secularisation	57
Meaning making in a changing world	58
PRINCIPLE 4: *The Contextual Principle*	59

5 Growing up in an era of deep change — 60

The worldview of young people: Looking at the big picture	60
Acquiring a personal worldview	63
Major studies into the worldview of young people	64
The Spirit of Generation Y	65
Putting Life Together	66
Something there	67
Young adult Catholics: Religion in the culture of choice	67
Studies into the worldview of young people: Some common themes	68
Popular religious beliefs of young people	68
Young people's construction of knowledge	69
PRINCIPLE 5: *The Life-world of young people principle*	71

PART C
CATHOLIC CURRICULUM:
THREE KEY CONSTRUCTS 73

6 Culture and the worldview of culture — 76

Culture and its pervasive influences	76
History of a concept: Classicist and modern conceptions of culture	77
The classicist understanding of culture	77
The modern understanding of culture	79
Understanding how culture works: Working models	81
How cultures function: An analogical explanation	81
The worldview of culture	84
Understanding culture: The postmodern turn	84
Culture as a battle between themes and counter-themes	85
Educating in the context of advanced cultural pluralism	85
The postmodern challenge from an anthropological perspective	86
Re-contextualising cultures	86
PRINCIPLE 6: *The understanding living cultures principle*	87

7	**Faith and culture: Missiology meets education**	**88**
	Faith and culture: Sharing the journey through history	88
	Relationship between faith and culture: Source documents	89
	Faith and culture in Catholic mission theology	90
	Ecclesiam Suam: A seed is sown	90
	Faith and culture in *Gaudium et Spes*	91
	Faith and culture in the *Declaration on Christian Education*	92
	Faith and culture in the mission theology of Pope Paul VI	93
	Theology of faith and culture: John Paul II	95
	Theology of faith and high culture	95
	John Paul II and 'living cultures'	96
	John Paul II's mission theology	97
	Faith and culture in the documents on Catholic schooling	99
	Integration of faith and culture	99
	PRINCIPLE 7: *The expressive principle*	101
	PRINCIPLE 8: *The faith and culture principle*	102
8	**How we see the world: The worldview concept**	**103**
	Meaning making at the convergence of worldviews	103
	Modern understanding of worldview	105
	Postmodern understanding of worldview	106
	Articulating a worldview	108
	The postmodern definition and public worldviews	109
	Exploring worldviews	110
	Comparing traditional worldviews	110
	Postmodern critique of worldviews as 'packages'	111
	Finding the right starting point and	
	the right starting question	112
	There is no worldview-free position	112
	PRINCIPLE 9: *The Public Meaning Principle*	113
9	**Making sense of life: Traditions of meaning**	**115**
	Worldviews and traditions of meaning	115
	Traditions of meaning: Worldview of culture	116
	Traditions of meaning: Worldview of the age	116
	Traditions of meaning: Worldview of faith	117
	Traditions are mediated by communities	118
	Traditions are interpretive maps	118
	Worldviews as ideologies	119
	How we make sense of the world:	
	What it means to interpret experience	119
	Making sense of everyday life: Advanced working model	121
	Working with traditions of meaning	123

Traditions of meaning and the role of language	123
Role of self-reflection in meaning making	124
Fragmentation of meaning and the reconstruction of personal worldviews	124
Traditions of meaning: Implications for a Catholic curriculum	126
PRINCIPLE 10: *The personal meaning principle*	127
PRINCIPLE 11: *The hermeneutical principle*	128

PART D
THE WORLDVIEW OF THE AGE AS A PUBLIC SOURCE IN MEANING MAKING 129

10 The worldview of modernity — 131
Modernity within the Western intellectual tradition — 132
    Genesis of a tradition — 132
    Late Middle Ages: Dialectic reaches its limits — 133
    Church control of knowledge systems — 134
    Rise of the modern academy — 135
    Sustaining a 'Shared and accountable enquiry' — 136
Modernity takes definite form — 137
    Descartes' unintended revolution — 137
    Descartes' intended revolution — 139
    Kant and the structure of the human mind — 140
    Classical modernity and instrumentalism — 141
Nature as a closed system — 142
    Naturalism becomes the ideology of modernity — 142
    The world understood as a closed-system: Working model or ideology? — 144
Beyond modernity where? — 144
PRINCIPLE 12: *The working model principle* — 146

11 The postmodern critique: Prophets of deconstruction — 147
Meanings of 'postmodern' — 148
    'Postmodern' as an era in history — 148
    'Postmodern' as a sensibility — 148
Postmodern thinkers — 150
Prophets of deconstruction — 151
    Nietzsche: Pushing modern thinking to its logical limits — 151
    Jean-Francois Lyotard and 'Incredulity to meta-narratives' — 154
    Jacques Derrida and the birth of 'deconstruction' — 158
    Michel Foucault: 'Power is knowledge' — 161

Postmodernity's options: Understanding the world as an open system	164
PRINCIPLE 13: *The deconstruction principle*	165

12 Postmodern critique: Prophets of reconstruction — 167

Jurgen Habermas:	
Knowing inter-subjectively	168
Modes of knowing: Subject to object	169
Modes of knowing: Subject to subject	169
Reconstructing modernity	171
Charles Taylor: The self and the search for authenticity in a secular age	171
Critique of Descartes' theory of knowledge	172
Authenticity as the moral ideal of modernity	175
Reconstructing modernity: Authentic education	178
John Thornhill: Re-launching modernity as a movement	178
Modernity: From movement to ideology	179
Modernity's quest for autonomy	179
Restructuring modernity: Re-launching the modern movement	179
PRINCIPLE 14: The prophetic principle	181
PRINCIPLE 15: The public square principle	182
PRINCIPLE 16: The nature of learning principle	183

PART E
THE WORLDVIEW OF FAITH AS A PUBLIC SOURCE IN MEANING MAKING   184

13 The worldview of faith — 187

The worldview of faith as a tradition of meaning	188
Contemporary tensions	188
Integrating the worldviews of faith, culture and the age	189
Genesis of the Christian worldview: Hebrew foundations	190
The Hebrew worldview: Three themes	191
The Hebrew worldview in outline: A tradition of hope within history	191
Israel's place among the nations	191
Israel's God as the God of history	192
Israel worships the God who liberates	192
Israel's God is a God who does justice	194
Between text and community: Dynamic by which the tradition was created	194
Dynamic by which the tradition is sustained	195

Biblical critique of the Western construction of knowledge	198
PRINCIPLE 17: *The dignity of difference principle*	201
PRINCIPLE 18: *The authenticity principle*	202

14 The Christian worldview — 204

Constitutive elements in the Christian worldview	205
The Christian worldview: Person, message, community, mission and ethos	206
Knowing Jesus: Between text and tradition	207
The message	207
The community	208
The mission	209
The ethos	210
The Catholic worldview: Two interpretations	211
Constants in Context	212
Challenges in articulating the Catholic worldview	212
The Catholic worldview: Rohr and Martos	213
The Catholic worldview: Bishop David Walker	216
PRINCIPLE 19: *The Sacramental Principle*	218
PRINCIPLE 20: *The Kingdom Principle*	219
PRINCIPLE 21: *The Pivot Principle*	220

15 The Catholic worldview: Developments in postmodern times — 222

Mission defines the Church	222
Concerns about the mission of the Catholic Church	223
'Evangelisation' and 'new evangelisation': The problem of meaning	223
Church mission and Church identity	224
Need for a 'new evangelisation'	225
A Church 'Missionary by its Very Nature'	225
God's Kingdom reaches beyond the Church	226
Modes and forms of the Church's mission	226
God's Kingdom as the central focus of mission	227
A horizon beyond the parish as spiritual service station	228
Reclaiming the mission orientation of the local parish	229
From maintenance to mission	229
'Doing theology' as a complement to 'learning theology'	230
Catholic schools and the mission of the Church	232
PRINCIPLE 21: *The Plausibility Principle*	232
PRINCIPLE 22: *The Integrating Principle*	233

PART F
TOWARDS A CATHOLIC CURRICULUM 235

16 Catholic curriculum: A mission to the heart of young people — 237
   A Catholic curriculum and its mission to the heart of young people — 237
      Worldview and the biblical 'heart' — 238
   Catholic curriculum and its mission to truth — 242
      Bringing the disciplines together in the search for truth — 242
      Dealing with distortions in the mission to truth — 244
      Meaning making goes on in all classes — 248
      A return to the beginning — 248
   Epilogue — 250

APPENDIX 1 Principles of a Catholic curriculum — 252

APPENDIX 2 Profiling tool for a Catholic curriculum — 256

APPENDIX 3 Mapping tool — 260

INTRODUCTION: REFRAMING THE CONVERSATION

The hope of this book is to re-invigorate discussion in Catholic schools about what it means to have a 'Catholic curriculum' as opposed to taking the school curriculum as largely circumscribed by the public curriculum with the 'Catholic' part dealt with in Religious Education, a range of faith development activities and social justice initiatives. The conversation is about 'a Catholic curriculum' rather than 'the Catholic curriculum' since, as we will argue, there are many ways for a curriculum to be Catholic.

A CONVERSATION IN CONTEXT

The immediate context for attempting to reframe discussion about a Catholic curriculum is the implementation in Australia of a national curriculum which has put curriculum, an often taken-for-granted aspect of school life, again in the spotlight. All curricula are based on a set of theoretical assumptions and principles, and the advent of the national curriculum has highlighted the fact that the different states in this country operate either from different curriculum models, or from different interpretations of the same model. As a consequence, the national curriculum represents *a negotiated compromise* in which not only educational interests play a part, but also power interests and ideologies as well. Understanding the dynamics at work in developing the national curriculum is important to understand the directions it will set for Catholic schools.

However, it is the broader context that interests us. This is the context of 'deep change' now engulfing education in most Western cultures. This broader interest encompasses the power interests and ideological movements driving deep change at the intellectual, moral, economic, social, political and religious levels of human experience. This is not just a local phenomenon, although it plays out locally; it is a global phenomenon. As a consequence, it is a brave educator who can predict the shape of the world that students entering primary school will inhabit by the time they complete their studies – 12, 15 or 18 years from now. Yet education, and within this the curriculum of the school, has to be planned in the students' interests at least with some such prediction in mind. If leadership often involves making decisions when you have only a fraction of the data needed to make truly informed decisions, it is not hard to see why educational leadership is so challenging, and why the public curriculum holds the place that it often does in the minds of school leaders. The uncritical adoption of the public curriculum can short-circuit the need to discern the future and so transfers this responsibility elsewhere. *Real educational leadership involves an inescapable dilemma – to plan for a future that can only be dimly discerned.*

RESOLVING THE CURRICULUM LEADERSHIP DILEMMA

One way to resolve this dilemma is to pose the question – *what capabilities do students need to develop to live effectively and well in an ever-changing world?*[1] The answer we can readily see will involve a certain stock of knowledge, skills in accessing and using knowledge, ways of valuing and judging, and a sensibility to what is happening around them that enables students to make sense of people and events as change, so characteristic of our society, continues to unfold. Such capabilities will give young people *the capacity to respond creatively* to the situation in which they will live their lives, not as victims of change, but as its shapers. In most cases this will involve working collaboratively with others and being able to communicate effectively with them.

The future is created not only by human action, however, it is also influenced by the creative action of God in the world as this plays out in human aspiration. We argue later in the book that a Catholic curriculum carries within it a mission to the heart of young people. We make the point at this early stage that, to be future-oriented, such a curriculum needs to promote a deep, intelligent and meaningful relationship with Jesus which becomes the axis on which all else turns. From this relationship springs the capability and drive to develop the skills and competencies to make the Kingdom of God, which was central to Jesus' life and mission, present in the complex world of family, society, culture and Church. It is in commitment to Jesus and his mission that the creative action begun in Jesus' earthly ministry, and continued by his followers through the empowerment of the Holy Spirit is brought to fruition. This creative action is achieved in collaboration with Jesus' disciples living and working in dialogue and hope.

---

1 Howard Gardner takes this question up insightfully in *5 Minds for the Future* (Boston: Harvard Business Press, 2008).

Developing such an outlook and capabilities in their students is the great hope of Catholic school teachers, the reason why we get up in the morning and look forward to re-engaging with our students. It is this hope that enlivens this book and provides the broader perspective in which a conversation about a Catholic curriculum needs to be reframed.

THE TARGET AUDIENCE

Curriculum is not only about students and what they learn; it is also about teachers and what they know, what they aspire to, what they value and are committed to. It is also concerned with the forms of support available to them as they go about their important task. In particular, it reflects *what they think and how they think,* since this determines how the curriculum is delivered, irrespective of what its designers may have prescribed. Since this book is addressed primarily to teachers at all levels in Catholic education it has to be concerned with 'what teachers think' and unashamedly seeks to influence this.

While our primary audience is teachers in schools, the issues we raise have clear implications for those *who influence the thinking of teachers* in schools – school leaders, Church leaders, those who teach teachers how to think about their profession and its meaning, Catholic tertiary educators, and those involved in various forms of teacher development.

TOWARDS A WORKING DEFINITION OF A CATHOLIC CURRICULUM

What is a 'Catholic curriculum'? In setting out the understanding that informs this book we do so using what Berger and Luckmann call the 'social stock of knowledge'[2]. Within this understanding:

> *A Catholic curriculum assists young people to engage constructively with the wisdom and faith of the community in a way that is meaningful to them, living as they do, in a particular cultural and historical setting, with the life chances this setting has to offer, and the constraints that it imposes on them, in establishing their identity as individuals and as members of the community.*

There are a number of key elements in this understanding that we will elaborate further as the conversation proceeds and its scope becomes more clearly defined.

---

[2] Peter Berger and Thomas Luckmann *The Social Construction of Reality: A Treatise on the Sociology of Knowledge* (New York: Anchor Books, 1967), 41.

DEVELOPING AN INTERPRETIVE MAP

If we are to present the 'wisdom and faith of the community' to students in a way that is meaningful to them, then we have to pay attention to the way in which people come to make sense of their world. They do this with reference to 'sources of public meaning'.

Public worldviews as sources of meaning

Education seeks to introduce young people to these sources in a way that ensures that they are passed from one generation to the next as a valuable inheritance. This inheritance is passed on as 'master stories'. There are competing versions of these master stories so the process of transmission is 'critical' in the sense that young people have to learn how to discern between authentic and bogus presentation of the 'master stories'. The master stories provide the means by which public worldviews are conveyed. A public worldview is one owned by a community which determines what are, and are not, authentic presentations of it. There are three such public sources of meaning in Western societies: the *worldview of culture* that is sponsored by a cultural community, in our case the Australian community; the *worldview of the age* which has currency across Western societies; and *the worldview of faith* that has currency within a particular faith community, in our case the Catholic community.

These three public worldviews – of culture, faith and the age – and their associated 'master stories' have cognitive, affective and evaluative dimensions that, when taken together, define for each *a coherent tradition*. These traditions, while meaningful in their own terms, also contain a wisdom that is partially shared with the other two traditions. The worldview of the age, for instance, influences that of culture and of faith. The worldview of culture moderates how the worldview of the age is understood in a particular culture. Put more concretely, 'being Australian' influences how we think of ourselves as 'being Catholic' because of the particular way in which the worldview of Australian culture shapes the worldview of faith among Australian Catholics.

There is an ebb and flow in the interaction between all three traditions, that causes each to flourish sometimes in sympathy with, and sometimes in opposition to, the others. We each construct our *personal interpretive map* against the background of such dynamics. Understanding these public worldviews is therefore important once the focus of education shifts to meaning making. However, as Hack has pointed out, meaning making has often been a by-product of education rather than an end-goal[3]. A Catholic curriculum now demands that this process become more intentional.

---

3 Joanne Hack *Meaning Making: A Key Pedagogical Paradigm for Schooling in the Third Millennium* (Sydney: Catholic Schools Office Broken Bay, 2011), 3.

The interpretive map that we create for ourselves to make sense of life, *our personal worldview*, can be imagined as a kind of personal *Lonely Planet Guide to the Familiar* which also provides us with our orientation in making sense of the unfamiliar. The process by which we create this guide lies largely out of our awareness. Its construction depends on our understanding of the three sources' maps: the three public worldviews. These stand behind its development whether we realise this or not. For most people the construction of this map is unproblematic. They call on what sociologists call 'the social stock of knowledge' or 'recipe knowledge' in negotiating meaning in everyday life.[4]

The situation becomes problematic only when the three public maps lose alignment, provide contradictory or competing conceptions, or make seemingly irreconcilable demands. It is at this point that we are required to move beyond the 'recipe knowledge' we use in negotiating everyday life, and are forced to look more deeply into the issues of life. However, being Western, *we are confident that we have the tools at our disposal in terms of knowledge bases, narratives, value sets, and methods of enquiry to do this*. We know that the major problems of life generally involve a shift in the equilibrium points that define our taken-for-granted view of the world and that a new equilibrium point will eventually be established that is more responsive to the demands of living.

We construe the immediate challenge as 'getting our head around' what is happening, the feelings this generates, why it is happening, and forming some idea of what should be happening, in order to get to 'the heart of the matter'. Once this is located, it becomes possible either to make a response, or at the least to evaluate the adequacy of the responses that others are making as a step forward.

The advantage of living within three tested, and often complementary, traditions each of which has an array of resources for negotiating change, and each of which has its own wisdom in negotiating change, is that we are confident we can work through problems to reach a solution[5]. We do not accept that this cannot happen, that the solution lies totally outside our capacities. We do not see ourselves as the victims of fate. This understanding is integral to 'the wisdom and faith of the community' into which Western people are born.

---

4 See Berger and Luckmann, 19–46, for a discussion of this phenomenon.
5 In many ways the present study reflects this confidence in accessing the resources available in sociology, history and philosophy of science, social philosophy, education, missiology, theology and cultural anthropology and bringing them to bear on the problem of a Catholic curriculum.

Having confidence in tested and living traditions

This belief, or axiom if you like, is the gift that we as teachers have received through our own education, and which we seek to share with a younger generation. How this gift is understood, and how it can best be shared, is central to reframing a conversation about Catholic curriculum.

Helping young people develop the capabilities and insights necessary to live in a changing world, means *projecting them beyond the imaginal horizon often imposed by the particular cultural community, and the particular faith community*, into the wider world encompassed by the three public worldviews we have been discussing with the hopes and possibilities this opens up for them. *It is teaching them to dream big and to find hope within history*. This is the responsibility of teachers, school leaders and system leaders. It is not a responsibility that can be delegated to the public curriculum, important though this is.

The task is one of interpretation in which the narrative of faith has an important place. This task cannot be carried by the Religious Education curriculum enhanced by faith development and social justice initiatives; *it is a responsibility integral to what Catholic schools do*, to the mission of the school, and to the identity of the educators caught up, sometimes willy-nilly and somewhat uncomprehendingly, in this mission.

In outline then, these are the major themes explored in this book. It offers little help in what you will be teaching in Period Six tomorrow, but on the other hand it may put what you are teaching in Period Six tomorrow in a totally new light. That, at least, is the aim!

STRUCTURE OF THE BOOK

In exploring the various themes outlined above we do so in a number of stages, starting with the immediate context, which is a redefinition of the public curriculum and the structures within which this is developed in this country. This provides the opening for a new conversation and so it is important that **Part A** sets out *the scope of the conversation*.

Our central problem – what is a Catholic curriculum? What does it look like? – has a human face, that of teachers and students, and this needs to figure in the conversation. **Part B** looks at the context of teaching and learning, in particular what we know about how students currently construct their world and, within this, how they construct knowledge. This introduces us to *the life-world of young people*.

In any attempt to systematically address any problem, it is necessary to secure the key concepts used and the language of discourse in which it is to be explored. In **Part C** where we look more deeply into the meanings of concepts such as 'culture', 'worldview' and 'meaning making', drawing on the insights of cultural anthropology, social philosophy, and hermeneutics.

These three disciplines help us delineate the three public worldviews central to meaning making – the 'worldview of faith', 'the worldview of culture' and 'the worldview of the age'. The 'worldview of the age' is shorthand for *the worldview dominant in the Western cultures in particular historical periods.* This worldview, encompassing the dominant hopes and view of what *constitutes knowledge* and *legitimates enquiry*, has taken different forms as the Western intellectual tradition has continued to develop. It bears repeating that all of these worldviews stand behind *dynamic living traditions which are embedded in human communities.* When these are explicitly articulated we speak of them as 'traditions of meaning'.

The traditions are not independent, since they *are all part of the one story.* They grow together, not only through the interaction of the ideas embedded in them, but also through interactions occurring in the communities that hold them as valuable. These traditions become *the sources of meaning making* to which we all turn to in creating the interpretive maps we use to make sense of our lives. How we access and use these sources as contexts change becomes important to our conversation about Catholic curriculum. We explore these themes in Part C.

Part D looks in some detail at the way in which the worldview of the age shapes meaning making. Here we trace the development of the modern worldview and its metamorphosis into the ideology of modernity. We then look at the emergence of the postmodern critique and the competing conceptions of what 'postmodernity' means. Of particular interest are competing conceptions of *where this development is heading* since this has an important bearing on what educators need to know in planning for the future.

In **Part E**, the focus changes to the worldview of faith as a public tradition of meaning. This tradition has its own internal dynamisms which enable the faith community to conserve, adapt and develop. These dynamisms are sourced in the life of the ancient Hebrew peoples and subsequently the Christian community. The relationship between the Hebrew and Christian worldviews is examined before exploring the developments in the Catholic worldview in the postmodern era, and the significance of this development for Catholic schooling and the Catholic narrative. We lay the foundation of mission theology on which a better conception of a Catholic curriculum can be established.

The aim of a Catholic curriculum is to engage students with a tested wisdom to which many come as uncomprehending and sometimes less than enthusiastic heirs. Across time young people acquire, or can acquire with help, the ability to integrate the traditions of the faith community, of their cultural community, and of the broader Western community to create *a personal worldview.* This interpretive framework acts as both a guidance system and a source of emotional depth in their lives which secures their commitments. In scriptural terms, the image that carries this meaning is that of 'the heart'. In the end *a Catholic curriculum seeks to effect an orientation of the heart to Jesus through the agency of the Holy Spirit*. The mission of a Catholic curriculum is a mission to the truth, but also a mission to the heart of young people. The final chapter explores these two themes.

Since the book is set out in sections, there is an introduction to each section which provides an outline of the chapters that immediately follow, and seeks to locate them within the overall structure, sometimes providing some brief but necessary recapitulation in the process.

METHODOLOGY

Methodologically, we oscillated between both a theme and a counter-theme that lie at the very heart of Western learning. The theme derives from the Greeks and their concern *to state knowledge in abstract propositional form*. The genius here was Plato. This is the path of philosophy. The counter-theme derives from the mostly unknown geniuses who constructed the Hebrew Bible and left the West with its *narrative tradition of knowledge*. This is the path of culture. There is a creative tension at work here which is very much part of the 'postmodern turn'. The philosophers criticise the storytellers for not securing their terms, so that the truth that their stories proclaim is difficult to locate precisely, and thus defies 'deconstruction'. The storytellers chide the philosophers for pretending that there is not a story behind the propositions they are putting forward, and that *their abstract propositions are not culturally and historically located*.[6] Clearly a balance is required here between narrative and analysis, and the most difficult task in writing this book has been to get this balance right. We leave the reader to judge how well we have succeeded.

As we chart our way through the agenda set out above, our methodology has been *to identify a set of defining principles* that emerges from the explorations we are conducting which, when taken together, map a Catholic curriculum. We spell these out at the end of each chapter. Here we do three things:
- locate the principle embedded in the main text
- provide a commentary linking the principle to school life
- provide some questions to 'continue the conversation' introduced by the text and bring it to bear in the milieu of the school.

School leaders might choose to use this three-part structure as the basis for a reflection process to explore the themes developed in the book and their application to the local school setting.

---

6 This critique can also be extended to the theologians.

HOW DO WE KNOW WHETHER OUR SCHOOL'S CURRICULUM IS CATHOLIC?

At a practical level, one question remains: *Does this book give us specific direction in addressing whether or not the curriculum in our school is Catholic?'* This is the sort of question teachers, the most practical of people operating in busy schools, are bound to ask and so it requires some response. The answer is both 'yes' and 'no'. 'Yes' in the sense that we identify and set out criteria for judgement in the form of principles to use in answering the question, and 'no' in the sense that our aim is to *reframe a conversation* and not to be prescriptive. In our view that would be premature, since it would tend to close rather than open a conversation which, once it has been opened, needs to run its course.

In the appendices, we provide three resources that may aid local reflection. Appendix 1 provides a list of the principles identified in the text in the order in which they appear there. In Appendix 2, we have grouped the principles into categories or 'maps' which provide the basis for a profile instrument that could be used to assess the local curriculum. There are five maps covering:
- contextual factors
- structures of meaning
- introduction to the sources of public meaning
- curriculum content
- curriculum processes.

In Appendix 3 the principles and their associated reflection questions are grouped to correspond to the five 'maps' found in the profile instrument. This may prove a useful 'mapping tool' which provides criteria in making judgements about local curriculum as 'Catholic curriculum'.

Finally, the idea of a Catholic curriculum has been something that we have both been wrestling with at the school system level for some time. We did think of including a chapter on some of the major attempts by Catholic school systems to address the problems it poses. The difficulty is that these attempts are necessarily confined to the curriculum of particular jurisdictions, and even here to particular strategies, so an attempt to describe them would be selective and outside the task we set ourselves.[7] The advent of a national curriculum, however, does open up the possibility of a national project but, as yet, the Church in Australia lacks a structure within which this could be taken forward.

Since the issues we raise here are capable of being taken *in a number of directions*, this puts something of a question mark over the desirability of a

---

7 For a summary of several projects in Australia see Therese D'Orsa 'In the Second Modernity it Takes the Whole Curriculum to Teach the Whole Gospel' Journal of *Catholic School Studies* (Vol. 80, No. 1, May/June 2008), 36–52.

national project. A more promising approach based on recent history would be for major Catholic school systems to take the matter up creatively within their own resources, and to share their experience with the smaller systems that lack both the personnel and expertise to develop major projects. These could participate as valued conversation partners. This approach could see the emergence of a number of projects.

Furthermore, Catholic schools and systems now generally have access to a framework for school improvement, which characteristically includes indicators of achievement related to educational goals. The principles introduced in succeeding chapters could form a basis for the development of goals and indicators to ensure that the school is indeed aspiring to evaluate its curriculum in terms of its quality as 'Catholic curriculum'.

At the level of the curriculum itself, a major strategy used to date has been *values integration,* but this by no means maps the field of possible alternatives. A second strategy has been to identify themes which can be studied across the whole curriculum. Each represents tested ways of 'putting one's foot in the water', and of gaining wisdom in the process. Our project in this book has been to attempt to bring some *conceptual clarity to a difficult field*, by setting down principles on which a school or a system can build its own project, in the hope that multiple approaches might open up. Within the principles we have identified, a Catholic curriculum is a challenge with many possible solutions.

Part A
CATHOLIC CURRICULUM: SITUATING THE CONVERSATION

The Catholic nature of the curriculum has been a challenging topic for Catholic schools for some time. The Vatican Congregation for Catholic Education sought to provide broad guidance with regard to this in *The Religious Dimension of Education in a Catholic School* (1982). The issue returns to the agenda in Australia with the implementation of a national curriculum. This development highlights a wider issue with salience in many other jurisdictions – *the place of the public curriculum in a Catholic school*. In particular, the stance of the Catholic school in relation to the public curriculum and the basis on which this stance is taken.

Any conversation about Catholic curriculum must address this issue because of the important place the public curriculum has in the actual curriculum of the Catholic school and the role it plays in creating life-chances for students. The goals of the public curriculum are set by public policy and Catholics are part of the civic community that shapes this policy. Public policy has to be attentive to public interests, which means Catholics need to be aware of what their interests actually are. This is a matter on which Catholic educators need to have fairly clear ideas. Hence, the need for a conversation about the issue. Secondly, in the development of the public curriculum, the broad parameters of public policy have to be translated into educational objectives and curriculum frameworks. In this process the various curriculum ideologies at play in the educational bureaucracies that make this translation need to be taken into account. Teachers need to be aware of what these ideologies are, the influence they exercise in the development of the public curriculum, and whether or not they are consistent with Catholic interests – particularly in the development of an education that is holistic that is, directed to the development of the young person as someone with a unique dignity and not as just another unit of production and consumption in a capitalist economy.

The conversation about a Catholic curriculum raises a number of important issues and has a definite scope. It needs to explore both dimensions, that of 'curriculum' and that of 'Catholic'. In Part A we set out to open up these themes. Chapter 1 deals with the situation in Australia, particularly the development and implementation of a new public curriculum. Chapter 2 deals with the contours of a new conversation about Catholic curriculum. Chapter 3 sets out the understanding of Catholic curriculum that is explored more fully and amplified as we proceed. This understanding is offered as a working definition that brings together what we see as the determining aspects of a Catholic curriculum in our postmodern context.

1
CATHOLIC CURRICULUM: THE CHALLENGE IN CONTEXT

The Catholic nature of curriculum is a matter that engages Catholic educators around the globe. This is because curriculum is a key determinant of education and as such is a critical component in the life of every Catholic school.

At the present time, curriculum is up-front and centre in Australian education as the country moves towards developing and implementing its first national curriculum. For teachers trialling and implementing the national curriculum, this is an exciting, demanding and challenging time. The Australian experience is not unique. For example, this country is retracing a journey made by Catholic schools in the United Kingdom in the late 1980s. The experience of Catholic educators there is particularly helpful to us as we negotiate our way through the issues that such a wide-ranging development entails.

The UK experience was not an entirely happy one for Catholic educators because, as Arthur points out,[8] Church authorities did not have adequate policies or structures in place to implement the ideal set out in the various documents issued by the Vatican Congregation for Catholic Education. In consequence, while it was acknowledged that Catholic schools were definitely 'more than state schools with statues',[9] Catholic educational authorities found it difficult to defend what this 'more' actually was.

Arthur goes on to argue further that the lack of clarity prevailing at the time about the 'Catholic nature of curriculum' meant that the Catholic school system in England and Wales failed to establish the information base needed to defend a position on the 'Catholic nature of the school curriculum'. Lacking this, the system was left to defend the position that ten per cent of school instruction time should be devoted to Religious Education.[10]

---

8 James Arthur 'Section One: Theological, Historical and Socio-cultural Perspectives' in *Can There Be a Catholic School Curriculum? Renewing the Debate* (University of London: Institute of Education, Centre for Research and Development in Catholic Education, 2007), 9.
9 ibid. Arthur is quoting B. Green, 'Church Schools in a Pagan Culture', *The Tablet*, 6 October, 1990, Education Supplement, 1271f.
10 For a full discussion of the introduction of the National Curriculum in England and Wales see James Arthur 'Theological, Historical and Sociological Perspectives', 1–17.

The allocation of at least a minimum of time to Religious Education has been the pastoral decision of bishops in dioceses beyond the UK, including Australia, in recent decades. The wisdom of this decision is not being questioned here. However, as becomes obvious on consideration, the Catholicity of the curriculum, and thus of the total teaching-learning process, is not assured by such a decision. The Catholic educational tradition holds that it is only by including the total curriculum in their consideration that schools can claim to engage students in a teaching-learning process that is Catholic. *It takes the whole curriculum to introduce students to the whole of the Gospel message.*

In Australia, this tradition was expressed publicly as early as the 1860s when the bishops present at the 1862 Provincial Council (the bishops of Hobart, Melbourne, Brisbane and Sydney) declared:

> *Catholics do not believe that the education of a child is like a thing of mechanism that can be put together bit by bit. Now a morsel of instruction on religion, and then of instruction in secular learning – separate parcels… We hold, that subjects taught, the teacher and his faith, the rule and practices of the school day, all combine to produce the result which we Catholics consider to be education…*[11]

The recent UK experience points up the pressing need in many societies to develop greater clarity around what the concept of a 'Catholic curriculum' can or should mean in our time. While admittedly ambitious, such is the goal of this book. We believe there is an urgent need to reframe the conversation to take note of major changes in the context in which contemporary Catholic education now occurs.

CURRICULUM IN THE AUSTRALIAN CONTEXT

In Australia, under a federal system of government, responsibility for schooling is shared between the Commonwealth and the states with the latter being mainly responsible, up to now, for determining the nature of the school curriculum.[12] For the most part, each state has gone about specifying curriculum in its own manner, with input from both the academic world and the teaching profession, within broad policy parameters set nationally

---

11 Quoted in Patrick O'Farrell *The Catholic Church and Community: An Australian History Revised Edition* (Sydney: New South Wales University Press, 1985), 149. The sentiments expressed echo those elsewhere attributed to Archbishop Polding, Australia's first resident Catholic bishop.

12 Until recently the Commonwealth curriculum input has been largely through special purpose and targeted programs which the Australian Government funds nationally, such as literacy, numeracy, special needs, values education, etc. In recent years, the Commonwealth Government has become referred to as the Australian Government.

by Ministers of Education. This has resulted in different curricula, different starting ages, different transition points from primary to secondary schooling, different levels of support for students with special needs, etc. The system that has evolved fails to serve well the interests of an increasingly mobile workforce, particularly those moving from state to state, seeking new or better employment opportunities.

National policy on education

The goals of publicly funded education have been stated in a series of 'declarations on the education of young Australians', collectively adopted by state and Commonwealth Ministers of Education on behalf of their respective governments. The first of these declarations was made in Hobart in 1989. This was followed by the *Adelaide Declaration* in 1999 and the *Melbourne Declaration* in late 2008. The *Melbourne Declaration* provides the charter for the Australian Curriculum, Assessment and Reporting Authority (ACARA), the body now charged by state and Commonwealth governments with developing the national curriculum.

The goals of the *Melbourne Declaration* set the trajectory for the national curriculum. The formal implementation process was scheduled to begin in 2011 and full implementation to be rolled out in subsequent years. The *Melbourne Declaration* is an important source document, giving direction to school education in all Australian schools, including Catholic schools. It poses important questions about the nature of the curriculum and its likely impact on schools. The introduction of the national curriculum has certainly raised the profile of curriculum from its often 'taken-for-granted' status in schools.

The *Melbourne Declaration* begins by noting that:

> *In the 21st century Australia's capacity to provide a high quality of life for all will depend on the ability to compete in the global economy on knowledge and innovation.*

and continues:

> *Education equips young people with the knowledge, understanding, skills and values to take advantage of opportunity and to face the challenges of this era with confidence.*

> *Schools play a vital role in promoting the intellectual, physical, social, emotional, moral, spiritual and aesthetic development and wellbeing of young Australians, and in ensuring the nation's ongoing economic prosperity and social cohesion.*[13]

---

13 Ministerial Council on Education Employment Training and Youth Affairs (MCEETYA) *Melbourne Declaration on Educational Goals for Young Australians*, 2008, 4.

The *Melbourne Declaration* recognises that increasingly this responsibility is shared with parents, carers, families, the wider community, business and other education and training providers which, in this country, include the churches.[14] In consequence, the education of young Australians needs to be discussed in a way that recognises a *collective responsibility* to face the major changes reshaping the world into which young people will move. The *Declaration* confirms Australia's commitment to excellence in education. While acknowledging that its young people perform creditably in OECD testing, it also recognises that the opportunity to succeed is not equitably distributed. Students from Indigenous and low socioeconomic backgrounds are under-represented among higher achievers and over-represented among low achievers. Against this background the ministers set out two broad goals for Australian schools. The first is the promotion of excellence and equity. The second seeks to ensure that all young Australians become successful learners, confident and creative individuals, and active and informed citizens.[15] The hopes that stand behind these goals are then further elaborated as 'intended educational outcomes for young Australians'. These are set out in full in the table below.

A solid foundation in knowledge, understandings, skills and values on which further learning and adult life can be built…
The curriculum will include a strong focus on literacy and numeracy skills. It will also enable students to build social and emotional intelligence, and nurture wellbeing through health and physical education in particular. The curriculum will support students to relate well to others and foster an understanding of Australian society, citizenship and national values, including through the study of civics and citizenship. As a foundation for further learning and adult life the curriculum will include practical knowledge and skills development in areas such as ICT and design and technology which are central to Australia's skilled economy and provide crucial pathways to post-school success.
Deep knowledge, understanding, skills and values that will enable advanced learning and an ability to create new ideas and translate them into practical applications
The curriculum will enable students to develop knowledge of the disciplines of English, mathematics, science, languages, humanities and the arts; to understand the spiritual, moral and aesthetic dimensions of life; and open up new ways of thinking. It will also support the development of deep knowledge within a discipline, which provides the foundation for interdisciplinary approaches to innovation and complex problem solving.

14 Catholic schools, for instance, educate one in every five Australian students.
15 MCEETYA *Melbourne Declaration on Educational Goals for Young Australians*, 2008, 7.

General capabilities that underpin flexible and analytical thinking, a capacity to work with others and an ability to move across subject disciplines to develop new expertise
The curriculum will support young people to develop a range of generic and employability skills that have particular applications to the world of work and further education and training such as planning and organising, the ability to think flexibly, to communicate well and to work in teams. Young people also need to develop the capacity to think creatively, innovate, solve problems, and engage with new disciplines.

TABLE 1.1 Intended educational outcomes for young Australians[16]

Translating National Goals into Curriculum Outlines

The ACARA policy paper *The Shape of the Australian Curriculum* provides discipline-based curriculum developers with guidelines for devising the K–12 national curricula for all key learning areas. The paper emphasises the need for

- *fundamental knowledge, skills and understandings* in each key learning area
- *depth* rather than breadth, where choice is possible
- *balance* between gaining knowledge and understanding the process by which knowledge is created.

The paper acknowledges, and hence opens up for further exploration, realities that are held to be important by Catholic educators.

> *Each discipline offers a distinctive lens through which we interpret experience, determine what counts as evidence and as a good argument for action, scrutinise knowledge and argument, make judgments about value, and add to knowledge.*
>
> *Rather than being self-contained and fixed, disciplines are interconnected, dynamic and growing, and a discipline-based curriculum allows for cross-disciplinary learning that broadens and enriches each student's learning.*[17]
>
> *... 21st century learning does not fit neatly into a curriculum solely organised by learning areas or subjects that reflect the disciplines. Increasingly, in a world where knowledge itself is constantly growing and evolving, students need to develop a set of skills, behaviours and dispositions, or general capabilities that apply across subject-based content and equip them to be lifelong learners able to operate with confidence in a complex, information-rich, globalised world.*[18]

16 Ministerial Council for Education, Employment, Training and Youth Affairs, December 2008, 13, quoted in *ACARA The Shape of the Australian Curriculum Version* v 2.0, 2010, 16.
17 ACARA, 17.
18 ibid, 18.

Developing these themes further, the document points out the need for students to acquire what, in many jurisdictions, are called 'key competencies', expressed as *general capabilities* to be acquired 'across the curriculum'. It is at this level that moral values enter the curriculum through the development of 'inter-cultural understanding', 'ethical behaviour' and 'social competence'.

The curriculum developers are also encouraged to move beyond traditional disciplines by incorporating 'cross-curriculum perspectives'. Three of these are identified: Indigenous perspectives, Asian perspectives, and environmental perspectives (with a focus on sustainability). In the context of these guidelines, religion could be viewed as a 'cross-curriculum perspective'.

A Discipline-Based National Curriculum

The proposed Australian national curriculum is essentially discipline based, and deals with matters of value mainly as these surface within academic disciplines. Additionally, values are introduced incidentally as 'competencies for living', through 'cross-curriculum perspectives' or as 'themes'. There is no provision for *dealing directly* with the 'moral and spiritual' dimensions of human growth as recognised in the *Declaration*.

It remains to be seen whether ACARA can produce within its own policy framework discipline-based curricula that win national approval. The draft History curriculum has been criticised for not mentioning Christianity as a formative influence on Western civilisation. This would seem, *prima facie,* a failure to meet the requirement that students 'appreciate Australia's social, cultural, linguistic and religious diversity, and have an understanding of Australia's system of government, history and culture'.[19]

Providing an education that is holistic

The preamble to the *Melbourne Declaration,* as in the previous declarations, acknowledges that the education of young Australians should be holistic. This corresponds with the Catholic understanding of the nature of education. However, as Australian educators Marissa Crawford and Graham Rossiter have pointed out,[20] public education bureaucracies in Australia have always struggled to translate the spiritual–moral dimension identified in successive national declarations into effective curriculum provisions.[21] As a consequence, and by default, the resulting school curricula reflect the worldview of modernity which sees the moral/spiritual development of students largely as

---

19 ibid, 8.
20 Marissa Crawford and Graham Rossiter *Reasons for Living: Education and young people's search for meaning identity and spirituality: A Handbook* (Camberwell: ACER Press, 2006), 243 ff.
21 These writers highlight the difficulty faced by public authorities in developing a language to deal with the 'spiritual' dimension of education from within a worldview which assigns the 'spiritual' to the sphere of private knowledge. In this context 'personal development' is often employed as code for 'spiritual development'.

a *private matter*, not to be confused with the transmission of *public knowledge* accessible through the curriculum.

The result is that, while education is concerned with the transmission of a cultural heritage, what is actually transmitted through the public curriculum is predominantly Western heritage *as this has been construed in modernity*. The situation seems little changed in the development of the national curriculum. We will devote considerable time to exploring the worldview of modernity and its implications for curriculum later in this book. ACARA seems to have side-stepped this thorny issue by simply ignoring it.

The difficulty for Catholic educators is that, over time, the national curriculum will come to define what is construed as *public knowledge* in Australia. Public knowledge in turn shapes *public discourse* and when religion is excluded from this discourse the exclusion impinges on both the public standing of religious bodies and their capacity to contribute to public life. It perpetuates the dilemma posed by construing education as secular, which bases it on problematic moral assumptions. Having only a secular basis for values, more often than not *encourages relativism in the process of justifying pluralism*, as sociologists Berger and Zijderveld have pointed out.[22]

The longstanding dilemma in Australian education is that while the worthy and declared national aim is to educate young Australians in a way that is holistic, the way in which the public curriculum is construed, and hence constructed, simply does not admit of this ever happening *in practice*.

Such a situation is unacceptable to Catholics who hold that the spiritual–moral dimension of life underpins the dignity of the human person, which in turn lies at the heart of morality and so must also lie at the heart of education. In an increasingly multi-faith Australia, neither Catholics nor other Christians are alone in finding this unacceptable. This situation seems set to continue and also to be perceived as problematic by an expanding segment of the population.

CORE CONCEPTS IN EXPLORING THE CATHOLIC CURRICULUM

To widen the conversation about the Catholic nature of the curriculum, we need to expand the range of concepts within which it is discussed. In concluding this introduction, we introduce three core concepts.

---

22 Peter Berger and Anton Zijderveld *In Praise of Doubt: How to Have Convictions Without Becoming a Fanatic* (New York: HarperOne, 2009). See for example Chapter 3 'Relativism', 49–68.

Worldview

If the Catholic school is to educate in a way that is holistic, then it will have to invoke ACARA's recognition, cited above, that '21st century learning does not fit neatly into a curriculum solely organised by learning areas or subjects that reflect the disciplines'. As we have indicated, the ACARA construction of curriculum is premised on the *modern worldview* and the 'traditional disciplines' most of which developed in modernity. Its stance implies an acceptance of modernity's construction of knowledge and meaning. However, both Christian and postmodern critiques challenge modernity's construction of knowledge and meaning. To understand the nature, strength and purpose of these challenges *it is necessary to understand the worldviews on which they are based*. 'Worldview' therefore becomes a key construct in what follows.

As Catholic educators, we need to be sure of the ground on which we stand in promoting holistic education, *not as an impossible ideal, but as a reality*. Put another way, if the mission of the Catholic school is to provide students with an education that is holistic, then we need to be able to articulate clearly what this involves and its *relevance* in our present cultural and historical setting. Unless this is done, parents and students will continue to settle for the limited understandings and hopes embodied in the modern worldview, with some espousing the more radical relativism that characterises the postmodern critique of modernity.

Worldview of the age

Our conversation about a Catholic curriculum is occurring in a Western context. It is framed, whether we realise in or not, within the hopes and aspirations alive in Western cultures and the characteristic ways in which knowledge is constructed in these cultures. For the two hundred years prior to the 1970s these were shaped by *the modern worldview*. Its hopes centred on the notion of 'human progress' and its construction of knowledge placed great emphasis on empirical verification of what was proposed as 'knowledge'. Since the 1970s, a new mood has arisen which challenges the modern worldview as a framework of meaning. 'The postmodern condition' is quite critical of modernity, pointing out that its great hopes have proved illusory and that its construction of knowledge is too narrow to solve the major problems now facing humanity.

Worldviews exist as coherent frameworks, which makes it difficult to construct a worldview solely on the basis of critique. The major postmodern critiques often know what they stand against, but are not quite as clear in outlining what they stand for. In consequence, the term 'postmodern' is difficult to define and so the worldview of the present age is quite ambiguous, caught as we are, between the modern worldview and the hopes of the present age which are often ill-defined. The postmodern critique has undermined confidence in science by pointing out that the modern worldview is built on axioms that are unproven and unprovable. The postmodern critique has major implications for curriculum in general, and Catholic curriculum in particular.

Worldview of culture

The most immediate worldview to influence our thinking is that of our culture. Culture and its relationship to worldviews becomes a second major theme in exploring Catholic curriculum. The modern worldview excludes the worldview of faith from public discourse, relegating it to the private sphere. Cultures have responded to the modern worldview in different ways. In Australia (and in other Western countries as well) the secular constructions of meaning are now taken for granted. Faith communities initially accepted the secular construction of the social world as serving the common good. They saw this as a way of avoiding the conflict resulting from the historical animosity between Christian denominations in Europe being imported into countries of the new world. However, the situation changed dramatically when the resultant secularisation became driven, not by concern for the common good, but by a secularist ideology which seeks to deny faith-based communities any place in the public square. This ideology is now under challenge in many Western countries as their societies become multi-faith.

The modern worldview, even in its more benign forms, privileges secularist positions at the expense of faith positions, usually in the name of tolerance. It is therefore necessary to understand the cultural dynamics at work as these continue to play out in the construction and implementation of something like the national curriculum. The major difficulty here is that people have very vague ideas about what 'culture' means or about how it works.

The Worldview of faith

There is a third set of questions to consider and these relate to the worldview of faith – What is the 'worldview of faith'? How is it best understood? How is it best delineated? Because the 'worldview of faith' is related to how we as Christians understand truth, it is often conceived in *static* terms, as something that is unchangeable. Many people have come to understand truth in the same way. *Our contention is that this represents a serious misunderstanding.*

There is a difference between the truth of faith and the way in which this truth is understood and expressed. While the first can in some sense be understood as invariant, the way truth is understood and expressed changes as culture expands to incorporate a wider range of experience, as history moves forward, and as languages evolve. In this sense, our understanding of the truth and our expression of it also changes as we gain insight into the deeper and truer meaning of things. We are heirs to a faith tradition *that seeks to hold conservative and dynamic tendencies in creative tension*. It is important therefore to articulate the key parameters of the worldview of our faith and the points of connection with the worldviews of culture and of the age in which we live.

Students living in this age and culture need to understand why the worldview of faith is a significant feature of their lives. It is the inclusion of the worldview of faith into the education program, both in terms of its *content* and its *process*, that takes Catholic education beyond the limited understandings of modernity and makes it holistic.

THE NATIONAL CURRICULUM – OPPORTUNITY OR 'BUSINESS AS USUAL'?

The development and implementation of a national curriculum in this country brings a number of important questions into focus, providing an important opportunity to explore an aspect of Catholic education which dedicated educators have wrestled with in various ways for generations. Key questions for Catholic educators are: How, within this new framework, can the spiritual/moral dimension of life be coherently addressed? As a key competency? As a perspective? As a value-set to be included in the curriculum? As a discipline additional to the prescribed key learning areas? As a framework of meaning? Some or all of the above? These are questions which now frame our discussion about the nature of 'Catholic curriculum'.

PRINCIPLE 1: *THE PIVOT PRINCIPLE*

A Catholic curriculum places Jesus, his message, his mission, his community and his ethos, at the centre of all learning, whether dealing with public meaning (teaching about public worldviews) or personal meaning (helping students develop personal worldview).

COMMENT

This principle informs all aspects of this book. It is discussed fully in Chapter 14.

PRINCIPLE 2: *THE PUBLIC CURRICULUM PRINCIPLE*

A Catholic curriculum endorses the public curriculum and understands its function, but in doing so adopts a critical stance to it.

COMMENT

The stance is critical on three major grounds:
1. With respect to its content and the curriculum theories at play in its selection of content. The critique is concerned with the *underlying ideologies and power interests* determining content.
2. With respect to the disciplines that stand behind the content. The critique is concerned with the *worldview endorsed by these disciplines* and the often unstated assumptions that are part of this worldview.
3. With respect to its aims. The critique here is that these aims are *quite limited in terms of what a Catholic curriculum seeks to achieve*.

CONTINUING THE CONVERSATION

2.1 Is the public curriculum simply taken at face value at your school or is it adapted in some way?

2.2 If it is adapted, on what basis does this occur? Who does it?

2.3 What is your reading of the dominant curriculum theory behind the design of the public curriculum? On what assumptions is this theory built? Whose interests does the public curriculum serve? What does this mean for the school's clientele? Who benefits and how loses out?

2.4 What implications do the above questions have for how your school implements the public curriculum? How well are these thought through? How well are they addressed?

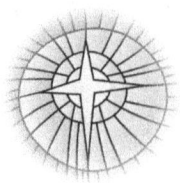

2
CATHOLIC CURRICULUM: SCOPE OF THE CONVERSATION

Any conversation must have a starting point and then usually proceeds within certain boundaries. In this chapter, we wish to outline what these are.

OPENING UP LINES OF ENQUIRY

Our starting point is the perspectives commonly encountered among teachers in Catholic schools when the subject of 'Catholic curriculum' is raised. These perspectives are informed by a range of views about the nature of the curriculum. They in turn reflect the worldviews, often unacknowledged, that teachers access in making sense of their work and determining what is in their students' best interests when they plan the activities which nurture learning.

A second line of enquiry looks at the Catholic curriculum as 'Catholic' and what this might mean. If teachers are divided over the meaning of curriculum, the situation is little different when the emphasis changes to their understanding of 'Catholic'.

In beginning to develop meaning around the term 'Catholic curriculum', we have found it helpful to think of it as a map directing us to a goal. This map is put together from a number of sources and in the course of opening up a conversation about Catholic curriculum we wish to interrogate these sources to assess their contribution. We can specify the goal as passing on a valuable cultural and faith heritage in a meaningful way, that is in a way which helps students make sense of their life-world and also of their context.

Furthermore, we seek to pass on this composite heritage in such a way that not only are students empowered to live meaningful and happy lives, but in consequence are enabled to make their own contribution to this heritage as contexts continue to change. We see the goal of Catholic curriculum as being achievable only *through an ongoing dialogue about the nature of what we are attempting and the process by which we intend to accomplish it.*

Meeting such a challenge is demanding because context is always *complex territory*, and the young people we lead may be quite resistant to travelling in the direction we indicate. Catholic curriculum has to face up to this situation. Our strategy therefore needs to take into account the fact that young people today *experience the world in highly subjective ways*. Theirs is a world qualitatively different from that of their parents and many of their teachers, which was post-PC, but pre-internet and pre-social media. It is a world in which the flow of information cannot be easily contained, in which people are generally wary of received wisdom, in which there are multiple options, and in which *the need to choose is an existential imperative*. It is a world defined by modern pluralism which has cultural, ideological and religious dimensions. Catholic curriculum, if it is to be effective, has to assist students to *understand and negotiate this reality*.

CURRENT PERSPECTIVES ON 'CATHOLIC CURRICULUM'

'Catholic curriculum' is a challenging concept for many teachers. We have discovered that, when it is introduced into tutorial sessions or staff discussions, it draws a range of responses that reveal *five commonly held perspectives*. Three of these view the topic positively, and two sceptically. The positive perspectives track along the following paths.

1 Religious Education as intellectual discipline

The curriculum of the school is 'Catholic' because Religious Education has a central place in it. In this perspective R.E. is seen as an intellectual discipline alongside other school disciplines. The study of religion is in this way *objectified*, while the subjective side of Religious Education is handled through separate 'faith development' initiatives in order to take into account the highly diverse levels of faith development found among students.

2 Values-integration approach

The curriculum is 'Catholic' because it integrates values central to the Gospel 'across the curriculum' either directly into specific learning areas, or as part of a thematic study centred on social justice, peace, the environment etc., and so embeds these values in the total life of the school. In this approach the aim is to incorporate Catholic values into the processes by which students construct knowledge, irrespective of the academic discipline involved.

3 Teachable moment approach

The curriculum of the school is 'Catholic' because it specifically addresses the spiritual–moral development of students in a way not possible within the conventional curriculum. It does this is in a variety of ways, but primarily through the 'teachable moment'. Recognising and utilising these when they occur is a hallmark of good teaching. Deliberately creating them is also an important aspect of curriculum planning. Activities such as liturgy, retreats, social service activities, student advocacy etc., play an important role in this perspective and these activities in turn *utilise the knowledge and skills developed in the traditional curriculum as a resource*. The expressive and creative arts, in particular, play an important role in creating 'teachable moments'.

Two other commonly encountered perspectives are sceptical about the value of the above approaches.

4 Colonial perspective

In this view 'Catholic curriculum' is regarded as a rhetoric by means of which Religious Education seeks to colonise other school disciplines either by introducing 'Catholic' material into them or by using them to promote 'Catholic values'. Teachers seem divided on the *authenticity* of such approaches because of what they see as their *partisan nature*. If 'Catholic' content and values, why not 'environmental' content and values? or content and values associated with some other worthy causes?

5 Agnostic perspective

Teachers holding this view raise questions like – can there ever be such a thing as 'Catholic Maths', or 'Catholic Science' etc., without distorting the notion of what these subjects are about? They hold that *these disciplines have a legitimate autonomy* in the pursuit of knowledge and that this needs to be respected. Imposing 'Catholic stuff' seems to them to ignore this autonomy. This position finds endorsement in Catholic Church teaching[23] which affirms the autonomy of academic disciplines in the pursuit of truth.

Each of these five reactions contains an implied understanding of curriculum and its purpose, the nature of knowledge, how meaning is created, the process of learning and what 'Catholic' can, or should, mean in relation to all these matters.

'CATHOLIC CURRICULUM' AS CURRICULUM

Any discussion about Catholic curriculum needs to be framed within the context of *current educational thinking about curriculum*. American educator Michael Schiro provides helpful discussion in dealing with the range of approaches. He observes that the nature and purpose of the school curriculum has historically proved inherently problematic, with at least four schools of thought, or four 'voices', shouting for dominance.[24] Educators and policy makers, by training or inclination, generally align themselves with

---

23 For example *The Religious Dimension of Education in a Catholic School* (1988),#53.
24 Michael Schiro *Curriculum Theory: Conflicting Visions and Enduring Concerns* (Thousand Oaks: Sage Publications, 2008), 4–6.

one or other of these voices and this makes curriculum a controversial issue in schools. This observation has an important bearing on our conversation.

Schiro proposes four categories or *ideal types* that enable him to map the field of curriculum theory. As ideal types they are not mutually exclusive and all four have a valid claim to make in the shaping of curriculum in particular schools or school systems. Schiro's major contention is that it is competition among those holding these four views of curriculum that generates the *creative tension* needed to foster sound curriculum development in a school. Schiro's categorisation of curriculum theories is now briefly summarised.

Scholar academic perspective

Defining idea: The purpose of the curriculum is the transmission of knowledge. In this perspective educators construe curriculum as introducing students to the paradigms of the *academic disciplines*. (This is the framework adopted for the national curriculum in Australia.) The focus in this approach is on the *construction of knowledge seen as rational* enquiry pursued within the methods and ethical framework appropriate to that enquiry. There are right and wrong ways to proceed.

Social efficiency perspective

Defining idea: Curriculum must be at the service of the society that funds education. In this perspective, curriculum is designed to address *the needs of society*. How these 'needs' are determined makes the approach problematic. If social problems arise, then they need to be addressed through school programs since schooling provides society with a mechanism by which it can reach all young people. The social efficiency model often finds a home among government policy makers. The 'needs of society' are primarily construed in either social or economic terms, although in Australia there is also a strong social justice element concerned to re-address the disadvantage faced by many young people due to disability, socioeconomic and cultural factors.

Learner-centred approach[25]

Defining idea: Curriculum is designed to meet the learning needs of the students so that they become active agents in their own learning. In this perspective, curriculum is student-centred rather than subject-centred. The approach characterises much of primary education. This philosophy has also been the driving force behind school-based curriculum development. It is an emphasis to which many teachers most readily respond. It places great emphasis on the contextualising of learning.

---

25 The learner-centred approach embraces a 'broad church' which includes Dewey's pragmatism, Piaget's constructivism, and Catholic foundationalism all of which approach 'learner-centred education' from a different direction.

Social reconstruction approach

Defining idea: Curriculum is about transformation and freeing young people to become active agents in the transformation of their society. The final perspective sees the purpose of education, and hence of curriculum, as the *transformation* rather than the reproduction of society, *making it more just and equitable*. The aim of education is not construed so much in terms of meeting needs, as of *creating needs and empowering people to act* to meet their expressed needs. Education is seen as having a transformative effect on society.

Even this brief overview makes it clear that the various perspectives that teachers hold on the Catholic curriculum discussed in the previous section reflect their commitment to one or other of these perspectives. Importantly, as Schiro points out, the perspective a teacher holds can change across a career and with changes in context.

If each model carries its own degree of legitimation, then developing the school curriculum must involve an ongoing *dialogue among competing voices each proposing a worthwhile end*. This is a theme to which we will return in later chapters. This dialogue may result in somewhat different conclusions being drawn in different contexts. *Local aspiration, framed in the context of local needs, therefore becomes an important part of any conversation about the Catholic curriculum.*

Curriculum in the perspective of critical theory

Schiro's categorisation distinguishes between curriculum theories by examining *the ends that people seek to achieve* and this tends to *objectify* the process of learning. In another treatment that we continue to find illuminating, Shirley Grundy uses a more subjectively oriented classification system based on *the motivation for learning*. She adroitly uses the philosophical framework of Jurgen Habermas to explore curriculum from a 'postmodern' perspective. Her argument, based in critical theory, is that curriculum can be conceptualised as a *product*, a *process*, or a form of *praxis*, depending on the 'human interests' it serves.[26]

In Habermas' framework,[27] 'human knowledge interests' do not refer exclusively to 'personal' or 'corporate' interests,[28] but to *the things that make us quintessentially human*. He identifies three 'human knowledge interests' based on why people seek to know:

1 *in order to control* (technical interest)

---

26 Shirley Grundy *Curriculum: Product or Praxis?* (London: the Falmer Press, 1987).
27 While Habermas moved away from this theory in the early 1980s, it has continued to provide the foundations of critical education theory. See for instance David Smith and Terry Lovat 'Towards Critical Reflection in Curriculum Work' in *Curriculum: Action on Reflection Fourth Edition* (South Melbourne: Cengage Learning, 2003), 135–168.
28 This understanding of 'interests' is used in social analysis often employed within the curriculum of Catholic schools to explore social justice issues.

2 *in order to make sense of things* (practical interest)
3 *in order to be free* (emancipatory interest).

These three interests impact on curriculum thinking at both the system and individual levels. For instance, if a society begins to feel insecure, or under economic pressure, then exercising *greater control over the school curriculum* becomes an important goal of public policy. The focus moves to discipline-based learning which views the curriculum predominantly *as a product to be consumed*.

In other circumstances, for instance when faced with unrelenting change, or with a sense that bureaucratic or social controls are becoming oppressive, another curriculum emphasis emerges, one that stresses *the creation of meaning*. People adopting this view of curriculum tend to see it *as a process used to help people interpret and make sense of a situation so that they can engage more fully with it*. Schiro's Social Efficiency and some learner-centred curriculum theories fall into this category.

Brazilian educator Paulo Freire is an example of an educator pursuing an emancipatory interest. His aim was *not to meet the needs* of the people he was working with, but through education to *create new needs* that would motivate them to learn and so become empowered to meet these needs. He pointed out to illiterate farmers, for instance, the ways in which they were hampered by not being able to read, how this denied them the information needed to discuss matters of import in a constructive way, and how this in turn reduced their capacity to act. He then taught them to read. The result of this intervention was so successful that it created major social tensions and caused his contract to be terminated prematurely! Freire was clearly defining curriculum *as praxis* in this example. This is an example of the Social Construction curriculum theory. The emancipatory interest also motivates those approaches to learner-centred curriculum that promote social justice. The *Radical Math* movement in the United States of America (USA) is an example of this approach as is the *Peace Builders initiative* sponsored by Catholic Theological Union in Chicago.

At a deep individual level, we all want to know not only how to *make sense of life*, but also how to take *control of our lives* so as to maximise the life-chances available to us. We want to *live free from what otherwise would oppress us*. Context more often than not determines the relative emphasis we give to pursuing these three human interests. Grundy's analysis suggests that discussions about a Catholic curriculum need to balance the *objective considerations* of curriculum theory (dealing with means and ends) with the more *subjective considerations highlighted by critical theory* (dealing with interests and motivations).

The history of curriculum development in Australia over the past four decades has seen a constant ebb and flow between school-based development and central prescription. This has reflected the waxing and waning of enthusiasm for the various models of curriculum noted by Schiro as contexts have changed and as people have pursued their different human interests. The development of a national curriculum brings the curriculum models discussed above and the interests which drive them again into focus. While ACARA has opted for a particular model, discipline-based learning, *this does not de-legitimise the claims of other models*. It does suggest that it will prove difficult to implement the national curriculum if the legitimate claims of other models are not adequately addressed.

CURRICULUM AND WORLDVIEWS

Australian educators David Smith and Terry Lovat[29] highlight the fact that definitions of 'curriculum' are context dependent. Using a selection of these definitions the writers show how each reflects, implicit or explicitly, an underlying *worldview* that can be sourced to a particular historical or social context. They further argue that in most cases these worldviews often go unrecognised. Their advice is that when discussing curriculum issues *it is important to identify the worldview that plays in the background*. We take this advice as axiomatic to all that follows.

A worldview represents *a coherent way of looking at the world justified by the traditions of a community*. That community can be as narrow as the family, or as wide as a whole society. Worldviews form what philosophers call the *background* to our thinking and meaning making. No person has the capacity, or indeed the time, to check out all the propositions which he or she needs to know in order to make their way in life. We have to take a lot on trust. In practice, whether we realise it or not, we put our trust in the traditions that underpin our culture as these are held in the communities that make up our life-world. We will discuss the concept of 'worldview' in more detail in Chapter 7.

If we want to pass on the wisdom and faith of our community to the younger generation in a way that is meaningful to them, we have to take into account at least two worldviews – the *worldview of the faith community* and the *worldview of the culture* in which they live and learn. However, that is not the whole story. Cultures do not exist in the abstract; they exist in historical contexts and share in the aspirations of a particular era. These aspirations themselves flow from a third worldview – *the worldview of the age*. It is at this level, however, that the complexity of our contemporary situation reveals itself because, whilst the worldview of modernity is still dominant, its hegemony is called into question by the 'postmodern' critique.[30] As a consequence, we find ourselves living in an age of competing aspirations

---

29 David Smith and Terence Lovat, 9–12.
30 We side with those authors who claim that this critique is too diverse, inconsistent, and lacking in coherence to be classified as a 'postmodern worldview'.

and expectations. This creates anxiety and uncertainty because we are no longer sure which tradition to appeal to in making sense of our experience. To make things even more complicated, the three worldviews noted above interact with and reshape one another.

While we will return to this issue in some detail later, it is sufficient to note at this stage that a major effect of the 'postmodern' critique has been *to lower confidence in the traditions that serve as background in making sense of experience.* As a consequence, people lose key points of reference in meaning making and drift into a soft form of relativism in which everything becomes 'a matter of opinion'. Science is just 'scientists' opinions' and religion, 'well that's just God's opinion', as one of the authors' young charges once put the matter! If the Catholic curriculum is going to achieve its goal then it must free young people from the oppression of a soft relativism in which 'anything goes'. As a minimum condition it must present them with meaningful mooring points in their intellectual and moral lives.

There is another question that we need to pose in this initial consideration of worldviews *–how do we as teachers discover the worldview from which we operate, given that our worldview sits in the background operating, as it were, from behind our backs?*

Empirical approach to curriculum

One very useful approach is to view curriculum as an *empirical phenomenon*.[31] In this perspective, it is possible to talk about:

- curriculum as *intended* – what we want students to learn
- curriculum as *enacted* – pedagogy that engages the student with the intended curriculum
- curriculum as *experienced* – how students experience the curriculum (which differs from student to student)
- curriculum as *assessed* – what students learned about what teachers intended them to learn
- curriculum as *achieved* – what have students actually learned intended or not
- curriculum as *reported* how well students are deemed to have learned what was intended.

---

31 For an expansion on this perspective see *P–12 Framework: Policy, Principles and Guidelines for Queensland State Schools* (Department of Education, Training and the Arts Queensland 2008),1.

Viewing curriculum from the empirical perspective tends to highlight the *values and meanings* that we as teachers bring to our work, and so surfaces the *worldview that stands behind our efforts* on behalf of students.[32] What we actually think and do when it comes to teaching and learning speaks volumes about our worldview.

The thrust of the argument from curriculum theory is that *there is not, nor is there ever likely to be, a clear-cut conceptualisation of 'curriculum'*. As contexts and ideologies change, shifts in emphasis occur in an existing balance between competing understandings of curriculum, all of which have some legitimate claim on the concept. For this reason 'a Catholic curriculum', because it is curriculum, shares in this dynamic. The concept of a Catholic curriculum is therefore an open one, requiring ongoing reflection and discernment, and one capable of taking a number of forms.

To say this is not to excuse us from the task of exploring its contours. It is to suggest that we need to recognise that our understanding is bounded by the state of an ongoing conversation that can, and will, take different directions in different eras. The question before us is this – w*hat directions does it need to take in our era?* Some elements in an answer are already beginning to emerge.

CATHOLIC CURRICULUM AS 'CATHOLIC'

As Catholic educators we stand heirs to a long tradition, forged by those before us who have also sought *to pass the faith and wisdom of the community on to the younger generation in a way that is meaningful for them*. This has been a constant challenge for Christian leaders dating back to post-apostolic times when this particular challenge first arose.

Utilising a received wisdom

Given the difficulties we presently encounter in achieving this goal, we can easily think our position is unique. While this is to some extent true, we are not the first to find our task demanding. The challenges faced by early Church leaders in passing on a wisdom and faith whose roots were buried deep in the soil of Judaism to young people immersed in Greek culture within the Roman empire were also acute! The task has become progressively more complex, however, as societies and cultures have become more diverse. Contemporary globalisation simply exacerbates an already difficult situation. The process is further complicated by the fact that in our time knowledge has expanded exponentially and, as a consequence, has become fragmented so that the concept of an education that is holisitic,

---

32 This model of analysis places great emphasis on the formative and summative roles of assessment and is integral to the outlook of ACARA and to NAPLAN (National Assessment Program Literacy and Numeracy) testing.

able to help people hold the pieces together, is perceived in many quarters to be a very difficult ideal to achieve in practice. One current tendency is to see education, not in terms of the development of the person, but as a commodity. In an individualistic world 'you go to school to get what you can out of the experience for yourself'. This conception is challenged by a Christian view of life which proposes the service of others, rather than self-interest, as the moral ideal.

In seeking to clarify the nature of curriculum in Catholic schools, we are guided by *a received wisdom* that has grown out of the experiences of previous generations. The wisdom of the Catholic faith community with respect to schooling is now set out in a number of Roman documents.[33] The trajectory found in these documents was set in the mid-60s. They reflect a positive assessment by Church leaders of the mindset that developed in the historical period we call 'modernity'. In this sense the documents are written in a different register from those that preceded the Second Vatican Council (1962–65).[34]

The documents consistently present the goal of the Catholic school as 'the integration of faith and culture and faith and life'.[35] 'Culture' is a key referent, but the use of the term is not defined with any precision and this leaves its meaning as an open question. The documents also refer also to 'the mission of the Catholic school', but have been developed with quite limited reference to important themes in the Church's own official teaching on mission. As a consequence, they present a quite narrow understanding of evangelisation, which is now officially understood as encompassing all those elements that, taken together, make up the evangelising mission of the Church.[36] The Vatican documents on Catholic schooling are meant to be interpreted in local contexts, but this is made difficult by the fact that the socio-cultural location of the texts themselves is undeclared. The content appears to reflect the situation and interests of North Atlantic cultures.

---

33 See *Vatican Council II Declaration on Christian Education (1965); Sacred Congregation for Catholic Education The Catholic School* (1977), *Lay Catholics in Schools: Witnesses to Faith* (1982), *The Religious Dimension of Education in a Catholic School* (1988), *Catholic Schools on the Threshold of the Third Millennium* (1997), *Consecrated Persons and their Mission in Schools* (2002).
34 One of the achievements of the Second Vatican Council was the effort made by the assembled bishops to come to grips with the positive aspirations embedded in the modern worldview. Prior to this, the Catholic emphasis had been on what was wrong with this worldview, as we shall see later.
35 C.f. Sacred Congregation for Catholic Education *The Catholic School* #44.
36 For an overview of post-Vatican Catholic teaching on mission and evangelisation see Jim and Therese D'Orsa *Explorers, Guides and Meaning Makers*: Mission Theology for Catholic Educators (Mulgrave: John Garratt, 2010), Chapter 10 'Befriending a Living Tradition'.

Our conversation needs to *engage this received wisdom* and explore how it is helpful in responding to our core task – passing on the faith and wisdom of the community to a younger generation in a way that is meaningful to them. A received wisdom is a mixture of enduring truths and time-conditioned insights. Sorting one from the other requires careful discernment. This requires that the present engages the past in dialogue. This is how a living tradition actually sustains its life!

The Kingdom dimension

The Catholic curriculum has both an *educational* and a *theological* dimension. *We therefore need to establish the theological locus of our conversation.* Our contention is that this is as a pilgrim community journeying towards the Kingdom of God. As taught by Jesus, the Kingdom of God is God's creative presence within history, which has its fulfilment beyond history.[37] If, as Benedict XVI points out, Catholic faith is 'the path the faith community walks together',[38] then the 'Catholic curriculum' in an important sense maps a key element of that pathway as traversed by teachers and students in a shared journey towards the Kingdom. This needs to be a central consideration in our conversation for two reasons.

Firstly, there is the renewed realisation within the Catholic community that the Kingdom of God embraces Jesus' core teaching about our relationships to God, to fellow humans and to the whole of God's creation. Throughout history, faith communities, including Catholic school communities, have walked together on a journey towards God's Kingdom and this has been central to the mission of those faith communities. Most important for our conversation is the reminder that the Catholic faith, of which Catholic curriculum is an immensely important expression, *is not a closed system*; it is not a complete, or completed intellectual project. It is, first and foremost, a path we walk together with others, a path which opens up and becomes more fully recognisable *only in the process of actually walking along it*.

Secondly, Jesus' vision of the Kingdom is pursued in *local contexts* as the expression of a *global commitment by Christians to carry on his mission*. Theologian Richard McBrien reminds us that Catholicism is 'a way of *being human*, a way of *being religious*, and a way of *being Christian*'.[39] This 'way' has been lived out in many cultures and through a number of ages. It has a quality which *transcends the particular worldviews and contexts in which it is actually lived out*. As we proceed, our conversation needs to hold this truth in place – *the worldview of faith is quite a different type of reality from that of our*

---

37 Francis Moloney *Mark: Storyteller, Interpreter, Evangelist* (Massachusetts: Hendrickson Publishers, 2004), 126–7.
38 Joseph Cardinal Ratzinger (Pope Benedict XVI) *Truth and Tolerance: Christian belief and World Religions* (San Francisco: Ignatius Press, 2004), 145.
39 Richard McBrien *Catholicism* (HarperSanFrancisco, 1994), 6.

culture or of the age in which we live. It has a unique source and in a sense its own power supply! It is capable of enriching other worldviews.

The theological locus of Catholic schools challenges teachers' grasp of the 'worldview of faith' and how this informs our understanding of what 'being Catholic' means in practice. For instance:

- What does 'being Catholic' have to say to the way in which we are human?
- How aware are we of our Catholic faith tradition as a *living tradition*?
- What are the points of connection between 'being Catholic' and 'being Australian'?
- How do we identify ourselves with the local and global faith communities?
- How does the worldview of faith impinge on the worldview that teachers bring to the classroom?
- How does the worldview of faith shape the way teachers understand their mission as teachers – as part of God's mission? the Church's mission? the school's mission? or as something unrelated to all of the above?

The fact that people teach in a Catholic school engages them, implicitly or explicitly, in all of these questions. Students have a right to expect that their teachers are developing a *coherent* set of answers to them. While this may seem an unrealistic expectation to some teachers, it is part of the contemporary challenge of teaching in a Catholic school. The difficulty is that, given the path many teachers take to their position in a Catholic school, 'Catholic' may be understood more as a workplace brand, rather than as a collective identity. The conversation about Catholic curriculum is going to be largely meaningless if people have little understanding of the theological locus of the Catholic school.

PRINCIPLE 3: THE MISSION PRINCIPLE

While Catholic educators acknowledge that the curriculum can legitimately serve a number of purposes, the essential contribution of a Catholic curriculum to the mission of the school is meaning making.

COMMENT

In the critical theory of education, people pursue knowledge to gain greater control over their lives, directly and indirectly, and so maximise the life-chances this creates. They also pursue knowledge to escape various forms of marginalisation. However, both these objectives presuppose making sense of their situation in the first place, so that meaning making becomes a condition of either control or emancipation. It is the crucial process around which a Catholic curriculum needs to be planned.

This principle applies not only to students but to teachers and parents as well.

CONTINUING THE CONVERSATION

3.1 Does the school's curriculum include a coherent theory of meaning making? If so, how is this articulated and by whom? If not, what steps need to be taken to develop a better understanding of this process and its pedagogical implications?

3.2 How do you think students construct meaning? What are the sources they depend on?

3.3 What are the recurring biases in their thinking that they seem to draw most frequently from 'the common stock of knowledge'? How does the curriculum seek to address these?

3
CATHOLIC CURRICULUM: A WORKING DEFINITION

We have proposed the following as a working definition of a Catholic curriculum:

A Catholic curriculum assists young people to engage constructively with the wisdom and faith of the community in a way that is meaningful to them, living as they do in a particular cultural and historical setting, with the life-chances this setting has to offer, and the constraints that it imposes on them in establishing their identity as individuals and as members of the community.

The statement is fairly dense in that it brings together a number of elements which will be explored separately in the following chapters. It will be helpful therefore to do some preliminary 'unpacking' in light of the previous discussion about the 'scope of the conversation' and the issues raised there. In the sections that follow we expand each element in the working definition. Before doing so however, we add a caveat. We are talking about 'a Catholic curriculum' not 'the Catholic curriculum' because it is our contention that there are a number of ways in which a school curriculum can be 'Catholic'. Our definition is a 'working' definition because it keeps these options open, allowing a number of different interpretations *within agreed principles*. We set out to identify what these principles are as we proceed in the following chapters.

'A CATHOLIC CURRICULUM ASSISTS YOUNG PEOPLE TO ENGAGE CONSTRUCTIVELY...'

The wisdom and faith of the community do not exist in the abstract, but as traditions that have been *tested in the life of the community* and, as a consequence are 'canonised' by it, albeit to different degrees by the various groups that make up any community. Being able to respond creatively to future developments only has meaning against the background of a tradition and, in practice, this response serves to extend the tradition so contributing to its growth.[40] Secondly, 'engaging with a tradition' involves action on the part of the student and that action needs to be constructive. 'Engaging with' involves more than just 'passing on'. Students have to become *active participants in shaping the future*, not passive recipients of a tradition shaped by others. This is particularly important in the Catholic faith community whose young people have for too long now been socialised into the community in a way that renders them passive. It is a mode of socialisation against which many are now clearly rebelling.

Traditions can develop either organically or disruptively and in this context 'engaging constructively' may involve both forms of development. Rebellion can be interpreted as a disruptive form of engagement but only if its causes are identified and then addressed.

'…WITH THE WISDOM AND FAITH OF THE COMMUNITY…'

The concepts of 'wisdom' and 'faith' are integrally linked to that of 'community'. Wisdom and faith have meaning only in the context of a community which tests them, values them, affirms them, celebrates them, and passes them on. Wisdom has to do with 'living well'. It implies a notion of what Canadian philosopher Charles Taylor calls 'human flourishing'[41] understood in its broadest sense. It is attached to the biblical ideal of 'living in right relationship'. Wisdom is the possession of a people and, although philosophers may articulate it in proposition form, it is passed on as a guide to everyday living *in narrative form* from one generation to the next with the stories that make up this narrative taking on more elements as the experience of the community unfolds and as its insights into the meaning of its historical experience expand and deepen. Cultural wisdom has its heroes and heroines and these acquire mythic status in the processes by which it is transmitted. In our own day, Nelson Mandela has taken on the mantle of cultural hero, and with good reason.

Faith likewise is about 'living well', and so has its own wisdom, but this depends on having access to a source of knowledge that lies outside everyday human experiences. Faith is learned as sacred narratives that offer a particular interpretation of human history. This interpretation is preserved in texts, teachings and rituals held to be sacred by the community, because they collectively encompass in human symbols and language a

---

40 As three star Michelin cook Marc Veyrat once commented 'My cuisine is creative… But I am also traditional. To create you need a tradition on which to build' quoted in Donn F. Morgan *The Making of Sages: Biblical Wisdom and Contemporary Culture* (Harrisburg Pennsylvania: Trinity Press International, 2002), xv.
41 Charles Taylor *A Secular Age* (Cambridge, Massachusetts: The Belknap Press, 2007), 16.

meaning sourced in the divine. The texts stand behind and justify a faith tradition which, because it has its own conception of 'living well', has its own wisdom.[42] The wisdom of faith, like that of culture, has its heroes and heroines and these too acquire mythic status within the community of faith. Jesus is the *hero par excellence*. Others achieve heroic status because they are recognised as manifesting the qualities of Jesus in an exceptional way. Mary MacKillop is a heroine of faith whose narrative has great relevance within the contemporary Australian Catholic Church which is our immediate focus of interest. It is noteworthy that, as her narrative is made accessible, more heroes and heroines surface within the memory of the community, and this further reinforces the wisdom carried within it.

These two forms of wisdom, that of culture and that of faith, live together in creative tension, constantly challenging each other in making sense of everyday life. When students fail to understand this, they sometimes see them as alternatives, and feel pressured to make a choice between them, often prematurely. It is this that a Catholic curriculum seeks to offset by exploring the creative tensions inherent in this relationship, and showing how the relationship functions in making sense of life.

'...IN A WAY THAT IS MEANINGFUL TO THEM...'

Our contention is that the essential role of Catholic schools today is *to help young people make sense of their lives*, and that the dimensions of this task *need to be mapped by Catholic educators to a much greater extent than has been the case up until now.*[43] Young people are called on to make sense of their lives in difficult times. While making sense of life is a goal in its own right, it takes on added significance in the face of deep change and the often dysfunctional ways in which many young people attempt to cope with the demands this now places on them in Western societies. Too many accept the intellectual and moral fragmentation and associated relativism encountered in everyday life as defining a 'normal' state of affairs. It is not enough for an older generation to wring their hands about this; the challenge is to do something about it. If the Christian concept of mission, and its attendant demand to make God's Kingdom present within time, is to have any meaning, then it must include addressing this problem, not *for the young*, but *with the young*. This is the great moral challenge now facing the older generation who have the experience to know that 'normal' does

---

42 For an insightful treatment of the wisdom of the Christian faith community see Pope John Paul II 'Credo Ut Intellegam' Chapter 2 in *Faith and Reason*, 1998.

43 In saying this, we are indicating that we see the essential mission challenge here as one of hermeneutics (how people make sense of or interpret the world). In this we differ from Protestant missiologists such as Andrew Kirk and Lesslie Newbigin who see the mission challenge in epistemological terms (how people justify that what they know is true).

not necessarily have to be construed in the way young people think of it today. Young people do not, for example, have to remain with an unthinking acceptance that it is 'normal' for Australians to be excessive consumers of the earth's resources or for a significant proportion of their brothers and sisters to continue living in poverty and hunger. Such lack of understanding constitutes educational deprivation.

A state of meaninglessness is the antithesis of a search for wisdom, however inchoately this is understood. In this respect a Catholic curriculum has *a pastoral regard for the issue of meaning making* seeing it not as *a key competency*, but as *the key competency* in living wisely and faithfully.

'…LIVING IN A CULTURAL AND HISTORICAL CONTEXT…'

Students do not make sense of their lives with reference to abstractions. They are hard-wired to everyday life and the common stock of knowledge[44] needed to negotiate everyday life provided to them by their culture. They contribute significantly to developments occurring in everyday life as an older, less-technically literate generation now knows and has come to depend on, particularly when trying to exorcise the 'hazardous demons' seeking to inhibit and disrupt their access to the digital world! What students are not so aware of are the equally 'hazardous demons' embedded in cultural and historical dynamics at work in their society. These constantly reshape their everyday world and its taken-for-granted meanings and definition of 'normal', which adults know is 'far from normal' when judged against the tested traditions of meaning by which humans have come to make sense of their lives over the long haul.

A Catholic curriculum seeks to introduce students to these traditions in order to help them reinterpret the 'normal' and 'cool' of their everyday lives in line with a tested wisdom, aware that while this wisdom is itself under pressure as a source of meaning, it has within it the resources needed to withstand this pressure.

At the cultural level, globalisation and its consequent phenomena, urbanisation, mass migration and mass media, are forcing serious revision of the 'plan for living' that characterises every living culture – people's primary source of meaning and the repository of its practical wisdom. Equally, this plan is challenged by the religious pluralism of Western cultures and glaring deficiencies becoming evident in how 'the public square', so important in democratic societies, is now construed. The secular construction of the public square, a hallmark of modernity, is becoming less tenable as societies become multi-faith. This is providing not only a challenge for culture, but also for the way in which we understand faith itself.

---

44 Berger and Luckmann, 43–46 et al.

In terms of our present historical and cultural context much of the formal documentation dealing with the Church's understanding of the Catholic school is deficient, and this is for a number of reasons. Conceptually, it fails to secure its key terms so that it is difficult to discern what it actually means in practice. This fault is well illustrated in the statement that the task of the Catholic school is to 'effect an integration of faith and culture and faith and life'.[45] How is this to be interpreted in the absence of any clear understanding of what 'culture' means? Secondly, while the documentation is addressed to the global Church, it carries the presuppositions of a particular social location (the North Atlantic). To educators living in Australia, for instance, it often speaks to issues of an era that is now past. Thirdly, while the foundational document *The Catholic School* (1977) was formulated with reference to the documents of the Second Vatican Council (Vatican II), it ignores later developments in the Church's understanding of mission as this was formulated by Paul VI in *Evangelii Nuntiandi* (1975). Given that *The Catholic School* was written two years after the general synod on evangelisation, this seems inexplicable. However, having set off on its own path, no real correction has ever been made to alter course so that, as a body of teaching, the key documents on Catholic education still lack a coherent connection to Vatican II and post-Vatican II mission theology. As a consequence, the documentation is highly selective in its treatment of mission themes. Despite these limitations, it remains an important, if somewhat dated, source in any conversation about Catholic curriculum.[46] Historically, its trajectory was set in a world that was pre-PC, pre-digital, pre-global warming and does not engage the dilemmas of 'the postmodern condition' in a meaningful way.[47] This is part of the historical reality that Catholic teachers have to face in making sense of their lives in Catholic schools.

'…WITHIN THE LIFE-CHANCES THIS OFFERS AND THE CONSTRAINTS IT IMPOSES…'

Western cultures are currently caught up in two great movements. The first is *technological change,* occurring at an unprecedented rate, and bringing with it economic and social costs and benefits. One of the costs is global warming and the threat this poses to the whole natural order. Whether we realise it or not, global warming is *reshaping human consciousness* as people increasingly

---

45 Congregation for Catholic Education *The Catholic School*, 1977 #44.
46 The most accessibly written and contemporary of the documents is the 1997 statement by the Congregation for Catholic Education Catholic Schools on the Threshold of the Third Millennium.
47 Whilst also subject to the critique made above, *The Catholic School on the Threshold of the Third Millennium,* does provide some inspiring insights into the possibilities which exist when the connections between faith and life are taken seriously, and deserves close attention when dealing with the concepts and practicalities associated with Catholic curriculum (e.g. #14).

come to see themselves situated within the natural world and dependent on it, rather than as situated outside the natural world and consuming it. The wisdom and faith of the community have to be reframed to take note of this change in human consciousness and the aspirations that grow out of it. While technological change creates life-chances, it also imposes constraints that we now have to live within.

A second great movement has occurred in the intellectual order and is no less significant. This is the *dethroning of science as the major interpretive framework* in the Western intellectual tradition. The postmodern critique of the ideology dominant in modernity, that redefined 'knowledge' as 'science', equated 'reason' with 'scientific rationality', and classified 'faith' as 'irrational', has had an important impact on education at all levels. It is slowly redefining what is taken as 'the stock of common knowledge'.

Scientists are now pleading with politicians not to 'spin' the science of climate change because it is undermining public confidence in scientific research itself. Such a stance would have been unheard of even a generation ago. The dethroning of science also has costs and benefits. It creates lifechances by bringing to the fore a wider range of methods for exploring the complex problems that arise in modern societies, so moving enquiry away from the narrow focus on cause and effect that characterises scientific investigation. The scientific method breaks down when an effect, such as injustice, has multiple causes, or when a phenomenon cannot be 'objectified' as required by science as, for instance, happens when we study the culture of another people.

This second movement, however, acts as a constraint when it causes people to *lose confidence in the very notion of truth*, and, in particular, moral truth.[48] Without this confidence, wisdom loses much of its meaning and the idea of meaning itself becomes problematic. Such developments are part of 'the postmodern condition', the context in which young people now have to make sense of their lives. The status of 'truth', and the defence of truth, are particular difficulties in the West at the present time, and attract the attention of mission theologians, both Catholic and Protestant, who see *the construction of knowledge and the defence of truth as a new mission field.* This needs to attract the attention of educators as well.

Young people seek to make their way in life within a framework set somewhere between the life-chances and constraints of the dethroned, but still powerful ideology of modernity, and the often confusing, ambiguous and sometimes incoherent world of postmodernity. The allure of this latter world is that it canonises 'freedom from all traditions' as a serious option, without realising that this is simply creating a new and untested tradition

---

48 Pope John Paul II highlighted his concern about this in his encyclical letters Veritatis Splendor (The Splendour of the Truth) 1993 (which deals with moral truth), and Fides et Ratio (Faith and Reason) 1998.

that promises to be even more 'oppressive' than the traditions its seeks to replace. *There is no tradition-free place in which human life can be lived.* As Sociology 101 confirms, once a community forms, traditions emerge – that is the human condition!

'...IN ESTABLISHING THEIR IDENTITY AS INDIVIDUALS AND AS MEMBERS OF THE COMMUNITY.'

Every young person is caught up in the task of forming his or her identity. This developmental task is addressed while they are at school. Identity is both personally and socially constructed. Who I am is shaped by those around me in a process that goes on largely 'behind my back'. The process is tied to the phenomenology of the human person, to how human consciousness functions. If we could personalise this phenomenology it might run as follows:

> *As a Catholic, I think feel and behave in certain ways because I value the Catholic tradition as I understand it, and as it has been passed to me. My understanding is a product of my biography which includes not only my education, but also my experiences and those of my family, in living as part of this faith community with all the ups and downs this entails. While I hope the community will live up to its ideals, I am not totally surprised when it does not, and know the reasons why this is a possible outcome because the community is symbolic of myself. 'Being Catholic' operates at many levels as a consequence. It is part of who I am. It opens certain doors in closing others. It has led me to make choices many times over, and so has a taken-for-granted status that I live more or less happily with. I know that it does not provide me with the answers to all of life's challenges, but then nothing does. Its wisdom is enduring but provisional. It is a wisdom that underpins many of the things I value and am committed to and feel strongly about. Within this wisdom I have my heroes and heroines who for me stand as its legitimators.*

> *As an Australian, I think, feel and behave in certain ways. I value Australian culture and think of its plan for living as more or less successful, at least as I understand it. Being part of this culture provides me with a language of discourse and a common stock of knowledge, my 'recipe knowledge', for getting through life without having to think too much about it, for which I am grateful. Of course, I know there are deeper levels to our culture and occasionally pause to reflect on what these might be. These deeper levels seem to surface for me in celebrating the marker events of our culture, and when its norms are transgressed. This happens for me when refugees are demonised purely for political purpose and I realise this*

means they 'are not getting a fair go', yet a fair go is something intrinsic to Australian culture. Again, when someone represents the country in sport I do not expect them to come second because I have an innate belief that Australians will always 'punch above their weight', however unrealistic this belief might seem to outsiders. I also know that what is taken as 'recipe knowledge'[49] in my culture cannot be taken for granted overseas. This brings home to me that, as an Australian, I see the world in a particular way, that my construction of 'living well' is culturally located and while it is part of who I am, it is not necessarily part of who people are in other cultures. It makes us unique because we have our own wisdom and this is very important to us. If I want to convey this to others the easiest way is to tell them some of the stories in which it is embedded or to recount the deeds of some of my heroes.

I know that I am living at a given point in history of the West and understand this also as part of my biography. I have grown up in a Western culture at a particular time. I am heir to the history of ideas and dynamics that run through Western cultures and have shaped its amazing achievements. This is a common inheritance I share with people in many living cultures and it is not peculiar to Australian culture, although the way it is valued in Australia may well be unique. The defining part of this intellectual tradition is its academic disciplines which allow people to formally enquire into the problems and challenges of life, and arrive at some measure of 'living well', which is accepted across many societies and cultures. This enables me to think about what 'living well' means, both in itself and by comparison with the way people construe it in other Western cultures and in non-Western cultures. This form of exploration enables me to transcend the limits imposed by everyday living in Australia with its common stock of knowledge, and to put this in perspective. It also enables me to transcend the limits of being Catholic in a particular context, and to see myself as part of something much bigger. This sense of being part of a bigger story, and the options it opens up, is also part of who I am. It is something that I know and feel involved in, and as a consequence, it shapes what I value and what I am prepared to be committed to as a human person with a destiny, a story and something to offer others.

Education is concerned with how these three dimensions of human consciousness work together in a single biography, and in particular the relative importance they hold within that biography. At the phenomenological level, teachers in Catholic schools experience themselves, for better or worse, *as living in multiple worlds* – those of faith, of culture, and of the age in which

---

49 Peter Berger and Thomas Luckmann *The Social Construction of Reality* (New York: Anchor Books, 1967), 42.

they live. Each contributes to what teachers understand 'living wisely' can mean, because each of these worlds is defined by a worldview held by the communities that test, validate and value the traditions that shape them. The most accessible point of integration in these worldviews does not lie at the level of propositional knowledge, but *in the way the narratives through which they are transmitted overlap* and create meaning in the lives of individuals.

For young people the situation is slightly different caught up as they are in trying to understand how these public worldviews and their often complex inter-relationships function. In addition, they have to disentangle often competing positions as they try to develop their own interpretive framework. Teachers play a crucial role in helping them 'put life together'. It is important then that they not only have an understanding of the context and dynamics at work there, but also of what the situation must look like from the student's perspective.

Part B
CATHOLIC CURRICULUM HAS A HUMAN FACE

The starting point in any serious process of critical reflection is the *human experience of those involved* in it. Human experience defines a range of *facts* that our theoretical constructs have to address.

In our search to explain the facts of experience we generally attempt to construct a model capable of directing action. In Chapter 3 we argued that the Catholic curriculum can be thought of as a map. Examining the facts of experience determines *some important position markers* on that map. Our map is an example of a working model. Working models have two essential features:
- they are *sophisticated enough* to incorporate essential features of the phenomenon we want to understand
- they are *simple enough* to direct action.[50]

Our eventual aim is to create a working model of the Catholic curriculum. To do this, however, we need to bring together a number of matters besides the facts of experience.

One key fact in the Australian context is the introduction of the national curriculum. However, this is not the only factor, nor indeed the main one, determining why the Catholicity of the curriculum needs to be brought into sharper focus.

Our *starting point* in a new conversation is a survey of the different perspectives that teachers currently hold on the issue of 'Catholic curriculum'. We do this by looking at the context, or background, that shapes the views which teachers hold in Chapter 4. The contention is that

---

50 Gerard Egan *Change Agent Skills in Helping and Human Service Settings* (Moneterey: Brookes/Cole Publishing, 1985), 6.

teachers are living and teaching in an era of what sociologists call 'deep change', where something fundamental is changing in the culture that people rely on in order to make sense of their lives. Teachers have to respond to the reality of teaching in an era of deep change, so understanding the nature of this deep change is relevant to our conversation and provides important markers in reframing a conversation about Catholic curriculum.

Our students are growing up in this era of deep change. For them this does not represent a new situation. It is all they have ever known, and so is taken as defining what is 'normal'. As a result, their responses can often puzzle us, particularly if we have limited appreciation of what their life-world looks like *from the inside*. The ways in which they make sense of the situation, which for them is 'normal' is clearly important to our project. Their experiences have been tracked in a number of important studies and we survey the findings of these in Chapter 5. There are two important elements in a conversation about Catholic curriculum in this research – how students 'see the world' and how they understand the construction of knowledge.

As we move through the issues raised in Part B, three concepts come into focus. These are 'culture', 'worldview' and 'meaning making'. In Part C we seek to secure the meaning of these terms by calling on the insights of cultural anthropology, psychology and mission anthropology.

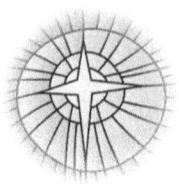

4
EDUCATING IN AN ERA OF DEEP CHANGE

The many conversations we have had with Catholic teachers working across a range of schools in Australia, New Zealand, the UK and the USA have played a significant part in shaping the contents of this book.

THE LIVED EXPERIENCE OF TEACHERS

As these teachers have reflected on the factors that shape their contemporary experiences, they have commonly spoken in terms of the following:
- the *multiple, and increasing, demands* of shouldering responsibility for redressing the impact of social inequality
- the development of the view within society that *education is another product* to be consumed within the marketplace
- pressure as government policy demands from schools *greater educational 'accountability'*, and a degree of frustration at the crude methods used in achieving this
- the demand by government that schools address *'public values'*, as determined and expressed by government
- issues that arise from the *greater role technology plays in education* wherein teachers often feel themselves to be less capable than many of their students
- the recognition that *students think and learn in different ways*, reflecting differences in their gifts and abilities and the implications of this for classroom practice
- the expanding range of *problems encountered in the classroom* arising from medical conditions or caused by poor parenting in unstable homes
- the increasingly *diverse range of attitudes* parents bring to their partnership with schools
- a more *litigious and combative attitude among parents* with a consequent narrowing of the activities in which schools are prepared to engage
- the *increasing number of students with developmental disorders and special learning needs* presenting in schools

- the importance of *clarifying expectations within the Church community about what is possible* in Catholic schooling
- the strategic demands created by *the different levels of religious faith among staff* and the impact of this in pursuing the mission of the school
- *differing understandings about curriculum and pedagogy*
- the *powerful influence schools* have when they function *as learning communities* involving staff, students and families.

These factors combine to make teaching a challenging and intellectually demanding profession. The list reflects in large measure the consequences 'on the ground' of the changes that are occurring in the life-situation and worldview of all involved in Catholic education– students, parents and particularly the teachers themselves. It is this theme that we want to explore.

THE EXPERIENCE OF DEEP CHANGE

The experiences noted above often contribute to a sense among teachers that *things that were once seen as being together are breaking apart*, that something fundamental is changing which, while it is hard to put your finger on, is nonetheless real. Some educators find this situation exciting, others disconcerting, but an increasing number find it overwhelming.

Sociologists describe the situation in which the fundamentals holding a culture or a community together begin to erode as the experience of *'deep change'*. This experience is generated by the mega-phenomena shaping our present age – globalisation, advanced pluralism and secularisation. There seems little doubt that the changes underway are reframing the fabric of teachers' lives by redefining what we now accept as 'normal', both in the classroom and in teaching. These three mega-phenomena constitute a primary 'given' in any attempt to give meaning to an authentic Catholic curriculum.

The experience of leading and teaching in a situation that is demanding, complex and at times very confusing, forces people to respond creatively, particularly when they are faced almost daily with the demands of educating in what is often uncharted territory. In order to cope with new demands, many experienced educators find themselves re-examining *the foundational beliefs and values that underpin their commitment to teaching* and that make their work meaningful.[51] It is perhaps not too surprising in this context that Parker Palmer's book *The Courage to Teach* became a best-seller.[52]

---

51 See, for instance, the work of Robert Starratt in *Centering Educational Administration: Cultivating Meaning, Community, Responsibility* (New York: Routledge 2003) and in *Building an Ethical School* (New York: RoutledgeFalmer, 1994).
52 Parker Palmer *The Courage to Teach* (San Francisco, California: John Wiley, 1998).

THE MAIN DRIVERS OF DEEP CHANGE

The driving forces of 'deep change' are secularisation, globalisation and the rapid rise of pluralism, (cultural, religious and ideological), all phenomena with far-reaching consequences. Deep change impacts on the framework within which we interpret and make sense of our lives, our worldview, causing it to change in ways that we often struggle to comprehend. It affects how we feel, how we see the world and what we value. It adds new chapters to the narrative by which we identify who we are.

Historians, sociologists, cultural anthropologists and educators argue over whether the experience of deep change is causing *human consciousness itself to undergo a significant transformation*. In this context, 'postmodern' remains a controversial term. What is certain is that deep change leads to new levels of human uncertainty on the one hand, and aspiration on the other.

The three mega-phenomena named above as drivers of deep change are reshaping the social and ideological environments in which we live and teach. They are also reshaping our culture in important ways,[53] and this projects schooling, along with the other institutions of society, into a new space.

Many teachers find the experience of being in this 'new space' disorienting, some find it oppressive, while others see in it the seeds of a new hope, a call to human ingenuity and creativity. For many Australian teachers, the real hope of the national curriculum is that it will bring some stability into what they see as an inherently unstable situation. While it will certainly help, it seems doubtful that such a hope can ever be fully realised in the foreseeable future. The experience of deep change is forcing school and school system leaders to re-contextualise, re-conceptualise and re-affirm their mission.[54]

We now briefly review each of the three phenomena that generate deep change, focusing our attention on the impact they have on teaching and learning.

Globalisation's many faces

Globalisation refers to the complex ways in which the world is now networked together economically, socially and intellectually through modern technology. It has many faces. Here we consider three which have an increasingly important impact on education: the knowledge economy; living in a globalised world; and the impact of globalisation on the migrant experience.

---

53 We find mission anthropologist Louis Luzbetak's definition of culture as 'the more or less successful plan for living' developed by a people in order to flourish in their environment to be a useful one. Louis Luzbetak *The Church and Cultures Revised Edition* (Maryknoll, New York: Orbis, 1988), 156.
54 This theme is developed by Robert Starratt in *Refocusing School Leadership: Foregrounding Human Development Throughout the Work of the School* (New York: Routledge, 2010).

Globalisation and the knowledge economy

One of the immediate consequences of globalisation is that schools are asked to take on a new role – that of main driver of the *'knowledge economy'*. They are asked to do this for a number of reasons not least because the life-chances of young people are now shaped within this economy.

The locus of the knowledge economy is the city, or the large provincial town. As a consequence, urbanisation is now a global phenomenon, and it is estimated that by the end of the first quarter of this millennium, three quarters of the world's population will live in cities.[55] A major consequence of globalisation in Australia has been a 'flight from the bush' which, given the cultural significance of 'the bush' in Australian culture, has already resulted in the loss of an important element in the local cultural heritage.

While globalisation creates life-chances, it often does so outside traditional patterns of employment and job security. The global nature of modern economies reduces people's sense of security and in consequence *they feel vulnerable*. This is because their employment prospects and job security are seen as controlled by forces outside their control. While this has been a default condition in the developing world, it is now becoming the case in the developed world as well. The global financial crisis of 2008-09 heightened this sense of vulnerability. This condition has an impact on how people see themselves and what they aspire to. Teachers play an important role in helping young people source their inner wealth, discover their talents, and thus develop the robust identity needed to counter the pervasive sense of personal vulnerability.

Globalisation creates inequity particularly for those *who lack access to the technology that drives it*. It entrenches privilege. It opens up opportunities for the well educated, but reduces life-chances for those most in need of them. As a counter-balance to this trend, educational policies and programs seek to provide *equity in opportunity*. Teachers are on the frontline when it comes to effective action to address this important social justice concern.

The technologies that drive globalisation enable *young people to live in virtual communities where once they lived in real communities*. This change brings with it new threats such as the internet predator and the cyber bully, while the ready access students now have to pornography via the internet has the capacity to distort their understanding of human sexuality. These emerging factors pose significant new challenges for teachers committed to providing them with an education that is holistic.

---

55 Benigno P. Beltran 'Searching for God in the Asphalt Jungles: Towards a Trinitarian Theology of the City' in Thomas Malipurathu and L. Stanislaus *The Church in Mission* (Gujarat: Gujarat Shaitya Prakash, 2002), 28.

Living in a globalised world

Young people are aware that they now live somewhere between the *global* and the *local*. While some find this unsettling, others find it exhilarating. One consequence has been that overseas exposure and exchange programs are now seen as part and parcel of secondary schooling. Overseas travel has become a rite of passage for an increasingly large number of young Australians. When taken together with a growing realisation of the need to protect the environment, these developments promote an understanding among young people that they are 'global citizens'. They are more conscious than older generations, who were denied such opportunities, that they live in a globalised world. Teachers play a significant role in ensuring that the opportunity to travel is open to students, thus facilitating the broadening of perspective that travel brings. This provides an important way of shaping the worldview of young people, because the purposeful encounter with new cultural situations really *challenges the presuppositions we rely on in making sense of the world in our local context.*

The impact of globalisation on the migrant experience

Globalisation inverts our sense of distance and time. Distance is now thought of in terms of the question – how long to get there,? rather than – how far away is it? Modern transport systems, particularly air transport, shrink distances and enable people from different cultures to mix on an unprecedented scale. As a consequence, globalisation has radically altered the *migrant experience*. When people migrate to a new country they are no longer cut off from their country of origin or their community of origin. By accessing the new communication technologies they have the means, through use of the internet, Skype and similar services, to remain in immediate contact with their families in the home country. It is thus possible for them *to live in two worlds simultaneously.*

While this sounds like a benefit, perceptive teachers have come to realise that for the many young people caught up in the migrant experience, the situation can be profoundly unsettling, distorting their sense of personal identity. Many young migrants now live suspended in a cultural no-man's-land, somewhere between the world they left behind and the new world they have entered, or to put it another way, between the worldview of their home and the worldview of their peers. They are often seen as being 'at risk' in the school setting. Teachers provide the pastoral care programs that seek to reduce this level of risk. *A good deal of the dignity currently associated with the teaching profession derives from being on the frontline in addressing many of the new social issues created by globalisation.*

Modern pluralism: Loosening a grip on the foundations of certainty

The increasingly plural nature of our society is highlighted in public debates about migration, tolerance, religion and social values. Modern pluralism has both a *cultural dimension* and an *ideological dimension*.

Cultural dimension of pluralism

Australia is regarded internationally as a successful multi-cultural society.[56] There seems a genuine appreciation in this country that people from other cultures can, and do, make a positive contribution to national life. Schools have played a major role in contributing to this outcome. While Catholic schools exist primarily to educate Catholic children, this has never been an exclusive option. The 'mix' of students in Catholic schools in Australia has changed over the past two decades, particularly in rural settings where the proportion of Catholic students has generally declined. The composition of the school population is an important variable shaping curriculum, particularly in its religious dimension. This is a matter of concern for those responsible for the governance of Catholic schools.

Ideological dimension of pluralism

'Ideological pluralism' refers to the presence of competing worldviews in contemporary society resulting in a pluralism of values. This has proved highly problematic for Catholic educators because one of its consequences is that many students seem to experience life as living in a *values supermarket*. They work from the assumption that *they are free to choose their values as if such choices have no implications*. What the prevailing culture fails to prepare them for is that to opt for one value often means excluding another. It is at this level that a discipline-based curriculum starts to break down. Value is established by appeal to a moral ideal. This is why science struggles with the notion of value. Its focus on rational inquiry into nature is geared to the discovery of truth about nature, not to the discovery of values that transcend nature. By its own means of enquiry science cannot establish what is good. It can determine, within the terms of its own axioms and processes, whether propositions are true or false, not whether they are good or bad. The latter requires a different sort of enquiry.[57]

---

56 In Australian discourse the term 'multi-cultural' does not carry the negative connotations found in some European countries. This is because, as a social phenomenon, it has developed in a way that did not seriously polarise popular opinion. Opposition to multiculturalism was largely disarmed by Al Grassby, the colourful Commonwealth Government minister responsible for negotiating the transition from 'white Australia' to 'multi-cultural Australia' during the Whitlam Labor government in the early 1970s. His reputed quip, to the following effect, has passed into Australian folklore 'the first Australians were black, the first migrants were white, and not up to much, so what's the big deal?'

57 For a helpful discussion see J. Andrew Kirk *The Future of Reason, Science and Faith: Following Modernity and Post-Modernity* (Aldershot: Ashgate Publishing, 2007).

Values, however, do not exist in isolation; they are nested within a worldview which gives them a legitimation sourced in a conception of what 'human flourishing' entails. As a consequence, the 'freedom' apparently on offer in the values supermarket often proves quite illusory when its consequences eventually work themselves out in real life. Dealing with the challenges of ideological pluralism is a major task in the mission of the Catholic school and certainly a central concern in any discussion of the Catholic nature of its curriculum, precisely because *the worldview of faith adds a dimension to our understanding of 'human flourishing'*.

The search for social cohesion

In a pluralist society schools are increasingly being asked to become sources of *intellectual and social cohesion,* helping young people to understand their world, their place in it, and the responsibilities that flow from this understanding. This theme is taken up in the new national curriculum under the rubric of 'general competencies' and more specifically in Catholic schools through formal courses in Religious Education, and in some places, through an introduction to ethics or philosophy.

The case for developing intellectual and social cohesion in the face of modern pluralism is well argued by American educator Robert Starratt who suggests that public education today should help young people *cultivate meaning, community and responsibility*.[58] He argues cogently that these three elements are now integrally connected in any education that claims to be holisitic. In effect, Starratt is mapping out the elements in a worldview within which young people can flourish. This is a vital discussion since it is not possible to talk of human flourishing without reference to a worldview.

Our experience in both teacher and leader development programs in Catholic school systems suggests that many Catholic teachers are not clear about the worldview they appeal to in making decisions. Their trust in older religious certainties has eroded and some are quite suspicious of what have been proposed as alternatives. Many clearly share a view, widely held in the community, that institutional authority is to be treated sceptically on matters of belief and value. This awareness has been heightened among Catholics by the sexual abuse scandal where the wrong represented by the abuse seems compounded by the way certain Church leaders have subsequently responded to it. In the context of deep change, institutions are seen to struggle to distinguish clearly between the good they wish to advance and institutional self-interest. The challenge identified so clearly in this case pertains to all institutional life including that of the school.

---

58 Robert Starratt *Centering Educational Administration: Cultivating Meaning, Community, Responsibility* (Mahwah: Lawrence Erlbaum Associates, 2003).

Just as our *educational context* is forcing teachers to look at their foundational beliefs about teaching and learning, the *cultural context* is also forcing many to reappraise the presuppositions on which they think and act. This is a defining characteristic of the 'postmodern' experience. Elsewhere we have argued the case that developing skills in theological reflection, that is being able to 'do theology', is important in reappraising the way in which we understand and engage with our world.[59]

The advent of modern pluralism highlights a challenge faced by Catholic educators in helping students identify, analyse, critique and reshape the worldview into which they have been socialised by virtue of growing up in a certain community, so that they can determine truth from falsehood, good from bad, and right from wrong. This is a further important element to consider in discussing the shape of a Catholic curriculum.

Secularisation: Friend or foe?

Secularisation is a particularly complex notion because it operates at multiple levels and is understood in a range of ways. One common construction of secularisation is as *the process by which institutional religion loses its authority in public life and religion becomes a matter of private choice*. The claim is that secularisation weakens institutional religion by denying it space in public life and as a consequence institutional religion is in decline.[60] This construction of secularisation is often generalised to claim that 'the Church' and 'religion' are in decline. Data on church attendance in the West tends to supports this view. While the claim may be true in the West, it can by no means be substantiated universally.

Secularisation is a complex phenomenon that has three major facets: the secularisation of knowledge, the secularisation of social institutions, and the secularisation of politics. All three have implications for education and impact on the classroom.

Secularisation of knowledge

The disciplines schools teach, the curriculum content, and the values teachers are asked to inculcate as part of the public curriculum, are *secular by design*. The Christian churches have no in-principle objection to this situation, since academic disciplines follow their own recognised methods

---

59 This theme is expanded in some detail in our book *Explorers, Guides and Meaning Makers: Mission Theology for Catholic Educators*. See also Evelyn and James Whitehead *Method in Ministry* (Oxford: Sheed & Ward, 1995) or Clemens Sedmak *Doing Local Theology* (Maryknoll, New York: Orbis, 2002).

60 This understanding of secularisation conflates religion with particular forms of institution. The evidence of several recent studies indicates that while some contemporary Catholics are somewhat disenchanted with the present institutional form of Catholicism, they still identify themselves as Catholic. They see the need for reform. Against this other Catholics see the present institutional form as a defining feature of Catholicism. For them reform is unimaginable.

in the construction of knowledge and the search for the truth of things. The autonomy of these methods is acknowledged.[61] In the modern academy the *secularisation of knowledge* is a presumed state of affairs. What often goes unacknowledged, however, is that the methods of modern scholarship *limit what is studied and this carries over into what is and can be known.*

The majority of teachers in Catholic schools are trained in disciplines which are methodologically secular in their construction of knowledge and operate from secular assumptions. When it comes to helping students construct knowledge many teachers simply fail to recognise that this is the case. They do not see that the assumptions they take as 'normal' have limits. Put another way, teachers as a consequence of their education and culture most commonly operate from the *modern mindset*. For most, this is a *default condition*. The postmodern critique of this mindset, as we shall see later is, fundamentally, that the modern mindset is selective in the questions it asks, and is oblivious to other important questions.

Conversations about Catholic curriculum must take into account the teachers' backgrounds. This means acknowledging the limits that the secularisation of knowledge places on the way they search for what is true, right and good. A Catholic curriculum seeks to pose *questions essential to living that the academic disciplines simply fail to address.*

Secularisation of social institutions

The second facet of secularisation is an inevitable consequence of the rising complexity of modern societies. At the beginning of modernity popular political expectations about health, education and social welfare were quite limited. The provision of such services was understood to fall within the 'charitable activities' carried out by the churches which Christians supported through almsgiving and tithing. The churches viewed the provision of these services as integral to their mission.

However, as political structures developed with the creation of the modern state, and as populations expanded, the demand for services grew, particularly in the expanding cities. The state became the only agency in society capable of providing mass education, health and social welfare services.[62] The state took over major responsibility for providing these social functions by developing its own institutions. Public institutions formed in this way were later split up due to increased specialisation. This occurred generally on *the basis of specialised secular knowledge*. Today the three social functions – education, health and welfare – constitute the 'stuff' of political

---

61 See for instance Pope John Paul II's *Faith and Reason* or Vatican II's *Pastoral Constitution on the Church in the Modern World*, both of which cover this matter in some detail.
62 In revolutionary France, for instance, the cost of providing these services was initially paid for with income derived from selling monasteries and other Church property acquired compulsorily, or simply appropriated, by the newly formed French state.

life. The churches' mission work in these three fields has continued, but in a quite limited form, and often subsidised by the state.

In Australia, this 'face' of secularisation has been driven largely by pragmatic political considerations. As a consequence, one-fifth of the school-age population is now educated in Catholic schools substantially funded by the government. Consequently, Catholic education provides the Church with a substantial presence in the public square. The Catholic school is now sponsored by both the Church and the state, the latter exercising a significant influence over its programs, particularly its curriculum. This face of secularisation is more closely linked to the development of the modern political system than the decline of religion.

Secularisation as a political phenomenon

As a political phenomenon secularisation has roots deep in the early history of modern Europe and of the USA. It developed, in large part, to resolve long-lasting and ongoing tensions, firstly between the Church and leaders of modern political states, and secondly among religious groups within these states competing for influence and the allegiance of people as the modern world developed. A principal characteristic of the modern European state was that political decisions were justified primarily by appeal to the *authority of reason*, rather than by appeal to the *religious authority* of the King or of the Church. Politics came to be seen as an area with its own autonomy, operating independently of ecclesiastical control or influence.

This change represented a decisive shift from pre-modern times, one which Catholic Church leaders initially struggled to accept. The leaders of the Catholic Church, which had been a major political player in pre-modern and in early modern Europe, rather painfully came to the view that *as an institution it should exercise no direct role in the political decision-making process of governments*; rather, its role was to *establish the moral principles* on which practical political decisions were made.

Limits to secularisation

The secularisation of politics raises many challenges for Western leaders at the international level when the problems they are addressing *are religious in origin*. These often arise in countries that *do not hold the Western view that politics and religion should be disconnected*. Leaders in the West find that, in espousing secularisation as a political ideal, they have limited their capacity to resolve such international tensions, except by the use of force. They lack both an adequate framework and a language in which to conduct the dialogues necessary to bring about peace. Tony Blair's *Faith Foundation* has been set up, in part, to address this problem.

The secularisation of politics has pursued two distinct objectives: *freedom for religion* (soft secularism) and *freedom from religion* (hard secularism). The first form which is tolerant of religion is found in countries such as Australia and the USA; the second, which is often atheistic and anti-religious, is more commonly encountered in Europe, but has its advocates, the secularists, in this country as well.

Secularisation is not to be confused with *secularism* which is an ideology based on the premise that *all religion is an illusion, a form of superstition, or an earlier stage in our cultural evolution,* that should have no place in public life, including in education, health and social welfare. Secularists, while still a minority in this country, are increasingly strident in their well-publicised attacks on religions and religious faith, particularly the Christian faith. Since their views are highly controversial and divisive, they receive wide coverage in the media. Secularism is rapidly becoming the new form of bigotry.

MEANING MAKING IN A CHANGING WORLD

Political leaders of various persuasions, as well as educational leaders, struggle in responding to the demands of the changing context in which we now live. Faced with a complex and uncertain situation, they seek to provide leadership increasingly through the exercise of tighter bureaucratic control. The war on terrorism has exacerbated this dynamic. An important aspect of this response has been to reshape public policy on education within a narrow ideology which, implicitly or explicitly, seeks to take control of the curriculum under the guise of 'accountability'.

What now seems clear to many teachers is that *the agenda for schooling is increasingly being set outside the profession,* a situation which many see as unsustainable in the longer term. The new approach is offensive to many teachers who entered the profession to make a difference in the lives of the young people they teach. They envisaged doing this by helping them make sense of the world in which they find themselves, developing their talents in order to maximise the life-chances that education creates, so as to find fulfilment and happiness in their lives.

The meaning teachers give to their work is often incompatible with a view of education in which the goals of instruction are defined principally by testing and where *the critical skill is the ability to achieve well on tests.* In the eyes of many teachers an over-reliance on testing as the main driver of learning *trivialises both their profession and their lives.*

The great challenge facing teachers today is making sense of the context in which they find themselves in order to help their charges cultivate meaning in their lives at a time when the *very foundations on which meaning has been built for previous generations are shifting. Teachers have to make sense of the world in which they live and work if they are to help students make sense of their world.*

In this chapter we have looked at factors shaping the lived experience of teachers, the context in which they teach, and the forces driving deep change in that context. This adds an existential dimension to our discussion of a Catholic curriculum. We next look at how students are coping with learning in this era of deep change and the issues such an enquiry surfaces for our conversation about Catholic curriculum.

PRINCIPLE 4: THE CONTEXTUAL PRINCIPLE

A Catholic curriculum is formulated in response to an understanding of:
- the historical and cultural contexts in which it is implemented
- the dynamics shaping these contexts

A Catholic curriculum attempts to respond to the needs which arise as these dynamics are played out in local contexts.

COMMENT

A Catholic curriculum is geared to the context in which it is implemented. The current context is being reshaped by globalisation and the technologies that make this possible, by secularisation and the issues this raises in a multi-faith society, and by advancing pluralism. These are all complex phenomena which generate significant local needs, both in terms of understanding the phenomena themselves and the impact they have on people's attitudes, values and behaviours. A Catholic curriculum is responsive to these needs as they arise in local contexts.

This principle implies an ongoing need to *recontextualise curriculum*. It applies to the provisions of the public curriculum and to the Religious Education curriculum. However, it is not possible to re-contexualise curriculum if teachers lack an understanding of the context which generates the need to recontextualise it in the first place.

CONTINUING THE CONVERSATION

4.1 What are the most evident manifestations of globalisation in the lives of your students?

4.2 How are the needs, which these manifestations generate, addressed within the curriculum at present?

4.3 How does secularisation impact on the work of your school? How does the school seek to offset the influence of its more extreme form – secularism?

4.4 What are the faces of pluralism that most impact on the teaching-learning process in your school?

4.5 How are these addressed within the curriculum at present? How adequate is this treatment?

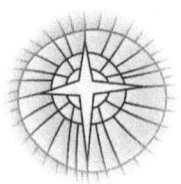

5
GROWING UP IN AN ERA OF DEEP CHANGE

If the contemporary world is complex and confusing for adults, including teachers, how does it appear to the students, and how do they customarily respond? What do we know about the way young people view their world? How should such knowledge frame the way we think about curriculum in Catholic schools? These are not simple questions but they are important to our conversation. We begin by outlining the macro factors that are shaping how young people see the world, then detail a range of research projects which explore the area, and finish by drawing together common issues identified in this research. The chapter draws attention to themes and topics that will be opened up in subsequent chapters.

THE WORLDVIEW OF YOUNG PEOPLE: LOOKING AT THE BIG PICTURE

There have been a number of important studies done in recent years in Australia, the USA and the UK exploring how young people see the world and react to what they see. While some deal with 'the worldview of young people' directly,[63] most address the subject tangentially under headings such as 'the spirituality of young people', 'the religious views of young people' or 'how young people put life together'.[64]

---

63 E.g. Walt Mueller *Engaging the Soul of Youth Culture: Bridging Teen Worldviews and Christian Truth* (Downers Grove: InterVarsity Press, 2006), and Leslie Francis and Mandy Robbins *Urban Hope and Spiritual Health: The Adolescent Voice* (Peterborough: Epworth, 2005).
64 Australian studies include Philip Hughes *Putting Life Together: Findings from Australian Youth Spirituality Research* (Fairfield: Fairfield Press, 2007); Michael Mason, Andrew Singleton and Ruth Webber *The Spirit of Generation Y: Young People's Spirituality in a Changing Australia* (Mulgrave: John Garratt, 2007); Marcellin Flynn and Magdalena Mok *Catholic Schools 2000: A Longitudinal Study of Year 12 Students in Catholic Schools* (Sydney: New South Wales Catholic Education Commission, 2002). US studies include Dean Hoge, William Dinges, Mary Johnson and Juan Gonzales *Young Adult Catholics: Religion in a Culture of Choice* (Notre Dame Indiana: Notre Dame University Press, 2001); Christian Smith with Melinda Lundquist Denton *Soul Searching: The Religious and Spiritual Lives of American Teenagers* (New York: Oxford University Press, 2005). UK studies include David Hay *Something There: The Biology of the Human Spirit* (Philadelphia: Templeton Foundation Press, 2007); Leslie Francis, Mandy Robbins and John

The churches have been major sponsors of this research carried out largely by researchers and academics whose field is sociology, particularly the sociology of religion. Taken together, the data from these studies paints a remarkably consistent picture.

Studies that explore the 'worldview' of young people tend to use the term quite loosely. While we will deal with the notion of worldview from the perspective of cultural anthropology in a degree of depth in a later chapter, some preliminary comments are called for at this stage. At the popular level 'worldview' is often taken to mean how people *perceive* the world in which they live, or as the 'lens' through which they see it. In this understanding worldview is a *subjective construct*. It is also a *cognitive construct*. Each person has a worldview and this is an important co-ordinate of his or her personal identity. For the present, we will accept this understanding as a useful, if somewhat inadequate, way of understanding *personal worldview*.

Worldview can be used in another sense as when we have talked about the *worldview of a culture*, the *worldview of an age*, or the *worldview of a faith tradition*. Here 'worldview' takes on a communal or corporate character. It is something held in common by a community or a society. The concept has a sociological and/or an anthropological meaning and indicates *a shared interpretive framework*. Its locus is objective, not subjective, reality because through it the community legitimates an interpretation of reality which makes a claim on things 'as they really are'.

Cultural anthropologists, such as Paul Hiebert, locate the *cultural worldview* at the very heart of a culture[65] where it confers communal identity, is passed from generation to generation, and is generally embodied in narrative form. The cultural worldview includes *presuppositions* that are thought to be true and which underpin important cultural values. The cultural worldview gains its legitimacy from the historical experience of a people, and is the most difficult level of culture to change since it is largely held below the level of consciousness and surfaces mainly when the culture is in crisis or under threat.

In Australian culture, for instance, there is an unshakable belief that everyone is entitled to 'a fair go'. This belief is transmitted via *a number of narratives* told in the many communities making up the society the convict experience, the goldfield experience, the experiences of Indigenous Australians, the post-war migrant experience, the Vietnamese boat people experience, and so on. Belief in 'a fair go' mobilises people to action in the face of manifest injustice. If a visitor asked an Australian in the street, why

---

Astley (eds) *Religion, Education and Adolescents: International Empirical Perspectives* (Cardiff: University of Wales Press, 2005).
65 See for example Chapter 2 'Characteristics of Worldviews' in Paul Hiebert *Transforming Worldviews: an Anthropological Understanding of How People Change* (Grand Rapids: Baker Academic, 2008), 31–69.

everyone should 'get a fair go', many would struggle to provide a coherent answer and find the question somewhat strange. The most probable answer would be something like 'because that's the way we are here!'

The *worldview of the age* influences most cultural worldviews in a particular historical period. Since the mid-18th century, cultures in the West have been under the influence of the *modern worldview*. Since the 1970s, this worldview has been under fire from proponents of the so-called 'postmodern worldview'. The vast scale of human migration at the present time brings many people into Western cultures from countries whose worldview has much in common with what can be described in terms of Western experience as 'pre-modern'. It is important to note that, when we are using terms like 'modern worldview' or 'pre-modern worldview', we are not making a judgement on the various merits of one compared with another. For the present, it is sufficient to say that all three – the pre-modern, the modern and the postmodern – proceed on *different sets of presuppositions and beliefs* which, for those who hold them, are taken as *self-evidently true*.

Finally, religions have a worldview – an understanding of what it means to be human, of human destiny and of the meaning of history that is presumed to be true. The shape of this worldview evolves over time as circumstances change. For instance, the changing human context created by globalisation is having an important bearing on how the Catholic Church understands its identity and mission.[66] Again, the Church community presently struggles to develop an appropriate theological framework to understand and address its mission in multi-faith Western societies particularly in regions of Europe, once the home of Christianity. This requires new developments in the Catholic worldview as older presuppositions have proved inadequate to the task.

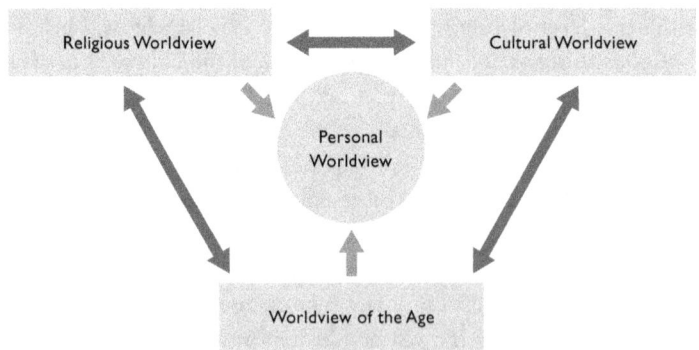

FIGURE 5.1 Influences at work in forming a personal worldview

66 Pope Benedict XVI addressed the implications of globalisation in his encyclical *Caritas in Veritate*, 2009.

One of the major challenges young people face today is attempting to *construct a personal worldview* at a time when there is *radical instability* in the three worldviews that we normally draw on as resources in this task. It is perhaps no wonder that many are quite confused about what they believe and are quite suspicious of offers of help in resolving this confusion, particularly from institutions in which they have only limited confidence. The complexity of the situation they face is represented schematically in Figure 5.1.

Today's young people are attempting to make sense of their lives in a world in which the cultural worldview, the religious worldview, and the worldview of the age are all under pressure due to the combined impact of globalisation, pluralisation and secularisation. As we noted in speaking of the situation of teachers, what makes the situation more complex is that these three worldviews tend to influence each other as they change.

ACQUIRING A PERSONAL WORLDVIEW

Young people initially gain a personal worldview as part of their enculturation. Without necessarily realising it, they acquire elements of the worldviews that shape the society in which they live – those of their culture, their age and, for many, the religious faith into which they were born. As they develop, the process of education helps them bring selected elements of these worldviews to consciousness in order to be examined, critiqued, better understood and consciously appropriated. Education plays an important role in consolidating a person's worldview. It is often construed in terms of 'passing on a cultural heritage'. This task is difficult enough in stable times. It is very complex in unstable times such as the present, and empathy for the situation of young people is a necessary pre-requisite in educating them.

A further difficulty arises from the fact that in the secular West *the legitimacy of all religious worldviews is called into question*. Many students grow up in an atmosphere in which a pervasive secularism inhabits the home, the workplace, their forms of entertainment, etc. The situation is represented schematically in Figure 5.2.

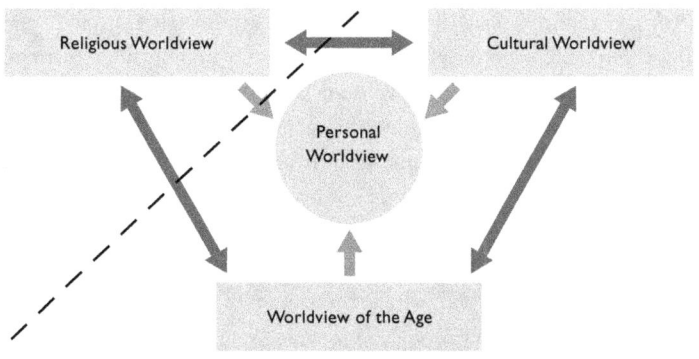

FIGURE 5.2 Personal worldview in the construction of modernity

Many young people now grow up in a cultural environment that ignores, represses, suppresses, or is often hostile to, any religious worldview, generally portrayed as 'conservative' or 'fundamentalist'. Religion is excluded from public discussion to such an extent that, for increasing numbers of young people, the language associated with religious traditions *loses its capacity to convey meaning*. It is foreign to them. They hear the words but take little note of them because this is not language they customarily use.

Nearly all major studies into the worldview of young people conducted in the last decade have noted the limited ability of young people to use traditional religious language to describe or even discuss experiences that they understand as 'spiritual'. This finding has bearing on how teachers present the worldview of faith to students.

MAJOR STUDIES INTO THE WORLDVIEW OF YOUNG PEOPLE

What, then, is the evidence base regarding the worldview of young people? What frameworks exist to understand their situation? While there have been a number of large-scale studies into how young people see the world, as cited above, two are of particular relevance in answering the questions posed. The first, the *National Study of Youth and Religion* (NSYR Project), was carried out in the USA under the leadership of Christian Smith, a sociologist based at the Catholic Notre Dame University in Indiana, and his associates. This is a longitudinal, three-stage project, the first stage of which was carried out in 2003–2004 and reported in 2005 as *Soul Searching: The Religious and Spiritual Lives of American Teenagers*.

The second project is the *Generation Y Study* conducted in Australia in 2003–2006 and reported in 2007. The *Generation Y Study* adopted a similar methodology to the NSYR study, even using some of its materials. The two studies differed in their target audience. The first stage of the NSYR Project focused on adolescents. The second and third stages of the study were completed in 2007 and reported in 2009 as *Souls in Transition: The Religious and Spiritual Lives of Emerging Adults*. This traced the religious and spiritual development of a large proportion of the young people who participated in stage one, but by then they were aged 18–23 were classified as 'emerging adults'. The composite study is able to map the views of adolescents and follow them as they make the transition to emerging adulthood.

The Australian *Generation Y Study* focused on young people aged 13 to 24 divided up into four groups for the purpose of analysis, two of these corresponding to the adolescent cohort in the NSYR study and two to the 'emerging adults' cohort.[67] Both studies used face to face interviews as a

---

67 The study incorporates some 260 personal interviews, 1200 telephone surveys, and 3000 surveys.

major data source. The comments of participants provided important clues in understanding the significance of quantitative data obtained through telephone surveys. The *Generation Y Study* had two components: a 'core project' and a 'schools' project'. The majority of respondents in the latter component were drawn from Lutheran and Catholic secondary schools, with a smaller sample from government schools.

The research team members were divided on the framework within which the data should be reported. As a consequence, the data is analysed within two quite different frameworks resulting in two reports: *The Spirit of Generation Y: Young People's Spirituality in a Changing Australia* (Mason, Singleton and Webber, 2007) and *Putting Life Together: The Findings from Australian Youth Spirituality Research* (Hughes, 2007). Philip Hughes' report, importantly for us, focuses on the school-age group which allows ready comparison with results from the NSYR study and studies in the UK.

The Spirit of Generation Y

The *Generation Y Study* was sponsored by a consortium of Catholic school systems.[68] *The Spirit of Generation Y* report suggests that youth spirituality can be best understood as comprising two elements: *how young people see the world* (their worldview) and *how young people respond to the world* (their ethos). Following the methodology of the NSYR report, the study classifies young people, based on their religious outlook, as falling into three categories – traditional (Christian), new age and secular.[69] It then traces the specifics of how young people in each group see the world.

The thesis defended by Mason, Singleton and Webber in their account of the *Generation Y Study* is that young people in Australia are becoming progressively more secular in their outlook. The authors postulate that this trend is irreversible, because the views of young people now closely track the increasingly secular outlook of their parents. They argue that the trend to a more secular outlook within Australian culture began in the late 1960s and early 1970s and that this represents a point of discontinuity with the past. They propose that the parents of current students *did not inherit their secular outlook from their own parents.* For these authors, current-day grandparents represent the last generation in many families with a 'traditional religious outlook'. Many of them now play a significant role in 'passing on the faith' to their grandchildren, a task they found overwhelming when dealing with their own children in the turbulence of the 1960s and 1970s. *The Spirit of Generation Y* views the data as supportive of this 'narrative' and so arrives at a

---

[68] Within the Catholic sector the project was sponsored by the Catholic Education Commissions of Queensland, Tasmania, Victoria, and Canberra and the Catholic Education Offices of South Australia, Parramatta, Sydney, Lismore, and Broken Bay and by the Salesian order.
[69] In *The Spirit of Generation Y* the breakdown of young people into these categories is as follows: Traditional (Christian) 46%, New Age 17% and Secular 26%. 9% were unclassifiable.

quite sombre assessment of the situation of young people and the Church's ministry to them, particularly through Catholic education.[70] While there is much of value in this report, we reject the determinism which seems predicated on the acceptance of secularisation theory by its authors.

Putting Life Together

In his account of the *Generation Y Study,* Philip Hughes distances himself from both the understanding of spirituality and the 'narrative' set out above. He looks to the UK rather than the USA in developing a framework within which to interpret the data.

Hughes explores the worldview of young people by mapping *the web of relationships*[71] within which they 'put their lives together'. This web or life-world is made up of five key relationships: to self, to family and friends, to the wider society, to the natural environment, and to 'the big questions of life'.[72] Secondly, he proposes that the five relationships may be lived at *three distinct levels*: 'living in the here and now' where the focus is on enjoyment and excitement, 'living ethically' where the emphasis is still on enjoyment, but lived responsibly, and 'living spiritually' which involves both a love of, and commitment to, what one believes. His model is set out in Figure 5.3.

		DIMENSIONS OF LIVING		
		Here and Now	Ethical	Spirtual
LIFE-WORLD RELATIONSHIPS	With Self			
	With Family and Friends			
	With the Wider Society			
	With the Natural World			
	With God and the Transcendent			

FIGURE 5.3 Model for analysing how young people put life together (Hughes 2007)[73]

70 The authors seem to have gone to great lengths to prove, on the basis of their statistical analysis, that Catholic schools have no measurable impact on the spirituality of their students.
71 Specifying the worldview of young people in this way has a long provenance in UK studies. See for instance Leslie Francis and Mandy Robbins *Urban Hope and Spiritual Health: The Adolescent Voice* (Peterborough: Epworth, 2005).
72 In a traditional framework Hughes' final category would logically have been 'God', and for the most part he interprets it this way, but he is also reporting the views of young people who have a totally secular outlook and how these wrestle with 'questions of ultimate concern'.
73 The diagram is adapted from Hughes, 2007, 35.

'Spirituality' in Hughes' frame of reference is *a quality people bring to their relationships*. In setting out his framework, he makes a further point: relationships unfold in life stages, so that each relationship can be lived at different levels – being spiritual in the way one lives a particular relationship does not imply being spiritual in any of the others. He suggests therefore that young people can be 'spiritual' *in quite selective ways*.

The shaded areas in Figure 5.3 suggest a profile of young people commonly encountered in interview data reported in both *The Spirit of Generation Y* and *Soul Searching*. Finally, Hughes suggests that young people have *an orientation to life*. For a minority, who 'hurt inside' or who lack 'inner peace', this orientation is *negative*. This shapes how they see life and put it together, often in self-defeating ways. Figure 5.3 represents a model covering the majority of young people whose outlook on life is *positive*. This model enables Hughes to achieve two aims:
- to map the worldview of young people by scanning their relationships
- to explore the level of commitment they bring to these relationships.

This is the unique feature of his work.

Something there

Hughes' approach receives empirical support in the studies of David Hay in the UK. Hay delineates 'spirituality' as 'relational consciousness' – an openness to explore the 'spiritual' in human experiences, the 'spiritual' being understood as *that which takes a person beyond the self*. His concept of 'relational consciousness' corresponds closely to the ethical and spiritual levels in Hughes' model of the life-world of young people. Hay's research aim was to understand the counter-intuitive situation encountered in the UK where, *as the society has become more secular in its outlook, people's interest in spirituality has risen*. As a Christian, and as a scientist, he is interested in how people, including young people, process their experience of the spiritual in a culture that suppresses or represses its expressions. Such knowledge, he suggests, is important for the future mission of the Christian churches.

Young adult Catholics: Religion in the culture of choice

Another important study is that of Dean Hoge and his associates published in 2001 as *Young Adult Catholics: Religion in the Culture of Choice*. While this earlier study focuses on the religious worldview of emerging adults, its findings have a wider relevance. Hoge worked with a national sample of young people all of whom had been confirmed as Catholic adolescents. Writing in the American cultural context, Hoge notes that the young people in his national sample 'liked being Catholic' and that the markers they accepted as defining 'Catholic', if somewhat circumscribed, are theologically valid. However, they chose to be 'Catholic' on their own terms.

They understood their Catholicism in terms that were personal, moral, sacramental and devotional. Few, for example, had any real knowledge of the Church's social teaching or its commitment to a 'social Gospel'.

The study did not support anecdotal reports, current at the time, that young adult Catholics in the USA were 'alienated from the Church'; rather, the situation seems best described as their 'being distant' from it. For many, religion is seen as 'something for the future', but not necessarily for the 'now'. The small number who had 'left the Catholic Church' since their confirmation (circa 8%), had mostly moved to other religious denominations where some held significant ministry roles.

The study concluded that young people now grow up in America's 'culture of choice', where there is a high expectation that they will choose for themselves. As a consequence these young people *construct their Catholicism* on the basis of personal choices, not according to institutional parameters. The majority of Hoge's sample had no intention of being anything other than 'Catholic'. His findings are confirmed in large part by both the NSYR and *Generation Y* studies.

STUDIES INTO THE WORLDVIEW OF YOUNG PEOPLE: SOME COMMON THEMES

The recurring theme in studies that touch directly and indirectly on the worldviews of young people is that *in putting their lives together young people are quite uncertain about their personal beliefs*. This does not mean that they do not believe in anything; rather it means that in response to a pervasive uncertainty about what one can believe, many have constructed a form of *popular religion*, which in many cases they now share with their parents.

Popular religious beliefs of young people

Christian Smith examined this phenomenon in reporting the first stage of the NSYR study. In exploring the religious beliefs of young Catholics and mainstream Protestants he found that many identified with five core religious beliefs which he articulates as follows:

1. A God exists who created and orders the world and watches over human life on earth.
2. God wants people to be good, nice and fair to each other, as taught in the Bible and by most world religions.
3. The central goal of life is to be happy and to feel good about oneself.
4. God does not need to be particularly involved in one's life except when God is needed to resolve a problem.
5. Good people go to heaven when they die.[74]

---

74 Christian Smith and Melinda Lunquist Denton *Soul Searching: The Religious and Spiritual Lives of American Teenagers* (New York: Oxford University Press, 2005), 162–3.

Smith argues that this belief set constitutes a *parasitic form* of religion in that it survives on the beliefs structures of Christianity, without being Christian.

He suggests it arises from self-constructing a religious worldview on the basis of Christian remnants still alive in the popular culture, and its prevalence is the consequence of the poor religious education that young people receive from their families and faith communities in the USA.

Hughes found evidence of this same belief set among Australian young people. However, he disagrees that it arises from a poor religious education. He notes in his interviews with students from Catholic schools that, while many demonstrated a quite sophisticated understanding of religious topics and could discuss issues such as science and religion quite intelligently, there was often a significant gap between what these young people *knew about religion* and what they *really believed*. He suggests that it is the latter which determines how they 'put their lives together', not the former. His findings suggest that *more goes into constructing a personal worldview than simply knowledge*. Put another way, *a personal worldview contains dimensions other than what we know*. We will take this matter up again in discussing the nature of a worldview.

YOUNG PEOPLE'S CONSTRUCTION OF KNOWLEDGE

Hughes' account of the *Generation Y Study* explores a question unique in the literature on how young people see the world – *how do young people understand knowledge and the way it is constructed?* As we have noted earlier, young people undergo two levels of socialisation in the course of growing up – the first corresponds roughly with their primary education where the dynamic of learning involves a *hermeneutics of trust*. Children learn on the basis of their own experience and by trusting in what their parents and teachers tell them. As their late primary and early secondary education unfolds they are introduced to another learning dynamic, *the hermeneutics of suspicion*, and so are taught to question what they have learned as well as what people present to them in class, at home and through the media.[75] It is in this stage in their development that the gap noted above begins to open up between *what they know* and *what they really believe*.

---

75 Many senior primary teachers tell us that the hermeneutics of suspicion is alive and well in their classes so this division may not be not as clear as outlined above.

FIGURE 5.4 Young people's construction of knowledge (Hughes 2007)

Hughes sought to delineate how young people understand knowledge and its construction. The model he constructed is set out in Figure 5.4.

At the heart of this construction is the idea *that knowledge is created by consensus*. For the young people in his sample there are *two kinds of knowledge*. The first is held in common and agreed on – *core knowledge*. Students identified Physics and Geography as examples of this form of knowledge. However, they also recognised that this core knowledge *has a fuzzy boundary*. This was evident in discussion about the relationship of science and religion. They see the academic disciplines they study at school as fitting into core knowledge generally well clear of its fuzzy boundary.

There is another area of knowledge, however, where there is little consensus and about which people have to make up their own minds. Astrology and psychic phenomena were seen as clearly falling into this category. Religion, for most young people, is also seen as fitting into this second category. In young people's understanding, knowledge that lies outside the core area is seen as *a different kind of knowledge* and needs to be processed differently. With regard to this form of knowledge they have to *make up their own minds* about what to accept.

If Hughes' picture is accurate, one reason for the high level of uncertainly that young people express about their personal beliefs may be that they are unsure where key religious concepts, such as God and Jesus, fit into their understanding of knowledge! As he points out, the matter has important implications for how religion and its attendant concepts are addressed not only in Religious Education,[76] but in other subject areas as well.

The model set out in Figure 5.4 indicates that young people's view of knowledge is implicitly shaped by the modern worldview. This is not surprising, since it is this worldview that stands behind most of what they

---

76 Hughes, 172–3.

study, and is the worldview of the majority of their teachers and parents! The modern worldview in the West, while challenged by the postmodern critique, remains the predominant 'worldview of the age'.

The purpose of this chapter has been to explore how students see the world and put life together. If the Catholic curriculum is to present the Catholic worldview in a way that makes sense to students, then it is important to understand something of the worldview they bring to this project and the influences which shape this worldview. As the evidence of the studies outlined above makes clear, a person's worldview *is not just a matter of what he or she knows*; it involves *something much deeper*. We now move on to explore what this might be, first by considering the concept of culture and its influence on how we make sense of things, and secondly by looking in more detail at how personal worldviews function in the way that people make sense of their world and relate to it in order to 'put life together'.

The case we will argue in future chapters is that young people do not in fact construct their personal worldview *from scratch* as is sometimes suggested. In reality, they put it together *with reference to the established meaning traditions they encounter in their culture* as these are mediated by the communities in which they live, including their school community. It is this process which the Catholic school seeks to understand and to influence. The Catholic curriculum is developed in response to this understanding. Efforts to create a 'Catholic curriculum' embody an understanding, either explicit or implicit, of how this process operates. In Part C we seek to establish the conceptual base necessary for this process to be more fully understood, explored and addressed.

PRINCIPLE 5:
THE LIFE-WORLD OF YOUNG PEOPLE PRINCIPLE

A Catholic curriculum is formulated in response to:
- the ways in which young people understand the major sets of relationships that define their life-world
- the progressive way in which this occurs
- their ongoing struggle to determine what is 'right' in these relationships as seen from within this life-world.

COMMENT

Young people come to define their identity relationally. The relationships that define this life-world are built up over time and take on importance as personal values are consolidated. Relationships depend on habit formation which can occur in both structured and unstructured ways. A Catholic curriculum seeks to provide a range of opportunities for students to experience at first-hand what 'living in right relationship' is like. It also seeks to ensure that the message is modelled particularly in the way teachers and leaders conduct themselves, which is part of the learning experience. This principle applies to the four sets of relationships that define the life-world of young people – living with family and friends, living in society and a civic community, living as part of a faith community and living as part of the natural environment. The life of the school is an important resource here, but only if it is used intentionally to achieve well-articulated goals for putting this principle into effect. Since students enter into these relationships progressively and often by 'trial and error'. Catholic educators are called on to extend a certain level of tolerance to the students in their efforts at implementing this principle.

CONTINUING THE CONVERSATION

5.1 As teachers we look at the life-world of young people from the outside; they live it from the inside. How is this difference in perspective best understood? What are the curriculum implications of such an understanding?

5.2 What level of importance do the four sets of relationships that define the life-world of young people (with the social world, with the natural world, with family and friends, with the faith community) have in the curriculum? Which relationships receive most emphasis? Is the treatment balanced?

5.3 What concept of 'living in right relationship' is promoted across the curriculum? Is this theme handled developmentally? If so how?

Part C
CATHOLIC CURRICULUM: THREE KEY CONSTRUCTS

In making sense of things, we access the worldviews of the faith community, our culture and our age. In doing so, we worked largely from an intuitive understanding of 'culture', worldview' and 'meaning making'. In official Church documentation, the task of the Catholic school is described as 'integrating faith and culture and faith and life' (e.g. *The Catholic School* #44) and as transmitting 'a specific view of what it means to be human, of society and of history'[77] in other words to formally introduce young people to their culture, but seen from the perspective of the worldview of faith. However, these two concepts are quite vaguely delineated. As concepts with *explanatory power,* the meaning of both 'culture' and 'worldview' has undergone significant revision in the past twenty years. Their meaning has expanded with use and this needs to be taken into account in conversations about Catholic curriculum.

A similar case can be made for 'meaning making'. While making sense of the world is clearly very important to human life, the process by which this happens is little understood. If, as we suggest, this is now core to a Catholic curriculum, it is important to develop at least a working model of the process by which we make meaning. We do this with reference to hermeneutics, the science of interpretation.

---

[77] Cf Congregation for Catholic Education *The Catholic School* (1977) ##8, 13, 27,36; *Lay Catholics: Witnesses to Faith* (1982) ##30,39; *The Religious Dimension of Education in a Catholic School* (1988) #57; *The Catholic School on the Threshold of the Third Millennium* (1997), ##10,14.

As the concepts of 'culture', 'worldview' and 'meaning making' provide the key to all that follows, so we now explore them in some depth. Their meaning has to be secured if our conversation is to advance.

Culture

In Chapter 6 we explore the notion of culture within the understanding of cultural anthropology, as this is applied to Christian mission. In this field there is broad ecumenical agreement, between Catholics and mainstream Protestant and Evangelical denominations. Our aim is to arrive at a more complete understanding of the 'worldview of culture', which recognises both its benefits and its limits as an interpretive map. The worldview of culture is important as it sets the 'imaginal horizon' beyond which we cannot normally see. In so doing it sets a limit to hope. The worldview of culture is the worldview we are born into, the one that most sharply defines who we are, and the one that most commonly determines how we will interpret our experience.

Faith and Culture

Chapter 7 takes the theme of culture further, looking at the nexus between 'faith and culture'. The aim of the Catholic school is often stated as 'integrating faith and culture and faith and life'. What precisely does this mean? Vatican II, and recent popes, have been quite forthright in teaching about *the relationship between faith and culture* and its importance to the mission of the Church. Unfortunately, this teaching is rather poorly translated into Church thinking about the Catholic school. We look at the mission of the school, in the light of this teaching and its implications for Catholic curriculum.

Worldview

Chapter 8 examines the concept of 'worldview' and adds some precision to what we mean when we talk about a 'worldview'. 'Worldview' has a provenance in three disciplines – philosophy, psychology and cultural anthropology. In philosophy, it is used to mean a 'self-contained system of thought'. In psychology and cultural anthropology, it means 'an orientation of life' which can be articulated as a 'framework of meaning' that people access in interpreting the world about them and making sense of their lives. They do this with reference to three public worldviews, that of their culture, that of the age in which they live, and that of their faith community. These worldviews are articulated as 'traditions of meaning' which we invoke when making sense of the world. How we understand these is determined by the way in which they are alive in the communities in which we grow up.

Meaning making

In the final chapter of this section, Chapter 9, the focus shifts to the ways in which people make sense of their lives – *how they put things together.* In Protestant circles meaning making is seen as a critical issue in Christian mission. The mission imperative there lies in meeting the challenge that radical relativism now poses for the churches. If the concept of truth is widely held as relative, then what certainty can be placed in Scripture? The latter is robbed of its authority as bearing witness to God's definitive communication to humankind. Some Protestant missiologists seek to address the central problems of epistemology seeing them as a new field for mission.

The Catholic mission concern lies in another direction – that of hermeneutics. It centres on three questions: *How do we make sense of the world about us? What constraints and possibilities are inherent in this process? What place does faith have in this process?*

Hermeneutics brings together two important strands of thinking that impact on education – *critical theory*, which we met briefly in discussing curriculum in Chapter 2, and *the postmodern critique*. There are at least four schools of thought in contemporary hermeneutics, three of which make claims on education. We follow the 'moderate' path of hermeneutics forged by Hans Georg Gadamer.

Theories about how people make sense of their lives quickly translate into theories about how people learn, since the two activities go hand in glove. Curriculum is underpinned by theories about learning. The program for Part C is both demanding and ambitious, but essential to the task of mapping the terrain through which we must pass on our journey towards a clearer delineation of principles underpinning 'a Catholic curriculum'.

6
CULTURE AND THE WORLDVIEW OF CULTURE

As one of the principal factors shaping how we see the world, culture is important. The problem is that culture is such a 'taken-for-granted' aspect of who we are, that we consistently underestimate its influence. It comes as something of a surprise to most people that, as a concept, 'culture' is of quite recent origin, having come to prominence only in the early part of the 20th century. The word is now used so frequently and in so many ways that its meaning requires clarification in scholarly discourse.

CULTURE AND ITS PERVASIVE INFLUENCES

There are three main reasons for examining culture in this treatment of Catholic curriculum:

1. Culture is the primary resource that we use, explicitly or implicitly, in making sense of our experiences.
2. Education is often construed as involving the passing on of a cultural heritage and how we understand this task depends on how we understand 'culture'.
3. The stated aim of the Catholic school in Church teaching is 'to integrate faith and culture and faith and life'.[78] Given that 'culture' can be understood in a number of ways, it is appropriate to ask the question – what understanding of culture stands behind this much-quoted aim?

The purpose of this chapter is to give the concept of culture a clearer meaning, particularly by reference to its use in the social science of cultural anthropology. In exploring culture from the perspective of cultural anthropology, we will encounter the concept of 'worldview'. Clarifying more fully what we mean by 'worldview' is the task of Chapter 8. At this stage, however, it is helpful to note that worldviews operate at two basic levels:

- each individual looks at life through the lens provided by his or her *personal worldview*

---

78 Congregation for Catholic Education *The Catholic School* ##44, 49.

- each individual is formed by the *cultural worldview* of the society in which he or she grows up, acquiring elements of it in the process of his or her enculturation.[79] We do not view the world from a neutral position; we always view it from a position *that is embedded in culture*.

We will highlight the relationships that exist between worldview and culture as we proceed.

HISTORY OF A CONCEPT: CLASSICIST AND MODERN CONCEPTIONS OF CULTURE

Our understanding of 'culture' has evolved through a number of stages. In this section we follow the 'narrative' of its evolution using US theologian Kathryn Tanner's work[80] as an authoritative guide.

The classicist understanding of culture

Culture as 'personal refinement'

The root meaning of 'culture' comes from the Latin word *cultivare* meaning 'to cultivate'. While the Latin root refers to horticulture, by the late 17th century the word had become associated with 'cultivating the mind'. The 'cultured person' was the one who, through assiduous effort and self-discipline, had achieved a level of *human refinement* through contact with what is deemed to be the highest level of intellectual, aesthetic and spiritual achievement attained in Western society. As the pre-modern feudal world began to disintegrate, claims to culture understood in this *classic sense* became claims to status. 'High culture', as this understanding is still popularly known, was socially constructed, and elitist. The elite decided who was 'cultured' and who was not! 'Culture' was understood as *a human sensibility*[81] that people acquire *in various degrees*.

The transition from this understanding to the 'modern' understanding took place in a number of independent developments.[82] Tanner skilfully traces these as they occurred in France, Germany and Britain in the eighteenth and early nineteenth centuries and also how these various strands joined together to give us the modern understanding.

---

79 Human beings do not *inherit* their culture, they learn it. This process begins in the family and is carried on more formally in school. The processes by which we acquire our cultural outlook are called enculturation. Enculturation combines both socialisation and education.
80 Kathryn Tanner *Theories of Culture: A New Agenda for Theology* (Minneapolis: Fortress Press, 1997), 3–24.
81 Culture understood as 'a level of human refinement' measured against the standards of European 'high culture' is still very much in use today. It retains its connotation of elitism.
82 The view of culture developed in cultural anthropology is referred to alternatively by the terms 'modern', 'empirical' and 'anthropological'. All three terms are used to refer to an understanding of culture as the possession or way of life of a people. For the sake of simplicity we adopt the term 'modern' to refer to this understanding of culture.

Culture as the characteristic of a 'civilised' society

In France, the development was shaped by the Enlightenment and its main project was to free people, through education, from the traditional ways of thinking and behaving that had dominated society. As this project proceeded, its leaders soon realised that their goal could not be achieved in a piecemeal fashion because the 'traditional ways' of thinking were knitted together as a whole. To change particular aspects of this popular culture two things were necessary: *to understand it as a whole* and to understand *how the parts function together*. Public education became a means to move the common people through stages towards the goal of 'civilisation' (as this was understood by the elite driving social change). This conception of culture was transplanted to the French colonies where native peoples were seen as being on the journey towards 'civilisation', a journey that the more civilised people of France had already made. French standards provided the criteria for judging how far along the track the native peoples were. Formulated in this way, the French concept of culture was highly ethnocentric. In the French understanding, 'culture' represented *a universal ideal towards which all people could aspire.*

The Germans took the classicist idea in another direction. For them, 'Kultur' referred to *a people's intellectual, artistic and spiritual achievements*. As Tanner notes, from the German perspective, the French had 'civilisation', but very little in the way of *Kultur*! The Germans developed the notion that *culture confers identity*. In other words, culture is what made the Germans 'German' and the French 'French'! It was not a cosmopolitan ideal, as suggested by the French, but rather something unique that separates 'us' from 'not us'. It was a small step from here to an understanding of culture as 'the way of life of a people'.

In 19th-century Britain, the classicist notion of culture evolved in a third direction. The promotion of a faux-version of 'high culture' was seen as an antidote to the breakdown in social order caused by the Industrial Revolution. The transmission of this 'high culture' through education was seen as having a potential *civilising effect* among the unruly lower classes through the promotion of a *moral ideal* – that of character formation.[83] This development gave a different impetus and direction to the development of public education in England from that in revolutionary France.

The British viewed the development of culture in *evolutionary terms*, with 'Western culture' standing at one end of the evolutionary scale and the culture of the 'savage tribes' encountered in its colonial enterprises standing at the other. First nation peoples in British colonies generally faired poorly under the concept of 'cultural evolution'. Effecting the required 'cultural

---

83 The British Governors and the Irish immigrant clergy in Australia in the 19th century agreed on this, if on little else.

improvement' made it necessary not only to understand Indigenous *culture as a whole*, as the French had discovered, but also to understand *the processes* by which the culture is transmitted. Anthropology developed as the academic discipline devoted to achieving these twin objectives.

Culture as a defining characteristic of a society

The colonial expansion of Europe enabled anthropologists and missionaries to describe the cultures of the new peoples they encountered by using *empirical observation*. Both languages and customs were recorded in detail. Their work initially helped colonial administrators co-opt the local culture in the cause of Western interests – commercial and religious. It later provided Indigenous peoples with vital resources in reclaiming their cultural heritage in the post-colonial period.

As cultural anthropology developed, it became clear that *no set of universal principles could explain the difference between cultures* because cultures arise in particular contexts and make sense only in those contexts. Attempts to evaluate cultures according to European standards were criticised because they *effectively made European history and experience the norm for all human development*. Such a position was recognised as untenable. Cultures had to be thought of as *entities in their own right*. Anthropology disconnected 'culture' from its classicist moorings.

As the 19th century moved into the 20th, culture was less seen as the *prerogative of a person*, and more commonly understood as the *prerogative of a people*, in fact a distinguishing characteristic of each people. However, the classicist understanding did not disappear, and 'culture' understood in this limited sense continues to be prized by many as a valuable human ideal.

The modern understanding of culture

Parameters of the modern understanding

This brief historical outline provides a background for understanding the genesis of the modern concept of culture. Tanner sums up this view as follows:
- culture is *a human universal*, a defining quality of all human life
- culture highlights the *diversity of peoples* and distinguishes among them on the basis of their way of life
- culture is the *shared possession* of people in a society which develops over time, and is the consequence of internal dialogues; it is carried as narrative
- cultures exist as *coherent wholes*, not as random collections of parts
- cultures are *socially constructed* over time; they shape the lives and character of their members.

In addition, she notes that:
- while people can change their culture, they do so *from the perspective of having first been formed by it*.[84]

Three understandings quickly emerged as the modern understanding of culture developed:

1. *Culture provides us with a way of seeing the world.* Every person views the world through the lens of culture since culture provides us with both the language and the conceptual framework within which we explore and make sense of our world, and that of other people. The corollary to this is that we can never have a 'God's eye' view of culture. We study it either as an 'insider' or as an 'outsider'. *There can be no culture-free perspective.*

2. *Culture provides us with blinkers.* Culture sets an *imaginal horizon* beyond which insiders cannot see. Outsiders are often perplexed by these limits. It is only in genuine dialogue with outsiders that the boundaries of this imaginal horizon are recognised, become open to challenge, and new possibilities seen. A 'fusion of horizons' occurs.

3. *Much of culture is held out of awareness.* Insiders often remain unaware of key aspects in their own culture, since culture is appropriated in a process that is, in the main, unconscious. On the other hand, outsiders do not always get the picture right either. They often struggle to give the correct meaning to what they observe. *It takes a combination of insiders looking out, and outsiders looking in, to map a culture with any degree of certainty.*

These three understandings work themselves out, for instance, when we read the Bible. We read the text as 'cultural outsiders'. In determining meaning for ourselves, we first need to ascertain the meaning of what the author *intended the text to mean for the insiders to whom it was addressed*.[85] To make sense of the text we have to know something of the culture in which it was written, and how the text would have been understood in that context.

When we read a biblical text from the perspective of our own culture, we most commonly treat it *as if it were written for us,* and so we are prone to misinterpret its meaning, or simply fail to make sense of it at all. Such a reading is naïve. To take the moderating influence of culture into account we have to proceed in *two steps*. In the first we consider what the text meant for the people for whom it was originally intended. In the second step, as heirs to the biblical tradition, we ask – what does God's communication hold for us, living as we do in an entirely different

---

84 Kathryn Tanner, 25–29.
85 The Old Testament texts, for example, are not just any texts from a historical period. They are special in the sense that they are determinative of Israel's faith of God's specific communication to humankind.

cultural context? Without the first step we are likely to impose only our own culturally conditioned meaning on the text.[86]

A working definition of culture

The literature on culture indicates no shortage of definitions. Reviewing how the concept developed historically enables us to identify key features that any useful definition must encompass. Accepting this constraint, we adopt Catholic mission anthropologist Louis Luzbetak's conception of culture as *a people's comprehensive and more or less successful plan for living together and meeting the challenges posed by their particular environment* as a good working definition.[87]

UNDERSTANDING HOW CULTURE WORKS: WORKING MODELS

As cultural anthropology advanced in the 20th century, a range of 'working models' was constructed to help convey the essential relationships that exist between the various components of a culture. Since many of these draw on analogies, they are called *analogical models*. We deal briefly with one of these models. In this class of model, culture is construed as *a system* made up of elements that are *ordered hierarchically*.[88] In the section below we employ the *onion model* of culture which, while simple, makes a number of important points about the nature of culture and how it functions in a society.

How cultures function: An analogical explanation

Internal structure of a culture

The onion model, set out schematically in Figure 6.1, identifies culture as having four layers, or depth dimensions. The analogy here appeals to the fact that culture has *an overall unity* which is built up in layers progressively distant from a core.

The surface layer of a culture is the *sensory layer*. It is what we see or come directly into contact with. It includes *cultural products*, such as housing, transport, cuisine, language, arts, etc., and *cultural patterns of behaviour*, how

---

86 It is a naïve reading of the biblical text that triggers the indignation of secularist celebrities like Richard Dawkins and Christopher Hitchens when they complain about the ills of religion.
87 Louis Luzbetak *The Church and Cultures: New Perspectives in Missiological Anthropology* (Maryknoll, New York: Orbis, 1988), 74. More formally, Luzbetak defines culture as 'a dynamic system of socially acquired and socially shared ideas according to which an interacting group of human beings is to adapt to its physical, social and ideational environment'. Luzbetak here shows his bias as a structural anthropologist. Structural anthropologists are primarily interested in the meaning of the systems that underpin a culture.
88 In *Explorers, Guides and Meaning Makers*, for instance, we employ two other models, the Iceberg Model (analogical) and Luzbetak's more formal functional model.

people gather, how they interact socially, the way they deal with space and time, the way members of a family relate, and so on. These two elements enable us to *describe the culture*. This description, however, does not penetrate the culture very deeply. It may tell us 'how things are done around here' but throws little light on underlying motivations – 'why things are done the way they are'. To understand this we need to move the point of investigation to a deeper level.

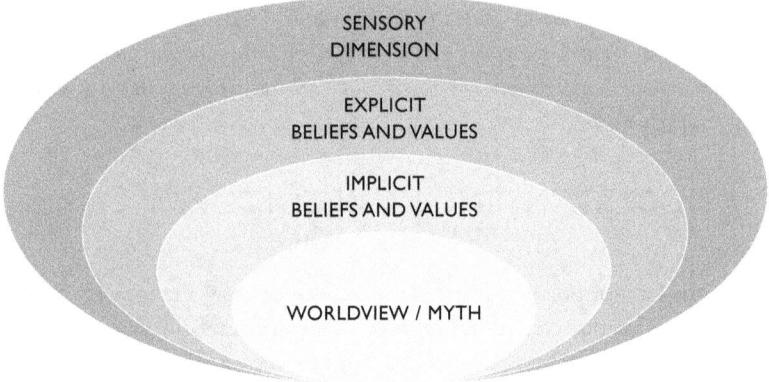

FIGURE 6.1 Culture: The onion model

The second tier of culture focuses on the *beliefs and* values that underpin overt behaviour and practices. Beliefs and values operate at two levels – an *explicit level* that insiders are aware of, and an *implicit level* which lies deeper in the culture and is often out of sight to insiders. This deeper level comes to consciousness when the culture is placed under stress due to major changes in the external environment, when rising internal tensions test the reliability of a society's plan for living, or when thinking and behaviour patterns are questioned by outsiders.

Culture at work: A case study

An example may help to explain how these two levels inter-relate in a culture. In Australia we have a public holiday on April 25th each year to celebrate ANZAC Day. If, as an outsider, you asked an Australian what is so special about this day, he or she would probably reply to the effect that it celebrates the valiant way members of the ANZAC Corps fought at Gallipoli during World War I. If you research the matter further you would find that the Australians were soundly defeated by the Turks at Gallipoli. As an outsider, the idea of a country celebrating a defeat would seem, objectively, to be foolish. So you pursue the matter further and ask the insider what is going on here! This forces the insider to look more deeply into the beliefs and values that hold the local culture together. Your questions may surface more substantial notions, such as Australian values and beliefs about comradeship, loyalty and courage in the face of adversity. These can then be cross-referenced to other aspects of the Australian narrative. This process of *insider/outsider dialogue* can tease out the underlying belief and value system of a culture. But it also raises another question – *why these particular beliefs and values?*

The core of a culture: Its worldview

In seeking the answer to this question your investigation approaches *the core of the culture*, the basis on which cultural identity is ultimately constructed. Sitting in the depths, below beliefs and values, and anchoring them, are *the taken-for-granted beliefs and presuppositions*, the unprovable assumptions that constitute *the worldview of the culture*. While we may attempt to analyse this worldview in terms of propositions, it is not held by people, nor is it transmitted in this form. Rather, it is held as what cultural anthropologists call 'myth' and is transmitted, from one generation to another in the form of revered narratives, that can be told in a number of ways. The form these narratives take reflects *the ways in which different communities living within the culture identify with them*. For some Australians, the narrative emerges from the events of *national history* – the convict experience, the Gold Rush, or the Eureka uprising; for others it is held within the *narrative of the family* – as for instance among migrants arriving after the Second World War, Vietnamese boat people, ex-servicemen etc.; while for a third group it is *tied to personal experience* – thousands of young people now travel to Gallipoli or Villers-Bretonneux in France each year to be present at the annual dawn service held there. As these different instances illustrate, people make contact with their cultural myth in a variety of ways.

The unique thing about the narratives that define cultural identity is that, while different, *they all point to the same myth*. While the narratives may differ from group to group, their underlying structure remains the same – *they spell out what is taken as unarguable in defining who we are as a people*. It is only through dialogue among groups that *we come to understand these points of convergence and the depth of the bonds that unite us as a people*.

The narratives of culture convey the worldview of the culture to both outsiders and insiders alike as 'the way things are for us'. We define who we are as a people, not by identifying with propositions, *but by identifying ourselves with a particular story,* one underpinned by cherished values, one that we feel committed to, one that we see as ongoing. And one in which we believe we have a part. *We believe this story to be true and reliable* (even if it is not always strictly historically accurate). This is because cultural narratives are constructed on two foundations – *historical experience* and *collective aspirations*, that is, what has happened and what we hope will happen!

The worldview at the heart of a culture, which is conveyed through cultural narratives, holds a strong *emotional resonance* for all who identify with it and it can be invoked to motivate action and win commitment to a cause, particularly a political, social or moral cause.[89] The worldview with its implied understanding of what it means to be human in a particular context represents *a point of stability, a conserving principle, the core of identity* when faced with the demands of a rapidly changing environment. The experience of 'deep change' discussed in Chapters 2 and 3 involves changes occurring at the *core of culture* induced by major changes in the external environment. Since it touches on our identity, we feel high levels of anxiety when confronted with 'deep change'. That is the power of culture.

THE WORLDVIEW OF CULTURE

The discursive outline above is put more succinctly by noted Protestant cultural anthropologist and missiologist Paul Hiebert in noting that any cultural worldview has three dimensions: an *affective dimension,* an *evaluative dimension* and a *cognitive dimension.* All three are brought to bear in the process of meaning making.[90] 'Meaning' involves not only making sense of what we know, but also of *how we feel* and *what we value*. In his view, with which we concur, it is a mistake to think of a worldview only in cognitive or ideational terms, as often happens in the literature. Culture is much more pervasive than a set of ideas; *it is an orientation of the whole person* brought about by living in a particular environment with its unique physical, social and ideational characteristics. Since the worldview of our culture provides most people with *a default frame of references in meaning making* it is necessary to understand it. The worldview of culture provides us not only with a model of reality (*how things are*) that operates at the level of ideas, but also with a model for action in affirming which values should guide our behaviour (*how things can be*). How the local cultural worldview is understood by parents, teachers and students, therefore, has major implications for faith-based schools.

UNDERSTANDING CULTURE: THE POSTMODERN TURN

The modern view of culture is based on an assumption: that *the world is divided into peoples each with their own culture*. This assumption was largely true in the nineteenth and early twentieth centuries. The situation changed after

---

89 As the people of Queensland were reminded by their Premier Anna Bligh, when the state was hit by major floods and then only weeks later by the biggest cyclone since records have been kept in Australia, 'We are Queenslanders, north of the border. If you knock us down we get up again and move on'. The appeal here is clearly to the motivating power of myth.
90 Paul Hiebert *Transforming Worldviews: An Anthropological Understanding of How People Change* (Grand Rapids Michigan: Baker Academic, 2009), 26.

World War II which resulted in the massive dislocation of peoples in Europe. The subsequent collapse of Communist regimes in Europe, and strife in the Middle East, Africa and Asia have added to the flood of refugees seeking a place to live that is peaceful and where their families can prosper. Added to this are the more recent phenomena of economic and environmental migration. The consequence of this mass migration, and the resultant intermingling of peoples in urban centres, is that many Western societies are being forced by circumstances on the ground to redefine the foundations on which 'their more or less successful plan for living together' is built. A massive process of social re-negotiation is underway. In this context a 'postmodern' concept of culture is emerging.

Culture as a battle between themes and counter-themes

Tanner points out that the formation of a culture has always been the consequence of a historical struggle within society between *competing ideas and values in which there can be no outright victor*.[91] Hiebert explains this situation by pointing out that, even within the modern period, there has been a constant struggle going on in cultures between 'themes' and 'counter-themes'.[92] For example, in most cultures *concern for the freedom of the individual* has had to be balanced against *concern for the common good*. If a society moves too far towards the first pole, the result can be individualistic anarchy. Moving too far in the other direction can result in either an overprotective 'nanny state', or some form of totalitarianism.

Because of the need to hold themes and counter-themes in balance, modern societies have to establish a basis for *the co-existence of agreement and disagreement with respect to beliefs and values*. If a society's 'plan for living' is going to be successful, it now has to provide a basis for pluralism, even if within clearly defined limits. *Cultures are now distinguished as advanced or not, depending on how this basis is determined.*

The mechanisms available differ. In some societies, tolerance is treated as a *moral ideal*. Here the 'plan for living' *is characterised by widespread agreement to engage in the processes of dialogue through which the limits to legitimate pluralism are negotiated according to principles of justice*. In other societies, legitimate difference is viewed primarily from a legal perspective (with rights spelt out in anti-discrimination legislation). Cultures which reject pluralism are now seen in the West as oppressive.

Educating in the context of advanced cultural pluralism

Education plays an important role in explaining and critiquing the options available to people living in a 'postmodern' society. The challenge is to

---

91 Tanner, 39.
92 Hiebert, 45.

educate in a way that preserves the essential tensions between themes and counter-themes without drifting into relativism which collapses these tensions and in the process not only compromises important values, but also robs the culture of its sources of creative vitality.

The modern view of culture assumed that cultures had tight boundaries which clearly distinguished the culturally 'us' from the 'not us'. In the postmodern situation *the boundaries of identity are understood as being quite fuzzy* because within society there are legitimately alternative values and beliefs systems now competing for influence in the public square. In this situation it becomes increasingly difficult to distinguish the 'not us' from the 'us', so 'identity' often becomes an issue at the personal and social levels, and people struggle to deal with the anxiety this generates.

THE POSTMODERN CHALLENGE FROM AN ANTHROPOLOGICAL PERSPECTIVE

The combination of anxiety about cultural identity and conflict within society over values are *bringing the deepest levels of culture to critical awareness*. People are forced to rethink what really holds things together in their 'plan for living' if it going to be 'more or less successful'. In this situation *cultural worldviews are being recontextualised*. Historically, this is a rare event in any culture. The fact that it is happening on a global scale may prove to be the characterising feature of a dawning 'global age'.

Re-contextualising cultures

In this new situation, the 'postmodern' understanding of culture *qualifies* the modern view in important ways; *it does not replace it*. Peoples are forced into the difficult task of reconstructing their culture to accommodate higher levels of difference and diversity, while not abandoning important tensions over values and beliefs or losing contact with the worldview that holds the culture together. People everywhere are caught up in a process of *cultural renewal* and are writing a new chapter in our cultural narrative in response to the triple challenge posed by a new cultural environment, a problematic economic environment and a deteriorating physical environment. In many respects 'deep change' is happening because of *the convergence of change at these three levels* and the impact this has on how we make sense of the world in which we live.

When the worldview of culture is recontextualised, so too is the personal worldview of people in the culture, whether they realise this or not. New levels of human aspiration surface in response. *School leaders and educators are challenged to reflect on and respond creatively to this situation in pursuing the best interests of their students.* The re-contextualising of culture, therefore, has important implications for how we think about the mission of the Catholic school and, within this, how we think about the Catholic curriculum.

If the purpose of the Catholic school is to help young people integrate faith and culture and faith and life, what does this translate to when culture is being recontextualised? How does the Church view the transition underway and how does it seek to respond? These are now important questions for Catholic educators to consider and highly relevant to any discussion of Catholic curriculum.

PRINCIPLE 6:
THE UNDERSTANDING LIVING CULTURES PRINCIPLE

A Catholic curriculum seeks to incorporate a coherent view of culture into the curriculum so that students can understand, and critically engage with, the strengths and limits of their own culture as a meaning system, and so discover the way in which it shapes how they see the world and make sense of it.

COMMENT

The focus here is on exploring Australian culture as a 'living culture'. A Catholic curriculum examines the structure of the local culture, particularly its depth dimensions – its dynamic values and the narrative structures that incorporate its worldview. Students need to be able to relate their own story and that of their family to the narratives that define cultural identity. Part of this exploration is finding the 'seeds of the Word' in Australian culture. It is to be regretted that few resources exist for this purpose as the topic is not generally included in the Religious Education curriculum.[93] The attempt to incorporate national values into the public curriculum is a help in implementing this principle.[94]

CONTINUING THE CONVERSATION

6.1 Is a cohesive understanding of 'culture' operative in the curriculum? If not, how can this be addressed?

6.2 How well is Australian culture as a 'living culture' developed as a theme within the curriculum? Does the treatment deal largely with the surface level of culture?

6.3 How are the depth dimensions of Australian culture explored? How are the cultural narratives that define Australian culture addressed?

6.4 What attempt is made to situate students within these narratives?

6.5 Is there any explicit attempt to relate the dynamic values of Australian culture with those of the Gospel? If not, why not?

---

93 An outstanding study is that by Australian theologian John Thornhill *Making Australia: Exploring our National Conversation* (Newtown NSW: Millennium Books, 1992).

94 The most extensive program to date to implement this principle has been conducted by *The Catholic Schools* Office, Diocese of Broken Bay in a project entitled *Our Values, Our Mission* (2009).

7
FAITH AND CULTURE: MISSIOLOGY MEETS EDUCATION

Faith and culture constitute the currency in which Catholic schools trade. How the relationship between them is understood is central to any understanding of Catholic schooling, and therefore of curriculum.

FAITH AND CULTURE: SHARING THE JOURNEY THROUGH HISTORY

The relationship between faith and culture has been an issue in Christian thinking since first Paul, writing thirty or so years after the death of Jesus, and later Origen (185–232), set out to provide *a rational account of faith* for their contemporaries. Thus began the long and complex encounter between faith and culture which is a central feature of the Christian story.[95] However, this encounter played out largely in the background of mission thinking in the modern period. It was not until the 20th century that the relationship between faith and culture began to be moved to the foreground as mission theology, both Catholic and Protestant, began to develop rapidly in response to a changing and challenging context. In this chapter, we look at the way in which faith and culture have become an integral part of mission theology, and then consider how this has played out in the development of thinking about Catholic education and the implications for a Catholic curriculum.

In this chapter we introduce some of the key themes in contemporary mission theology. We begin by exploring Catholic mission theology, with a particular eye to the role of culture, as mission theology develops from Vatican II (1962–65) to the present century. We do this by noting the major developments in a number of papal documents that have provided the basis on which the various Roman departments, such as the Congregation for Catholic Education, have based their own work. However, as is not so surprising in a complex organisation like the Catholic Church, there

---

[95] Stephen Bevans and Roger Schroeder provide the longer account of this story in *Constants in Context* (Maryknoll, New York: Orbis, 2003) and Susan Smith tells it from the perspective of women in *Women in Mission* (Maryknoll, New York: Orbis, 2005).

are often time lags before major developments in official theology are substantively translated into the thinking, and hence into the documents, produced by Vatican departments.

Our contention in tracing the development of faith and culture is that considerations about Catholic schooling have suffered from such a lag, and this has resulted in important issues around Catholic curriculum remaining unresolved. Later in the chapter we look in some detail at how the relationship between faith and culture is dealt with in the foundational post-Vatican II document on Catholic schooling *The Catholic School* (1977). We do not address all the official documents on Catholic schooling, as space precludes this. *The Catholic School* is, however, foundational to those that follow. Its conceptual strengths are their strengths, but equally its conceptual shortcomings are carried into the other documents. This has implications for consideration of curriculum as this is addressed both directly and indirectly in *The Catholic School*.

Relationship between faith and culture: Source documents

Papal teaching is carefully crafted. While the name and authority of the pope is attached to individual documents, they usually sum up a much broader conversation within the Church and give this conversation both a direction and a boundary. This has certainly been the case with the development of Catholic mission theology in the 20th century. Catholic thinking about faith and culture is an integral part of this conversation.

An important impetus for development came from Paul VI who wrote his first encyclical entitled *Ecclesiam Suam* (1964) during Vatican II. In this he set out the major issues he wished to pursue as pope (see below) which focused discussion at the Council on *the relationship between the Church and the modern world*. Faith and culture were integral to this discussion and are addressed at some length in the major Council document on this topic – *The Church in the Modern World* (1965).[96] The discussion also had a significant impact on the Church's understanding of its role in education which was also addressed at the Council and set out in its *Declaration on Christian Education* (1965). In 1974, almost a decade after the Council, Paul VI presided over a general synod to review the implementation of the agenda adopted at the Council under the broad heading *Evangelisation in the Modern World* (1974). Given the wide-ranging nature of the synodal discussions, the pope was asked by the synod to pull together the themes, and to draw out the implications for Catholic teaching. This he did in *Evangelii Nuntiandi* (1975), which provides the foundations on which modern Catholic mission theology now rests.

---

96 The Latin title by which this document is generally known and referred to is *Gaudium et Spes*.

A quarter of a century later, faced with a 'crisis in mission', Pope John Paul II further developed Catholic mission theology in *Redemptoris Missio* (1990). In the following year, in an important contribution to Catholic mission theology, and to the understanding of faith and culture within this, the Pontifical Council for Inter-religious Dialogue published *Dialogue and Proclamation* (1991), a document which provided rich commentary on *Redemptoris Missio*. In each of these *source documents* in Catholic mission theology, the relationship between faith and culture is a central topic.[97]

FAITH AND CULTURE IN CATHOLIC MISSION THEOLOGY

Contemporary Catholic mission theology has its starting point at the Second Vatican Council which represents the highest teaching authority of the Church. During the Council which took place in sessions over four years, Paul VI at the request of the assembled bishops, set out what he saw as the agenda for his time as pope.

Ecclesiam Suam: **A seed is sown**

In his encyclical *Ecclesiam Suam*, Paul VI set out the major policy goals that the Church needed to pursue following the Council. These related to:
- *the self-awareness of the Church* – the need for greater clarity among Christians about the identity of the Church, based on renewed awareness of its 'origins, nature, mission and destiny'
- *the renewal of the Church* – which would call for courageous change
- *dialogue with the world* – the need for the Church to enter into dialogue with the world in which it lives and in which it carries out its mission.

The last of these was taken up directly by the bishops assembled at the Council and has subsequently shaped the Catholic understanding of the relationship between faith and culture, which had been badly fractured in the modern period.

Prompted by *Ecclesiam Suam*, the bishops re-assessed both the achievements of modernity and the Church's judgement of them. They made a major effort to 'read the signs of the times' and so discern those contemporary issues that the Church needed to address in achieving its mission. One of these was engaging with cultures. The scope of their reflections is captured in *The Church in the Modern World (Gaudium et Spes).*

---

97 The documents cited do not exhaust the official corpus of teaching on mission, but simply those in which the relationship between faith and culture constitute major themes. For a fuller discussion of the Church's recent documents on mission see Jim and Therese D'Orsa 'Befriending a Living Tradition' in *Explorers, Guides and Meaning Makers*, 137–153.

Faith and culture in *Gaudium et Spes*

Those drafting *Gaudium et Spes* offered a *deliberately ambivalent* 'working definition' of culture, one that embraces both the classicist and modern understandings as outlined in Chapter 6.

> In its general sense the word 'culture' stands for everything by which human beings refine and develop their various capacities of mind and body (classicist understanding). It includes efforts to control the cosmos by knowledge and by work, as well as ways of humanizing social life within the family or civic community through the progress of customs and institutions (modern understanding) (#53).[98]

The document clearly attempts to balance the two meanings we discussed in the previous chapter, acknowledging each. Culture can be understood as *self-refinement*, but equally it can also be understood as the *way of life* lived by a community through which people may *become fully human* and by means of which they *express their freedom*. Later sections dealing with culture focus more sharply on the second of these meanings in order to embrace 'the plurality of cultures'. This 'plurality' was evident among the bishops themselves,[99] and was thus being immediately experienced as a factor shaping faith throughout the world.

In his analysis of Church teaching on faith and culture in *Gaudium et Spes*, senior Catholic theologian Michael Gallagher notes, as an important development, the acknowledgement that:

> ...each human community, with its specific history and geography, has its own inheritance of wisdom and its own way of fostering basic human values; hence, even if not stated openly, it is evident that there can be no 'uncultured' nations, and the monopoly exercised by the more aristocratic meaning of culture (in Catholic teaching) has been broken for good.[100]

While the monopoly to which he refers may have been broken, the classicist notion of culture is not rejected, nor should it be. Both conceptions appear in subsequent official statements, particularly on Catholic schooling.

---

98 Michael Gallagher *Clashing Symbols: An Introduction to Faith and Culture* (London: Darton, Longman and Todd, 2003), 42 (words in parentheses added). The passage is the author's own translation.
99 Vatican Council II was the most representative ecumenical council ever held with over 2000 bishops attending, representing all sections of the global church. Both in terms of numbers attending and areas represented the event was unique in Church history.
100 Michael Gallagher *Clashing Symbols: An Introduction to Faith and Culture* (London: Darton, Longman and Todd, 2003), 44 (words in parentheses added). The passage is the author's own translation.

Faith and culture in the *Declaration on Christian Education*

The Council's *Declaration on Christian Education (Gravissimum Educationis)* uses 'culture' almost exclusively in its modern sense. The document notes that each country has a culture and tradition, and that this is dynamic, constructed by the people, and capable of betterment. As public institutions, schools play an important role in both the transmission and 'betterment of culture'. Catholic schools make a particular contribution to this project, however, by *helping young people acquire knowledge in such a way that their understanding of the world, life and the human person is illumined by faith.* This key point, acknowledging that Catholic schools aim to communicate a worldview, provides an important foundation for later thinking about Catholic schooling.

The shape of the *Declaration on Christian Education* reflects the developments in thinking about faith and culture at the Council. The document began life focused somewhat narrowly on Catholic schooling. However, once the Council gave its attention on the modern world, the sorry state of educational provision for most young people in that world could not be ignored and required some form of response. This led to a major change in thinking, particularly about the Church's mission to address that which dehumanises.[101] The United Nation's *Declaration on Human Rights* (1948) provides an important backdrop to the Council's thinking about education. If God's Kingdom was to grow in strength in many parts of the world, then schools were going to be needed to facilitate this.[102] As the bishops wrestled with such ideas the focus of their thinking changed. If the Church was to respond to the global challenge which education now represented in a significant way, it was necessary first to establish *the principles* on which such a response could be built.[103]

In the seventh and final draft the authors settled on a brief document setting out twelve principles. The first of these recognises that *education is a universal right which flows from the dignity of the human person.* This principle sets the foundation for a subsequent development in Catholic social teaching. Since people can exercise this right only in the context of their culture, a universal right to education implies a universal right to culture itself. In Catholic thinking, education and social justice are *essentially connected* through this right to culture.

---

101 C.f. Vatican II *Gaudium et Spes* ##26,27.
102 The Roman document *Lay Catholics in Schools: Witnesses to Faith* (1982) for instance, argues that the work of all Catholics teaching in schools has a Kingdom significance that confers on teaching a special dignity.
103 This background is provided by Johannes Pohlschneider 'Declaration on Christian Education' in Herbert Vorgrimler (ed) *Commentary on the Documents of Vatican II*, Vol. IV (New York: Herder and Herder, 1969)

The concepts of mission and culture were linked at the Council through the participants' shared concern for 'humanising'. *People become more fully human only through their culture, which provides the milieu in which they live their lives.* Hence cultural activities, including education, have *an essential place in the mission of the Church.* This understanding, sown at the Council, took another decade to germinate and begin to flower in the mission theology of Paul VI, articulated in 1975 after the synod on evangelisation.

Faith and culture in the mission theology of Pope Paul VI

In 1974, Paul VI called a general synod of bishops to address the topic *Evangelisation in the Modern World*. The following year he summarised the discussions of the synod in *Evangelii Nuntiandi (1975)* which provides a comprehensive mission theology for the time, articulated in the light of a decade of experience in attempting to implement the Council's various decrees.

Jesus' mission and the Church's mission

Paul VI began his reflection on the mission of the Church by recalling Jesus' mission to announce the Kingdom of God and to be a witness to, and agent of, its breaking into human history. The Church continues this mission, having a responsibility not only to preach the Gospel of the Kingdom, but also to live it, to be a witness to it, and to be renewed continually by it. Credibility in mission depends on *the Church's willingness to renew itself as contexts change.* This was a challenge for the Church at the time of the Council, and remains so. The connection back to *Ecclesiam Suam* is clear.

Church renewal

The Church's mission is to make the Kingdom present *in its own life* through ongoing renewal, and *in the cultures in which Christians live*. Paul VI reclaimed Jesus' teaching about the Kingdom of God from the obscurity into which it had fallen, and made it *the central theme in Catholic mission theology*. He sought to 'evangelise' the Church in the process of teaching about what 'evangelisation' essentially means.

Having laid this foundation, he then discussed a number of forms in which the mission of the Church is carried forward. These include the pastoral ministry of the Church – the normal means by which the life of the faith community is sustained and nurtured – as well as works for human liberation, efforts to promote peace and justice, and attempts to promote socioeconomic development. This list has been extended subsequently to include efforts for reconciliation among peoples, care for God's creation, etc., as new mission needs emerge.

Constants in Missio: Proclamation

In all the actions to bring about the Kingdom there are some mission constants which are marks of authenticity. As individuals and as communities, Christians are called *to be witnesses* to the Kingdom and *to speak the hope that drives them on*. For Paul VI the 'proclamation of the Gospel' is the essential ingredient in any form of mission activity and this is done both *by word and by witness*. His much-quoted remark in this regard is: 'Modern man listens more willingly to witnesses than to teachers, and if he does listen to teachers, it is because they are witnesses'.[104]

Similarly, he saw that bringing about the Kingdom, which occurs not in some abstract way but in the context of cultures, involves co-operative action with others, and thus requires opening some form of dialogue with them. The Kingdom of God becomes present only through the willing co-operation of those who work to make it a reality in the context of their culture – it is either present in some form within culture, or it is not present at all. This is a major change in understanding. For many centuries Catholic theology held that the Kingdom was present *only in the Church itself*. This led to the world-Church dualism that sits behind the split between faith and culture which developed in modernity. It was now recognised as being in need of redress.

Evangelisation of cultures

Based on this understanding, Paul VI places the 'evangelisation of culture' on a par with pastoral ministry as a priority in mission. He speaks quite deliberately in *Evangelii Nuntiandi* about 'cultures' rather than 'culture', in order to avoid any misunderstandings about his usage of the term. The 'evangelisation of culture and cultures' means 'bringing the Good News into all the strata of humanity, and through its influence transforming humanity from within and making it new' (#18). This echoes the 'humanising' theme found in *Gaudium et Spes*. Transforming strata of humanity means 'affecting and as it were upsetting, through the power of the Gospel, mankind's criteria of judgement, determining values, point of interest, lines of thought, sources of inspiration and models of life which are in contrast with the Word of God and the plan of salvation'(#19). In other words, evangelisation involves what we called in the last chapter the depth dimensions of a culture, and in particular the worldview of the culture. The purpose of engaging with cultures in this way is to move the worldview, which holds them together and confers identity on individual peoples, closer to Jesus' vision of the Kingdom. This has to be done 'from within', that is by insiders. It cannot be imposed from without, a mistake commonly made in the past, and one which leads to shallow and unstable evangelisation.

---

104 Paul VI *Evangelii Nuntiandi* #42.

Paul VI's thinking about the relationship between faith and culture is very carefully delineated. It maps out the two-pronged strategy identified at the Council, to draw out and transform what is best in a culture and to discern, oppose, and if possible overturn that within a culture which dehumanises. If this broader mission program is to be pursued, the Pope suggests that a number of things have to be kept in mind:

- transformation needs to address *the depth structures of the culture* and not merely its surface features
- the mission to 'evangelise culture' applies to all cultures. There is no culture that the Kingdom of God cannot transform
- all cultures need evangelising – *there are no fully evangelised cultures*
- the *rift between culture and faith must be healed*
- the transformation of culture requires careful discernment, and will involve no small share of drama, as culture is an inherently ambiguous reality.

While Paul VI's mission theology moved Catholic thinking about faith and culture forward, its immediate reception was slow in the developed world because countries there considered themselves to be 'evangelised'. A further bias existed in the churches of the developed world which viewed mission theology as something for the 'foreign mission section' of the Church. This attitude has yet to be overcome in the structure of theological education.

THEOLOGY OF FAITH AND CULTURE: JOHN PAUL II

Paul VI was succeeded briefly by John Paul I and then by John Paul II who came to the papacy with a reputation as a 'man of culture'. He had a strong academic grounding in modern philosophy and the arts and a particular interest in resolving the disconnect between the Church and 'high culture', believing the Church to have been impoverished by this separation. Early in his papacy (1982) John Paul II established the Pontifical Council for Culture to promote a dialogue between 'people of culture' and the Church. On his many travels, his itinerary always involved meetings with 'people of culture'. These included artists, musicians, writers, and scientists, those who create and express meaning and beauty with and for others. These travels also gave him wide first-hand experience of cultures. His thinking about faith and culture, which also developed in the context of a mission theology, operates at two levels: *faith and high culture*, and *faith and 'living cultures'*.

Theology of faith and high culture

John Paul II seems to have given much thought to the theological significance of what we are calling here 'high culture'. According to Gallagher,[105] who

---

[105] Michael Gallagher *Clashing Symbols: An Introduction to Faith and Culture*, 51ff is the main source used here in summarising the work of John Paul II on faith and culture.

has made a study of his many addresses on the subject, John Paul II saw the behaviour of 'the artist' (here considered as representative of 'people of culture') as directed towards creating. But in this act he expresses who he is, not *ex nihilo* but from within a freedom extended to him by his culture, and using the rich resources of that culture. Art depends on culture, freedom and self-expression *being drawn together in the creation of beauty and meaning.* The act of self-expression central to art always speaks to the beauty and meaning of life as this can be understood within a culture. The artist therefore makes a crucial contribution to the quality of life in that culture through his particular human capacity to wrestle with, and express, the meanings that lie out of sight, the transcendental levels of meaning. Artists keep an awareness of the transcendent dimension of human life alive. Their creations add value to the culture and to the capacity of people within that culture to become more fully human.

Summing up this aspect of John Paul II's theology of faith and culture Gallagher notes -

> *If culture is where human beings become more human, and if different cultures represent different ways of facing the question of the meaning of existence, then the whole future of humanity is intimately linked with whatever happens in the field of culture...*
>
> *Every culture is an effort to ponder the mystery of the world and in particular of the human person. It is a way of giving expression to the transcendent dimension of human life.*[106]

The pursuit of high culture is therefore to be prized because of the artist's ability to communicate levels of meaning that transcend everyday interactions and perceptions.[107]

John Paul II and 'living cultures'

Having lived through the tragedies of successive invasions of his home country by the Nazis and the Soviets, John Paul II was well aware of the humanising and dehumanising potential in all cultures. A headline statement in his theology of 'living cultures' reads as follows:

> *(The Church has an important concern for) careful and far-sighted pastoral activity with regard to culture, and in a particular way with regard to what is called living culture, that is, the whole of the principles*

---

106 ibid., 55. The final sentence is taken from an address by John Paul II to the United Nations, 5.10.95.
107 The role and contribution of the artist in changing times is explored in some depth by Mark Hederman, Abbot of Glenstal Abbey, in *Underground Cathedrals* (Dublin: Columba Press, 2010). In particular he traces the place art and the artist have in the theologies of both Paul VI and John Paul II.

and values that make up what is called the ethos of people: 'The synthesis between culture and faith is not just a demand of culture, but also of faith. A faith that does not become culture is a faith which is not fully received, not fully thought through, not fully lived out'.[108]

This takes evangelisation a step beyond Paul VI's thinking in claiming that where faith and culture cannot be brought together, *there is a problem with the faith,* either in the way it is understood or is being transmitted! It is a small step from here to his call for a 'new evangelisation' in countries that consider themselves to have been evangelised.

For John Paul II, the mission question par excellence was: *How is the message of the Church to be made accessible to living cultures, to contemporary forms of understanding, and to new forms of human sensibility?* His answer to this question was that the Church needed to listen, and through dialogue, make sense of living cultures. This cannot happen unless the Church is prepared *to enter into dialogue with cultures.* Mission cannot proceed, the Kingdom cannot be built, without this form of interaction.

John Paul II's mission theology

John Paul II felt compelled to address the 'crisis in mission' that arose in the 1980s when a post-colonial mood took hold in newly independent countries and their governments began to ban or restrict entry to foreign missionaries. He also wished to head off the argument that, given that the Church is well established in every major cultural region of the globe, the responsibility for missionary activity should become a local matter – that is, the argument that the era of cross-cultural mission was over. The Pope responded to these developments in his encyclical letter *Redemptoris Missio* (1990) and in doing so moved Catholic thinking about faith and culture forward again.

The role of the spirit in mission

John Paul II's mission theology focuses on *the role that the Spirit plays in God's mission.* The mission of the Church, like that of Jesus, is God's work, the work of the Spirit. The Pope points out that this has been true from the beginning.[109] He highlights the meeting in Jerusalem at which Peter, Paul and the other early leaders attempted to resolve the question of who could become a member of the Christian community, and under what conditions. For John Paul II, the dynamic at work here is paradigmatic for all mission questions. The group carefully discerns the issues, seeks the guidance of the

---

108 John Paul II 'Letter Commissioning the Pontifical Council for Culture', 1982, quoted in Michael Gallagher, 59. In the last sentence, the Pope is quoting a statement he had made on an earlier occasion.
109 Pope John Paul II *Redemptoris Missio* #24.

Spirit, and then acts boldly. As a consequence of the Spirit's action in this particular incident, new insight was born and 'the Church opens her doors and becomes the house which all may enter, and in which all can feel at home, while keeping their own culture and traditions, provided that these are not contrary to the Gospel'.[110]

The Pope reinforces this point by referring to the subsequent efforts of the early missionaries to engage with people and their 'living cultures' noting how, in dialogue with these peoples, a common language and set of understandings emerged and was developed, and with them the Church's understanding of its faith. His contention is that there is a *common pattern of engagement between faith and culture* at work here with two distinguishing features:

- the Gospel takes root in a new cultural setting *because it speaks to that setting, particularly the hopes alive within it,* in a meaningful way
- the missionary, in making the Gospel known, comes to understand it in a new way, *not because he did not know it originally*, but because he knew it only *within the limited insights of his own culture*. By engaging with people in the new setting the missionary develops new insight into what the Gospel can mean.

That is, the process by which the Gospel enters into any culture is *reflexive* – it works both ways. In Catholic theology the process by which the Gospel enters deeply into a culture and becomes understood and expressed in terms of that culture is called *inculturation*. The main drivers of inculturation are the *aspirations of people* and *the power of the Gospel message to humanise* people in all cultural environments.

The power of the Gospel is not brought to a culture by the missionary; *it is already there* before the missionary arrives, because God's Spirit *is already at work in the culture*. Mission thus begins from a pre-existing starting point, and has its own dynamism which taps into the hopes people have about what the future can be.

Constants in mission: Dialogue

While Paul VI had raised the need for dialogue with the world in *Ecclesiam Suam*, it is only in the teaching of John Paul II that this becomes recognised *as a constituent element in the Church's mission. Dialogue is recognised as a second essential ingredient* in all the forms of evangelisation used to advance God's Kingdom.[111] Put another way, authentic action to advance the mission of the Church *always* involves both 'dialogue and proclamation'.[112]

---

110 ibid #25
111 When we deal with the Catholic worldview in Chapter 15 we will distinguish between *forms* and *modes* of mission.
112 See Pontifical Council For Inter-Religious Dialogue *Dialogue and Proclamation*, 1991.

The Kingdom of God revisited

John Paul II integrates his theology with that of Paul VI in pointing out that the *Kingdom of God develops under the action of God's Spirit* and so its coming always exceeds our ability to imagine what it can be. Our understanding of the Kingdom becomes clearer only in the act of living it and of being challenged by its possibilities in our particular cultural situation.

The core of John Paul II's mission theology seems best summed in the following passage from *Redemptoris Missio* (##28–29):

> *The Spirit... is at the very source of man's existential and religious questioning...*
>
> *The Spirit's presence and activity affect not only the individuals but also society and history, peoples, cultures and religions. Indeed, the Spirit is at the origin of the noble ideals and undertakings which benefit humanity on its journey through history... Again, it is the Spirit who sows the 'seeds of the Word' present in various customs and cultures, preparing them for full maturity in Christ...*
>
> *Whatever the Spirit brings about in human hearts and in the history of peoples, in cultures and religions, serves as a preparation for the Gospel...*[113]

FAITH AND CULTURE IN THE DOCUMENTS ON CATHOLIC SCHOOLING

The exploration of culture and its relationship to faith in the teaching of both Paul VI and John Paul II is nuanced and carefully developed. The implications for Catholic education are readily apparent. In this section we look at how themes addressed above have been handled in the documentation on Catholic education, taking *The Catholic School* as a case study. We focus on its treatment of the relationship between faith and culture in the context of curriculum.

Integration of faith and culture

The Catholic School views the essential *task* of Catholic schooling as bringing faith and culture together within the curriculum in a way that preserves both the integrity of the disciplines and the integrity of faith. The document argues for 'a systematic and critical transmission of culture' and for 'a living encounter with a cultural heritage' (#26) which is embodied in the subjects taught. This is done in the context of 'promoting a synthesis in the thinking and behaviour of the students' (#37) which operates at two levels:
- *a synthesis of faith and culture* through the way knowledge is acquired
- *a synthesis of faith and life* through the acquisition of virtue.[114]

---

113 John Paul II *Redemptoris Missio* (##28–29).
114 This is sometimes expressed as developing a 'Catholic worldview' and a 'Catholic character'. However, 'worldview' is understood here only in the philosophic sense, and as we will argue in the next chapter, this provides an unnecessarily narrow understanding of the term.

Because the school is seeking to achieve this aim in the context of 'cultural pluralism', it is necessary to assist students to acquire the critical thinking skills necessary to subject the range of worldviews on offer to personal and critical analysis so that they can choose what to include in their 'Christian human culture' (#48). The Catholic school therefore seeks to preserve and promote 'the spiritual and moral qualities, the social and cultural values, which characterise different civilisations' (#85) to all students. This can happen only if matched by a systematic presentation of Religious Education so that there is no 'distortion in the child's mind between general and religious culture' (#50).

While not disagreeing with the direction of the argument made here, it is obvious that a constant 'slippage' in the meaning and use of the word 'culture' muddies meaning. It is this lack of conceptual clarity which leaves some key questions unanswered and has turned the 'integration of faith and culture' into a rhetoric often devoid of precise meaning.

By failing to provide a coherent account of its key construct,[115] the document fails to address important questions that must be answered in devising a Catholic curriculum, such as:

- How is knowledge and its construction understood in our culture?
- More generally – where do the academic disciplines fit into the modern understanding of culture?
- How do you reconcile the 'evangelisation of cultures' with the counter teaching to 'respect the autonomy of disciplines'?
- How should 'high culture' and 'living cultures' come together in Catholic education?

To add to these difficulties, the concept of 'worldview' is employed in a way that implies that worldviews are 'sets of ideas' among which people can pick and choose. From the perspective of anthropology such an understanding is naïve.

Although published two years after Paul VI's primer on mission theology, *The Catholic School* fails to refer to it or draw out the implications of its teaching on 'the evangelisation of cultures' for Catholic education.[116] This seems inexplicable. If the evangelisation of culture' is a major mission priority for the Church, then *the role that knowledge systems play in the development and transformation of cultures* becomes an important mission issue.[117]

---

115 'Culture', or one of its referents, appears in 24 of the 93 paragraphs in the document. *The Catholic School* may employ 'culture' as used in *Gaudium et Spes*, but as this usage is far from precise, the matter needed to be addressed.
116 The existence of *Evangelii Nuntiandi* is not even acknowledged among the major documents referred to in the Introduction.
117 In Protestant circles this has long been recognised, and it has been missiologists such as Lesslie Newbigin, Paul Hiebert and Andrew Kirk, rather than educators, who have addressed the matter. In Catholic circles the current runs the other way.

These major weaknesses in a foundational document have bedevilled attempts to delineate and implement a Catholic curriculum. The passage of time has, however, served to throw the issues into clearer relief, which assists in the reframing of the conversation about the nature of a Catholic curriculum.

PRINCIPLE 7: THE EXPRESSIVE PRINCIPLE

In a Catholic curriculum faith and culture work together to provide expressive outlets for students so that they learn to manage the emotional depth of their experiences in constructive ways.

COMMENT

Young people invest great emotion in the way they negotiate their lifeworld. Sometimes this is well directed, sometimes not. Often through trial and error, they learn important lessons about the role feeling plays in human life and how to manage it. All cultures, if their plan for living is to be successful, provide expressive outlets through which young people can channel emotion constructively. Some of these are factored into the public curriculum, but many which involve collective performance, are part of the co-curricular program of the school. These include sport, the creative and performing arts, and in a Catholic school, liturgy, retreats, social justice initiatives and various forms of celebration. Parents also invest huge amounts of time and energy in this facet of their children's education which means it is an area in which home–school liaison is important.

The available research indicates that for many students the expressive opportunities provided by the school are their 'peak' experiences of schooling, the things students carry as important parts of their biography from their experience of the Catholic school. This aspect of school life often has a taken-for-granted status and is only partially integrated into what is seen as the 'essential' business of the school. A Catholic curriculum challenges this construction of the expressive, seeing it as having an important moral dimension. It is largely through these expressive outlets that a sense of identity is built up within the school and its status as a plausibility structure for faith established. It is also in this sphere that students discover their talents and learn to put them at the service of the community, which is a central aim of the school in promoting the moral and spiritual development of students. It is through bringing culture and faith together in personal biography and collective memory that the school 'evangelises culture'.

CONTINUING THE CONVERSATION

7.1 What are the major expressive opportunities provided within the curriculum?

7.2 Are these developed to achieve intentional goals? If so what are they and who decides what they are? What message is given to students about these goals?

7.3 How well do you think students understand this message? Why is this?

7.4 What level of home–school co-operation exists in this area? What are the major issues that need to be addressed in improving liaison on this matter?

PRINCIPLE 8: THE FAITH AND CULTURE PRINCIPLE

A Catholic curriculum draws on multiple knowledge bases and methods of enquiry to explore the changing relationship between faith and culture as this has unfolded in the development of the Western intellectual tradition, showing both the light and shade in the narrative of its development.

COMMENT

The narratives of faith and of culture in Western societies interweave and intersect as part of a single master story that is ongoing. Modernity is but one chapter in this story, and not necessarily the defining chapter. This story still has a very long way to run if what science tells us about the future of the planet is accepted. A Catholic curriculum does not shy away from this master story, even though it is not always pleasant in the telling. Students need to be grounded in terms of where they stand in the narrative of the Western tradition and what the challenges are that now face it. Similarly, they need to know where they are in the faith tradition and what are the challenges facing it. The related nature of these challenges also needs to be appreciated. In this way they come to know that they have access to living traditions and it is this vitality that underpins the confidence which people have that problems are solvable using the resources of these traditions.

It is the interdisciplinary nature of this project that gives the principle its salience as a curriculum principle.

CONTINUING THE CONVERSATION

8.1 In what specific ways does the curriculum seek to situate students within the Western tradition and the interplay of ideas that characterises this tradition?

8.2 How is the faith/culture theme dealt with as an across-the-curriculum issue? How does the school negotiate this theme in developing the curriculum?

8.3 How are major themes and narratives of Western culture addressed within the Religious Education curriculum?

8.4 Who are the major heroes and heroines presented within the curriculum? What do they stand for? How are they chosen? Are there any guidelines that apply here?

8.5 How is the 'narrative structure of all knowledge' dealt with as a theme in the development of the curriculum?

8
HOW WE SEE THE WORLD: THE WORLDVIEW CONCEPT

In previous chapters the term 'worldview' has been used in reference to three public worldviews – the 'worldview of culture', the 'worldview of the age', and the 'worldview of the faith community'. We have also used the term in another way in suggesting that each young person has a 'personal worldview'. Teachers consciously endeavour to shape this worldview in the process of education.

MEANING MAKING AT THE CONVERGENCE OF WORLDVIEWS

Our personal worldview is affected and moulded by the public worldviews which are in continual interaction with each other in response to the global forces acting upon them. The situation is complex and is summed up in Figure 8.1.

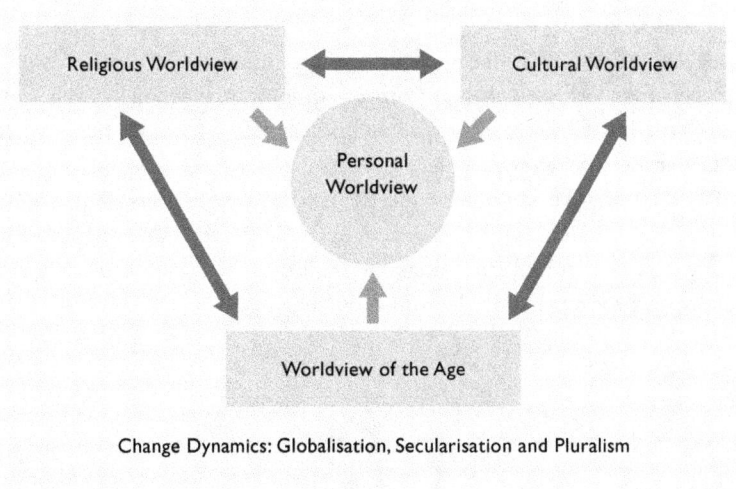

FIGURE 8.1 Context in which a personal worldview is formed

Teachers help their students understand these three public worldviews and the influences that shape them. The help on offer clearly depends on *how well teachers themselves understand the situation in which they live and teach* and how aware they are of their own worldview. The aim of this chapter is to secure the concept of 'worldview' which, like culture, has acquired a number of meanings in the popular and academic literature. This is important to our present project because Catholics do not look at the world exclusively through the worldview of faith. They recognise that faith is a gift and not all people have access to it or accept it. Thus, social and cultural life cannot be organised as if everyone had faith. Culture is recognised as having its own autonomy. The worldview of culture demands study because of the role it plays in how people, consciously and subconsciously, make sense of their lives. Understanding the worldview of culture and contributing to its development is, therefore, important.

A presupposition of the worldview of faith is that God is a creator to whose creativity there is no limit. Christian belief holds that God is active in the universe to achieve God's purposes and that God works through the hopes and aspirations of people in doing this. People identify with and pursue moral ideals and these give cultures a particular shape in a particular age. It is therefore important to understand the ideals current in the age, the dynamics that drive their development and the commitments they underpin, as well as the ways in which they are often subverted. The worldview of the age is another important area of study. Efforts to do so are a legitimate and timely response to faith.

There are two quite distinct ways in which students engage with the worldview concept in the course of their schooling:
- learning about worldviews and the academic disciplines that stand behind them
- developing the skills necessary to develop their personal worldview.

A person's worldview is their primary point of reference in making sense of life, which is why it is important to be clear about what we mean when we talk about worldviews.

'Worldview', like any other concept found to have *explanatory power*, has grown in conception as it has grown in usage. Today, as a consequence of its history, it carries multiple meanings. Like culture, it has a *modern meaning* and more recently it has acquired a *postmodern meaning*.

Modern understanding of worldview

The worldview concept was formulated and came to prominence in Europe in the high modern period.[118] It provided a way to understand and address differences in philosophical or cultural outlooks. In pre-modern Europe, people's outlook was shaped by the Christian faith. The worldviews of faith and culture largely coincided so there was no need to make any distinction between them. Other faiths were seen as either wrong or, at best, misguided. Furthermore, the idea that there could be more than one Christian view of the world simply lay beyond imagination. However, all that changed with the Reformation.

The expansion of Europe into the Americas, Africa and Asia greatly widened people's outlooks and demanded the development of a vocabulary appropriate to the new situation. It was in this context that the word 'culture' was coined. 'Worldview' emerged at a later date, first in philosophy as a way of distinguishing between philosophic systems of ideas, and later in anthropology to cover the different ways in which peoples outside Europe view the world.

In philosophy, 'worldview' refers simply to 'a coherent set of ideas'. A worldview in this early understanding is a cognitive category – *a thing of the mind*. James Sire, an influential writer on the topic, uses the word in this sense in examining nine 'worldviews' that have currency in Western society today: Christian Theism, Deism, naturalism, Nihilism, Existentialism, Eastern Pantheistic Monism, New Age Thinking, Postmodernism, and Islamic Theism.[119] These systems of ideas are often classified as *traditions* because they have been worked out over time, are sponsored by a community of adherents, and are both coherent and comprehensive. They all purport to explain how the world is.

In anthropology, 'worldview' quickly came to mean 'how people understand and engage with the world'. The meaning here has expanded and refers to *an orientation of the whole person*. It involves not only what people think but how they feel, what they value and how they react, since all these elements go together. All reflect different aspects of a person's worldview.

The initial presumption in modern anthropology was that it was possible to observe a new people and, by careful observation, determine the shape of their worldview. However, it soon became apparent that this approach did not work. The resultant observations told as much about the worldview of the person observing as they did about that of the people being observed. The conclusion was quickly drawn that *there is no worldview-free place from which to view worldviews*. We all interpret the world about us from a particular place whether we recognise this or not.

---

118 The German philosopher Immanuel Kant first coined the word 'weltanschauung' in the late eighteenth century, but it did not enter English vocabulary until quite late into the next century, and then in the context of theology and psychology.
119 James Sire *The Universe Next Door: A Basic Worldview Catalog* (Fifth edition) (Downers Lane, Illinois: Intervarsity Press, 2009). This influential book was first published in 1976.

Postmodern understanding of worldview

The initial critique by postmodern thinkers of the worldview concept as used in philosophy is that the proponents of 'worldviews' fail to acknowledge the *presuppositions* on which their 'systems of thought' are based. They point out that these 'knowledge systems' are built on axioms that are unable to be proven and so require an act of faith. Two examples illustrate this point. Nihilism denies the existence of objective truth, but if there is no such thing as truth, then why should anyone take the statement that 'there is no such thing as truth' as true! We would have to excuse this statement from the general prescription, for the statement to be true. Naturalism is based on the premise that nature forms a closed system and so, using the methods of science it is possible, if given enough time, to know and to control all aspects of this system. The axiom at work here is that nature is an intelligible system. However, science cannot prove that nature is intelligible.

A second important strand of postmodern thought focuses attention on *the axiomatic structure of all knowledge systems.*[120] This development has had a major impact on the study of worldviews. In this view, what really distinguished worldviews as knowledge systems is not so much the 'sets of ideas' they contain, but the *axioms or presuppositions* on which they depend. 'Worldview', used in the postmodern sense, denotes *the presuppositions or axioms on which a knowledge system is based*. For instance, James Sire's 1976 (early postmodern) explorations of the traditional worldviews referred to above was guided by the following definition:

> A worldview is a set of pre-suppositions (assumptions which may be true, partially true, or entirely false) which we hold (consciously or sub-consciously, consistently or inconsistently) about the basic make up of the world[121].

After exploring the development of the concept in subsequent years, Sire significantly modified this definition in his 2004 study, as we shall see.

The modern construction of 'worldview' implicitly portrays it as 'a thing of the mind'. Put another way, a 'worldview' was understood as 'a coherent set of ideas'. This view is challenged by the commonsense experience that people do not change their worldview simply as a consequence of superior logic or persuasive argument. Most religious educators dealing with adolescents can vouch that this is so! Other elements very obviously come into play. The question is what are they? Clearly presuppositions have a place.

As people responded to issues raised by the postmodern critique, a more comprehensive definition emerged that linked worldview not only to systems

---

120 'Knowledge systems' refers to both traditional worldview and to academic disciplines.
121 As quoted in James Sire *Naming the Elephant: Worldview as a Concept* (Downers Grove Illinois: InterVarsity Press, 2004), 19.

of thought and their *cognitive presuppositions*, but also included presuppositions about their *affective* and *evaluative* dimensions. In this perspective a worldview is a characteristic, or *orientation of the whole person* not just what he or she thinks. This understanding is also prominent in psychology as well.[122] According to Koltko-Rivera, Jung has been influential here. ·

> In Jung's thought worldviews are an integral part of each individual's psychological makeup and greatly influence volition, affect cognition and behaviour. Worldviews act outside consciousness and are part of the warp and woof of personality, rather than being deliberate intellectual constructions.[123]

Worldviews, however, are not confined to individuals; they are characteristics of collectives as well. As sociologists Peter Berger and Thomas Luckmann have pointed out, reality is not interpretable 'as is', it requires a hermeneutical framework. This takes the form of a culturally transmitted worldview that makes existence itself interpretable.[124] The 'worldview of a culture' then, denotes *a common orientation to life characterising people living within a given culture*.

The orientation characteristic of a worldview justifies *commitment – personal or communal*. In this sense what we are committed to, or care about, defines our worldview. This is true both of individuals and collectives.

We can recognise our commitments only by journeying inwards. How people rationalise their commitments, therefore, provides an important window into their personal worldview. From an educational point of view this means that helping young people extend their personal commitments (that is the range of people and things they care about) provides a prime means of expanding their worldview, *so long as commitment and meaning remain linked*. It is in this context that US educator Robert Starratt's injunction that teachers help young people 'put their talents at the service of the community' makes eminent sense. His further advice, which remains as relevant today as when originally given, is that young people 'need to develop a sense of the heroic'. This is something that wise teachers know instinctively to be the case.[125] Commitment provides the touchstone in determining the shape of a person's worldview. Real heroes and heroines model commitment. They are people whose narrative is built around service and caring.

---

122 Mark Koltko-Rivera traces the use of the worldview concept in psychology in a meta-study. See Koltko-Rivera 'Psychology of Worldviews' in *Review of General Psychology* (Vol. 8–1, 2004).
123 ibid. 9.
124 See Peter Berger and Thomas Luckmann *The Social Construction of Reality: A Treatise on the Sociology of Knowledge* (New York: Anchor Books, 1967), 103ff.
125 Points made in an address entitled 'The Religious Development of The Catholic School Teacher' delivered to the Superintendents of Catholic Schools, New Orleans, 1984.

Anthropologist Paul Hiebert employs the postmodern understanding of worldview defining it as:

> ….the foundational, cognitive, affective and evaluative assumptions and frameworks a group of people makes about the nature of reality which they use to order their lives.[126]

What people are committed to and care about determines the way in which they 'order their lives'. Worldview in this postmodern sense goes beyond the cognitive and includes the *moral and affective dimensions* of human experience as well. Put simply, worldview incorporates not only the questions we ask, but also how we feel about, value and utilise, the answers we give to them in responding to the demands of life.

Sire's most recent work also reflects this broader understanding. Here he amends his earlier definition, changing it to read -

> *A worldview is a commitment, a fundamental orientation of the heart, that can be expressed as a story or in a set of presuppositions (assumptions which may be true, partially true, or entirely false) which we hold (consciously or subconsciously, consistently or inconsistently) about the basic constitution of reality, and that provides the foundation on which we live and move and have our being.*[127]

His use of biblical language in the wording here reflects his worldview.[128]

ARTICULATING A WORLDVIEW

A personal worldview defines the *orientation* a person adopts in making sense of life and responding to its challenges. It can be expressed as a set of ideas and associated values that are meaningful to the person and in which he or she makes a personal investment – it is in Sire's words an 'orientation of the heart'.

---

126 Paul Hiebert *Transforming Worldviews: An Anthropological Understanding of How People Change*, 25–26.
127 ibid. 122.
128 The understanding above aligns well with that in psychology which Koltko-Rivera sums up as follows 'A given worldview is a set of beliefs that include limiting statements and assumptions regarding what exists and what does not (in actuality and in principle) what objects or experiences are good or bad, what objectives behaviours and relationships are desirable and undesirable. A worldview defines what can be known or done in the world and how it can be known or done. In addition to defining what goals can be sought in life, a worldview defines what goals should be pursued. Worldviews include assumptions that may be unproven and even unprovable, but these assumptions are super-ordinate, in that they provide the epistemic and ontological foundation for other beliefs within a belief system, 4.

An important distinction needs to be emphasised between *what a worldview is* and *how a worldview is expressed*. There can easily be a mismatch between what people say they are committed to, and what they are actually committed to. Self-reporting is not always a reliable guide in determining one's actual worldview. Most people are therefore hesitant to hold their worldview as a set of ideas; rather they *hold it as a story*, as a narrative with which they personally identify and to which they feel committed. This narrative is generally centred on what they really care about. It is only by exploring *the structure of this narrative* that the ideas, values and presuppositions that make up the worldview are revealed and come to awareness.

Teachers can help young people make use of personal narrative in helping them firstly access and then identify the contours of their developing worldview. *This process cannot be confined to particular classes, but needs to be done as opportunities arise across all classes.* It is a collective responsibility and a challenge open to all teachers, one that follows from the nature of worldview itself and of teachers' role in helping young people develop a personal worldview. It is a key indicator of a Catholic curriculum.

THE POSTMODERN DEFINITION AND PUBLIC WORLDVIEWS

Our discussion has been focused largely on personal worldview, but the postmodern understanding can be extended to cover public worldviews as well. A public worldview reflects what people collectively are committed to and care about and so is integral to their identity and how they engage with the world (their sense of mission). The worldview of culture reflects what a people is committed to and cares about. The worldview of an age reflects the concerns and commitments of peoples living in a particular historical period. The worldviews of Christian faith communities share a common commitment – Christian discipleship. Christian denominations, however, hold their worldviews within different narratives, and so express them differently.

Given its importance to all that follows, we conclude this section by offering the following working definition of worldview:

> *A worldview is an orientation of the heart that encompasses the commitments of a person. It is held and expressed either as story or as a set of beliefs and values that people feel strongly about because they underpin the commitments that guide their lives. A group can share a common 'orientation of the heart' which gives rise to public worldviews. These are mediated for individuals by the communities in which they grow up and in which they live.*

The converse of this definition also seems to be true. To the extent that people are unable to sustain commitments, they seem to lack a coherent set of beliefs and values with which to makes sense of their lives, and so find little meaning in their own narratives. A life devoid of commitment to others provides too narrow a focus for effective living.

EXPLORING WORLDVIEWS

Public worldviews, expressed either as narrative or more abstractly as a set of beliefs and values, are referred to as *traditional worldviews* or more simply as traditions. Christian Theism is an example of a tradition that is religious. Naturalism and existentialism are examples of philosophic traditions.[129]

Comparing traditional worldviews

Sire analyses and compares a selection of these *traditional worldviews* to see what they share, and how they differ, in making sense of life. His work is guided by the assumption that traditional worldviews have come to prominence because they provide a comprehensive set of answers *to life's basic questions*. While acknowledging that these questions can be formulated in a number of ways, he proposes that there are seven fundamental questions that a worldview must answer in a coherent way. Each of his questions has been expanded in the list below to illustrate its 'basic' nature. (The part in italics is Sire's question). The seven questions are:

1. *What is really real?* Why is there something out there rather than nothing?
2. *What is the nature of the world around us?* What can we say about the cosmos in which we live?
3. *What does being human mean?* What gives value to human life? How should we treat each other?
4. *What happens when we die?* Do humans have a destiny or is this it?
5. *Why is it possible to know anything?* How do I know things? What guarantee is there that things are true? What are the limits to what we can know?
6. *How do we know what is right and wrong?* On what basis can we establish our moral ideals?
7. *What is the meaning of human history?*[130] Does the human story have a direction? Does it have an ending?

These are philosopher's questions. They lack an affective dimension. However, the questions do highlight why traditional worldviews come in handy. People often adopt a traditional worldview *as a short-cut in making sense*

---

129 Scholars today argue over whether the set of ideas that are central to post-modern thought are sufficiently coherent to be considered as a tradition.
130 James Sire *Naming the Elephant: Worldview as a Concept* (Downers Grove, Illinois: InterVasity Press, 2004), 20.

of life. Because they value *some* of the answers offered by a particular worldview, they develop a degree of confidence in 'the total package' and so adopt it as their personal orientation.[131] Students in secondary classes often 'try out' these packages, sometimes to the exasperation of their teachers, particularly in Religious Education classes! However, as their experience continues to unfold, their confidence in a particular package can either grow or decline. As long as they have faith in 'the package' they have adopted, they feel no need to go elsewhere. Change becomes possible only when this confidence is shaken. Education, particularly the critical scrutiny of the packages, often plays this role. However, this can be a two edged-sword when the worldview of faith itself is put under a similar level of scrutiny. Then the way in which this worldview is articulated becomes an important educational issue.

Postmodern critique of worldviews as 'packages'

The principal characteristic of the 'postmodern condition' is that all such 'packages' are placed under suspicion and are challenged on the basis of *their unstated assumptions and overstated claims.* The underlying belief systems can fall victim to the 'hermeneutics of suspicion'. This form of critique has led to an erosion of confidence in many traditional worldviews, but especially that of naturalism which characterised the worldview of scientists in the modern period and is still present today. We will take this matter up in more detail in a later chapter.

Most people find it disconcerting to have to revisit the frameworks within which they make sense of their lives, and re-assess their value. Many Catholics have found this process difficult as it challenges the often naïve understanding they have of their faith. At the same time, many have learned to 'befriend' a faith tradition from which they have grown distant. They are engaged in what Paul Ricoeur famously termed the 'hermeneutics of retrieval', that is, finding they can make more sense of life after discovering that there are *new and unexpected depths within their own tradition.* This seems to be the situation for many teachers in Catholic schools today.[132]

A second aspect of Sire's list of questions is that it is far from innocent. *The order of the questions reflects a specific worldview.* The first question begs the answer – God – and this then shapes all the answers that follow. A modern philosopher conducting the same investigation would begin with the question – 'how is it possible to know anything?' for if we cannot be sure about what we know, then how we can know about God or, in fact have confidence in any of our answers.

---

131 This saves them working through all the issues. Culture plays an important role in this process. It is easier to 'go with the flow' than to go against it. It is easy to be a Christian when everyone is Christian! However, the obverse is also true.

132 We explore this theme in some detail in *Explorers, Guides and Meaning Makers: Mission Theology for Catholic Educators.*

Finding the right starting point and the right starting question

A comparable dilemma faces Catholic educators. While they aim to bring about an integration of the worldviews of culture, the age and the faith community, the success of this venture very much *depends on the starting point, and the questions that flow from a particular starting point*. Very often religious educators and subject teachers find themselves adopting different starting points – faith for the first group of teachers, the subject or discipline for the other. Without sincere effort the result can be a dialogue of the deaf with each group holding to the legitimacy of its starting point.

Working to a modus vivendi that will help students achieve an integrated understanding is not a matter that can be left to chance and so is a key matter for school leadership. The worldview approach offers a way forward. The worldview of culture has its own autonomy, but it also has its limits. These derive primarily from the fact *that most contemporary knowledge systems tend to interpret the world as if it were a closed system*. While in the secular context of academic study this may provide a credible working hypothesis, *it is in fact an unstated belief*, and not necessarily true. The worldview of faith views the *world as an open system*, albeit one which also has its acknowledged limits. The argument in Catholic teaching is that the worldview of culture and of faith are public worldviews that *complement each other* and it is this complementarity that teachers need to address with their students in the transmission of knowledge.

There is no worldview-free position

In dealing with worldviews it is also important to realise *that there is no neutral position* and so teachers, in particular, need to be conscious of *how their own worldview comes into play in teaching*. This is an important matter whether we are teaching students about public worldviews or teaching them the skills needed to construct a personal worldview and engage with life as a consequence. The problem, as we encounter it in our own classes, is that *few teachers in Catholic schools, even very good school leaders, seem aware of what their worldview actually is*.

The present chapter has sought to achieve two objectives:
- to give more precision to the concept of worldview by telling its story
- to trace the way in which the meaning of the concept has expanded over the past half-century.

In postmodern usage a worldview denotes a person or group's orientation to life. This orientation has cognitive, affective, and evaluative dimensions that rest on assumptions that often lie out of personal, or group, awareness and so goes unstated.

The key to a person's worldview is to be found in his or her story. Our stories are our most valuable assets, if only we realised it! We either discover God present in our stories, or we do not discover God at all. In discovering God in our stories we invite God to be part of our worldview and in return God invites us to be part of God's worldview and the mission that flows from this. This is true for individuals, for communities such as Catholic schools, and even for whole cultures.

PRINCIPLE 9: THE PUBLIC MEANING PRINCIPLE

A Catholic curriculum ensures that young people understand the major worldviews that act as sources of public meaning. It seeks to show the inter-related nature of these sources, their limits and their importance in meaning making.

COMMENT

The three major worldviews that shape meaning in the public square are the worldviews of culture, of faith and of the age. While it is possible to outline these in general terms, the important presentation of them is as they are understood and moderated *in local communities*. It is in this form that they influence the enculturation of young people. A Catholic curriculum seeks to introduce these traditions of meaning as public sources of meaning making, to clarify and critique the students' understanding of them, and to show the ways in which they are linked to the academic disciplines that stand behind the key learning areas that make up the public curriculum. Two key elements in implementing this principle are:
- situating Australian culture within the Western tradition and acknowledging the contribution of Australians to the development of that tradition
- situating the Australian Catholic community within the development of Australian culture and acknowledging the contribution that this community has made to the development of our cultural tradition.

These are important stories to tell since our students are located within them as they continue to unfold.

CONTINUING THE CONVERSATION

9.1 How is the 'worldview of culture' and its status as a public source of meaning addressed within the curriculum?

9.2 How are the variety of cultural worldviews alive in the narratives of the families that make up the school community acknowledged and celebrated?

9.3 How does the school curriculum seek to show the connections between the Australian narrative and the Western narrative and acknowledge the Australian contribution to this narrative?

9.4 How does the curriculum link the Australian narrative with the narrative of the Australian Catholic Church and so acknowledge the contribution the Church has made, and continues to make, to civic life in this country?

9.5 What understanding do staff have of the transition from a modern to a postmodern sensibility occurring in our society? How aware are they of the impact this has on debate in the public square or its translation into school curricula? Does this issue need to be addressed? If so, how?

9
MAKING SENSE OF LIFE: TRADITIONS OF MEANING

Worldviews provide us with the traditions we appeal to in making sense of the realities of life. These traditions are *the interpretive maps* we use as individuals, groups and even whole cultures, to chart a course through everyday life. The content of these traditions is important because they raise matters that have been the subject of struggle, and that people have come to value. Because these traditions embody the wisdom of a community, they are communicated from one generation to another. As providers of traditions, the worldviews of culture, of the age, and of the faith community, are sources of wisdom that we ignore at our peril.

WORLDVIEWS AND TRADITIONS OF MEANING

Our personal worldview is an interpretive map shaped by the *worldview of the culture* in which our communities are embedded. This in turn is shaped by the *worldview of the* age in which we live. Our personal worldview defines the *horizon of understanding* we bring to the task of making sense of the world and our place in it. This horizon is the boundary of our *personal map* for negotiating life. We chart our course through life, and expand this horizon in the process, by accessing other maps. The sense we can make of everyday life *depends on the confidence we have in the reliability of these maps*. As we become more aware of what these maps have to offer, we are then able to adjust our own personal worldview. We can expand our horizon and in the process make more sense of everyday life. The most commonly accessed traditions of meaning have their home in the major worldviews we have discussed – the worldview of culture, the worldview of the age and the worldview of faith.

A tradition of meaning is a public worldview as articulated. It comprises a set of presuppositions, generally held as beliefs, as well as values and narratives that are open to public scrutiny. A public worldview, as the orientation of a community, always stands behind a tradition of meaning.

Traditions of meaning: Worldview of culture

The first of these, the worldview of culture, has its source in the *need people have to live together constructively* in facing the demands of life in a particular environment. This worldview has a primary role in our enculturation. As Berger and Luckmann point out in their classic work, human beings come into the world underdeveloped and unable to survive alone. We begin life in the context of a cultural community and this shapes who we will become.[133]

In the first few years of life we learn what it means to be human, not in a generalised environment, but in particular contexts. The process goes on largely out of consciousness and without intentionality, by observation and by trial and error, within the freedoms and limits of our immediate family and community. Of course it also occurs consciously through education. While enculturation takes many forms, we always experience the three public worldviews only as these are *moderated locally for us by the communities in which we live*. This can introduce distortions into our understanding of them, their relevance to life, and the values inherent in them. Education can act as a balance and a corrective here.

The worldview of culture conveys a sense of what it means to be human, and what it means to live successfully with others. While this worldview exists in a number of forms in any society, the dominant form acts as the primary *tradition of meaning* for most people. It provides the map to which they turn to make sense of life. That is what gives culture its power.

Traditions of meaning: Worldview of the age

The worldview of an age has exercised an influence, to greater or lesser degree, on all Western cultures in a particular historical epoch, and has generally defined that epoch. It has its source in *the human aspirations underpinning the publicly shared commitments* which determine what is possible given the knowledge resources at hand. It is a worldview that appeals to the imagination. In the history of Western ideas the geographical boundaries covered by the worldview of the age have progressively shifted as the Western concept of 'the world' has expanded. The modern worldview, which we deal with in the next chapter, was the first worldview of an age to be *truly global in its influence*.

The worldview of the age, like the worldview of faith, transcends particular cultures. In pre-modern Europe, the dominant worldview was that of Christendom. This worldview shaped all the cultures in Europe, then generally considered by Europeans with their limited grasp of geography, as defining 'the world'. The Greek and Roman worldviews had operated similarly in earlier periods of Western history.

---

133 Peter Berger and Thomas Luckmann *The Social Construction of Reality* (New York: Anchor Books, 1966), 47–49.

In its several configurations in the history of Western civilisation, the worldview of a particular age has always been characterised *by the search for excellence in intellectual enquiry and in the development of knowledge.* The worldview of our present age is closely tied to the prevailing understanding of knowledge and the aspirations this gives rise to. These form part of our interpretive map, whether we realise it or not.

Traditions of meaning: Worldview of faith

Like the worldview of the age, the worldview of faith is a frame of reference that transcends cultures and exercises a pervasive influence. Christian faith holds that the Holy Spirit seeks to shape human aspiration in such a way as to realise the hopes contained in Jesus' teaching about the Kingdom of God. The worldview of faith therefore *respects the hopes embedded in the worldview of the age.* In fact, it seeks to surface these, since it is an imagination fired by hope that is the driving force in human efforts to make the Kingdom of God present in history.

The Kingdom of God can, however, have meaning *only in the context of cultures,* otherwise it remains an abstraction. *Faith therefore seeks to put down strong roots into cultures* in order to play a constructive role in each society as people continually re-adjust their 'plan for living' in changing circumstances. The hope implicit in 'evangelising cultures' is to make them more human or, put negatively, less dehumanising. In this context globalisation presents new mission opportunities and challenges in our time, as cultures are re-configured under its impact.[134] Its potential to dehumanise is evident, for example, in the urbanisation of major cities around the world and in the treatment of refugees from poorer countries who aspire to the better life available in developed countries.

As an interpretive map, the worldview of faith speaks to the hopes and lives of people challenging them to push out their horizon of understanding beyond the narrow limits of the ideologies and dominant opinions that feature so strongly in other interpretive maps. Whilst very concerned with life as experienced in the here and now, it says there is more to life than a focus on immediate concerns.

---

134 The Christian Church's understanding of culture and its significance in evangelisation underwent a quantum shift in the 20th century once it was accepted that the Holy Spirit is at work shaping the human aspirations that guide the construction of all cultures. While cultures are human constructs, and hence reflect both human strengths and limitations, 'the seeds of the Word' are to be found in all cultures, as Justin Martyr taught as early as the second century.

TRADITIONS ARE MEDIATED BY COMMUNITIES

The worldview of faith, like that of culture and of the age, is mediated for our young people by other worldviews as these *have currency in the various communities in which they grow up*. The school and family are important communities in this regard, and need to work together to help young people develop *a coherent view of what human life is all about*. This is becoming an increasingly difficult task as the postmodern mood deepens. The fact that the worldview of faith is now mediated by families and communities with limited connection to the Church presents major challenges for Catholic schools not only in curriculum leadership, but also in the broader area of school leadership.

The worldviews of the age, of culture and of faith can exist either in harmony or in dissonance. Irrespective of what the situation is, all provide maps in the form of traditions that we use in charting our course through life. They constitute our primary frames of reference. It is vital to understand the relationship between them, and how this evolves over time.

The picture built up above is summarised schematically in Figure 9.1. The worldview of faith has something to say to each level in the diagram.

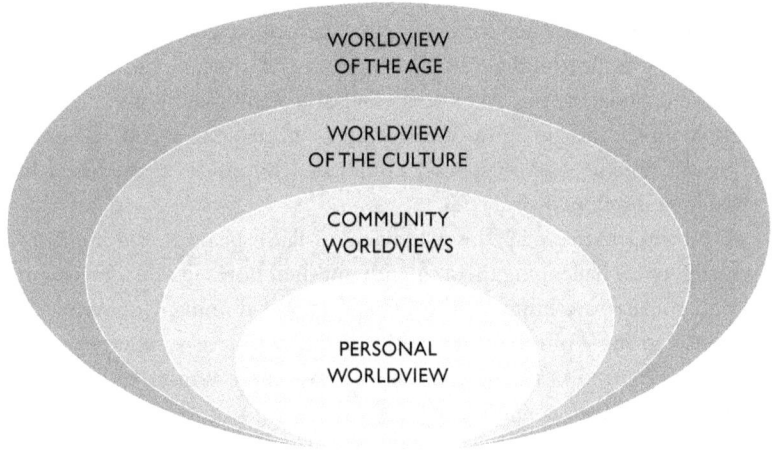

FIGURE 9.1 Worldview as an interpretive framework

TRADITIONS ARE INTERPRETIVE MAPS

Traditions of meaning deriving from worldviews are *maps* of reality. When we access the GPS in our cars, the screen provides us with selected information relative to our purpose, which is to get to our destination.

The map does not present us with all the details of the reality through which we drive, which would be unhelpful.

You can see the difference between a map and reality if you use Google Map to check out a holiday destination. Whereas the map-view gives you only a selection of the information needed to get from A to B, the satellite-view provides a much better impression of what A and B actually look like. While this is closer to reality than the GPS map, it too is still a form of map. Traditions of meaning operate in an analogous manner. They provide us with necessary knowledge *relative to our purpose*. The three worldviews are *constructed to serve different purposes*: that of the age inspires us with *hope of what can be possible*, given the tools at our disposal; that of culture tells us *how to live together*; that of faith reminds us that *life has a purpose* that transcends history but which also needs to shape how we live everyday life.

In making sense of the world we are like the medieval cartographers who compiled their maps of the world using information *drawn from a number of sources:* merchants, seamen, explorers, etc. Some of this information proved accurate and therefore reliable; some of it was simply fabricated. The quality of the input data controlled the capacity of a map to represent the reality it sought to portray. So too with creating a personal worldview; its usefulness depends on how we understand and use the sources available to us.

WORLDVIEWS AS IDEOLOGIES

Because worldviews represent reality but are not reality, all worldviews – religious and secular – have the potential to become ideologies. We use ideology here to mean *an interpretive scheme that seeks to explain all aspects of life from within its particular perspective without acknowledging the limitations of that perspective*. Communism, for instance, endeavoured to explain all of human life in economic terms. Scientism is similarly ideological and reductive. Even the worldview of faith can become an ideology, for example if it fails to acknowledge the limits to its own legitimacy. *A worldview becomes an ideology whenever its proponents forget its status as a map.* In teaching students about worldviews it is important, therefore, to *understand the limits inherent in them.*

HOW WE MAKE SENSE OF THE WORLD: WHAT IT MEANS TO INTERPRET EXPERIENCE

Drawing on the insights of moderate hermeneutics,[135] Shaun Gallagher proposes a useful model to explain how people make sense of their world. In hermeneutics 'to make sense of something' is 'to interpret it'. Hermeneutics

---

[135] Moderate hermeneutics is a post-modern development inspired by the work of Hans Georg Gadamer.

is concerned both with how the human process of interpretation works, and with what are its limits.[136]

One way to explain how we encounter new ideas or new situations and make sense of them is set out in Figure 9.2. In this picture we make sense of everyday life within a certain pre-existing horizon of understanding based in our personal worldview. We make sense of the unfamiliar by reference to the familiar and in this process our understanding grows. However, that is not the whole story, as teachers are well aware.

The unique ability of humans is not only to know something, but *to reflect on what they know and how they came to know it*. Thus, we can look at a new experience again but this time from within our expanded understanding and re-evaluate its significance.

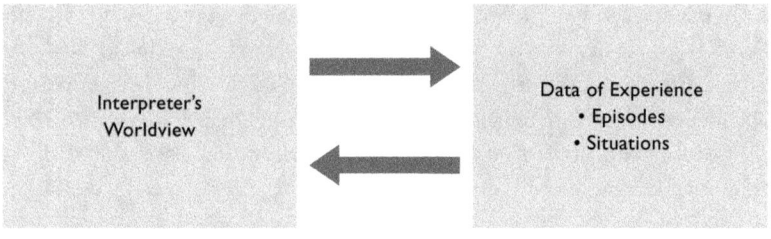

FIGURE 9.2 The simple model of interpretation

A good example of this process occurs when you travel to a new country, particularly if you go there to do business. Engaging with the local people involves a non-stop process of interpretation, both of what they are saying and how they are acting. Having absorbed this, you then have to reflect on whether or not you have 'read the signs' correctly. It is through this process of reflection that you may learn that the way the 'locals' do business is not quite the way you are used to, and you will have to adapt if you are to succeed.

Jesus makes much the same point to the Pharisees and Sadducees in Matt 16:3 when he points out that they are unable to interpret 'the signs of the times'. Our whole conversation about the Catholic curriculum is an exercise in reading the signs of the times, of becoming conscious that we have to take something new on board and that this has serious consequences for us.

---

136 Hermeneutics began as the study of the rules governing the interpretation of texts to uncover the meaning the author intended. The immediate focus was the Bible, but later extended to ancient authors and, more recently, to legal documents. In a post-modern development it was realised that we 'interpret' a whole range of entities as well as texts human behaviour being the most obvious so the notion of 'text' was extended, giving rise to philosophic hermeneutics. Moderate hermeneutics is the school of thought within philosophic hermeneutics which holds that it is possible to get to the meaning of a text, but that our capacity to do so is limited.

These are two instances of the broader process of meaning making in which our understanding of the world expands by *developing new insight into the meaning of a part in terms of a pre-existing whole* and then *reformulating that whole in terms of our new understanding of the part*. This then leads to greater insight into the part and so on. Our understanding grows through an iterative process. Philosophers refer to this cyclical process of meaning making as the 'hermeneutical circle'.[137]

However, Figure 9.2 simplifies what is actually a more complex situation. Our meaning making process functions in the background of thought, and becomes conscious, or intentional, only when we are confronted by experiences that perplex us. Such experiences challenge the adequacy of our 'interpretive map' to make sense of things, particularly when we are confronted by experiences which demand a lot of us. If we are able to interpret these experiences in a way that is meaningful, then we learn to value the traditions of meaning on which our interpretive map depends. We feel more secure in using it and more confident in dealing with our experiences. We also come to accept the larger traditions of meaning as reliable guides to what is real and authentic in life. To take this into account we have to expand our model.

MAKING SENSE OF EVERYDAY LIFE: ADVANCED WORKING MODEL

When we find ourselves unable to make sense of a new situation we tend to respond in either of two ways:
- we question the *reliability* of our reference maps
- we question *whether we are reading the maps correctly*.

In the first instance, we put questions to the traditions of meaning into which we have been enculturated. In the second we question ourselves. In this process we become aware of the limits of our maps, or of ourselves in making sense of them. This situation is more fully represented in the working model set out in Figure 9.3 which indicates that *sitting behind our personal worldviews* are the *traditions of meaning* which are always at work in the background of our thinking when we seek to make sense of things. Because they operate at the sub-conscious level and so are out of sight we often fail to notice how they affect our thinking.

---

137 While the term 'hermeneutical circle' is widely used, the iterative nature of the interpretation process makes it more spiral than circle.

FIGURE 9.3 The meaning making process (Gallagher 1992)[138]

When trying to make sense of new situations or events, we do so by unconsciously *employing pre-understandings embedded in the traditions of meaning that have shaped our personal worldview* (Arrow a). These are accepted as part of the 'package', or map, we routinely employ in making sense of the unfamiliar.

If a tradition of meaning has been corrupted in the process of its transmission through the family or local communities, this introduces distortions that generally appear in the form of biases in these pre-understandings. The whole point of questioning students in the process of learning is to uncover such biases and bring them to conscious awareness so that they can be tested. These biases often determine what students see as 'relevant' in learning. To sum up, we interpret our experiences *within a framework* of which we are, at best, only partially aware and of which we have only partial knowledge (Arrow b).

Through the process of reflection we are able to reshape our worldview, by recognising the limited nature of our *pre-understandings, or our poor grasp of them* (Arrow c). This can even lead to a change in our understanding of a tradition of meaning itself (Arrow d).

There are several options here:
- we can *'befriend' the tradition* recognising that the problem was not with the tradition but with our understanding of it
- we can abandon the tradition altogether because we now judge it to be inadequate
- we can see the tradition as valuable but incomplete, and decide to contribute to its further development.

Thus, the act of interpretation can place us in a new relationship to the traditions on which we come to depend in making sense of the world and our place in it.

This more complex model enables us to understand the situation our students face today as they try to make sense of their experiences. In a multi-cultural and multi-faith society their socialisation into the communities that shape their lives is often weak because of the *multiple traditions of meaning* now at play. Modern communication systems highlight the variety of options that exist so that it is now virtually impossible

---

138 Shaun Gallagher *Hermeneutics and Education* (New York: State University Press, 1992), 106.

to limit young people's access to the multiple traditions of meaning. As a consequence, students fail to develop confidence in any tradition of meaning and so fail to acquire a coherent map to assist in charting their way through life.

Limiting access to worldviews has been a key feature of traditional enculturation processes. Catholic schools, and indeed many faith-based schools, have sought to keep young people apart from other interpretive systems during their formative years in order to give them a sound grounding in the faith tradition of their families. This form of separation is no longer possible and this projects Catholics into a new and challenging situation in regard to the mission and process of Catholic schooling.

WORKING WITH TRADITIONS OF MEANING

Traditions of meaning are embedded in the very language we use. David Hay's work, to which we referred earlier, has highlighted this. In the secular culture of Britain, the suppression of religious language in society has been such that it now inhibits many young people's ability to articulate experiences that in other cultures would be described as 'spiritual' or 'religious'. When the young people encountered in Hay's research had such experiences, they were largely inarticulate when it came to describing them.

Traditions of meaning and the role of language

If a person lacks the language to describe experience, then the obvious course of action is to question whether the experience was real. This is because you seem to be operating outside what your culture defines as 'normal' in its use of everyday language. However, if the person is convinced that it is real, then he or she has to find a tradition of meaning *that has the linguistic capacity to make sense of it*. Today while it is possible to draw on the many options available – Christian, Buddhist, New Age, etc., – or some combination of these, in order to do this, for the most part, the language of a faith lies outside the common stock of language for most people. A secularisation of language has occurred, even for people of faith.

A common interpretation of the beliefs and worldviews of young people is that students today create a personal worldview by selecting their beliefs and values eclectically from the B&V Supermarket. If the moderate hermeneutics model outlined above is true, then such an interpretation is nonsense. Culture has determined the choices open to students long before they reach the supermarket, and even when they get there, what they find on offer is more a remnant sale than anything else.

Role of self-reflection in meaning making

When people live unreflective lives, the tradition of meaning dominant in their culture becomes their interpretive map, by default. Catholic education stands as a challenge to this happening. The ancient Greeks were well aware of the need for self-reflection. Socrates espoused 'know thyself' as his organising theme when leading his students on the search for wisdom.

If a central goal of education in a Catholic curriculum is, as we suggested at the outset, 'to make the faith and wisdom of the community accessible to a younger generation in a way that is meaningful to them' then, given how we make sense of everyday life, five things seem necessary:

- to encourage our students to be self-reflective in their learning
- to understand the major traditions of meaning that shape contemporary life and the dynamics by which each evolves since each is *a living tradition*
- to grasp the relationships that exist between them
- to understand the limits of each as an interpretive map
- to understand the major forces currently at work reshaping these traditions.

These five tasks constitute *a basic responsibility* for all educators committed to the development of their students. They raise issues central in any discussion about a Catholic curriculum.

FRAGMENTATION OF MEANING AND THE RECONSTRUCTION OF PERSONAL WORLDVIEWS

The fragmentation of meaning has become a major social issue in our time. Noted sociologist Leo Apostel and a group of academic colleagues, drawn from universities across Belgium, Holland and Germany, have endeavoured to address this problem. They initiated a project over a decade ago aimed at helping young people *become active agents in constructing a coherent worldview*. The motivation for their project was the realisation that the social world in Europe was fragmenting rapidly because the major religious and social movements that had previously provided the energy needed to build human communities, had largely collapsed. As they note 'outside of science, (European) sociologists seem to agree that the informed public feels intellectually, ethically and politically lost'.[139] In their view, ordinary people have lost confidence in traditional worldviews in making sense of the world and now attempt to make sense of their lives by appealing to the 'fragments

---

139 Leo Apostel et al. *Worldviews: From Fragmentation to Integration* 2007 Internet Edition, 4. http://pespmc1.vub.ac.be/clea/reports/worldviewsbook.html (accessed 1 June, 2011). Diederik Aerts is listed first in the alphabetical listing in the internet edition, but Apostel is the most widely quoted member of the team.

of these worldviews' that still have currency in society. They have become a people who have lost contact with the narratives that give life meaning.

To address the situation, Apostel and his colleagues sought to establish a way in which young people could begin to reconstruct a personal worldview that was *coherent* and that would *enable them to make sense of their experience* (including the experience of feeling lost). Their project did not pretend that there is such a thing as *the* worldview; rather, it sets out to establish 'a new starting point for an important human endeavour' by proposing a number of questions that need to be answered in formulating a coherent personal worldview. These are:

1. What is the nature of our world? How is it structured and how does it function?
2. Why is our world the way it is, and not different? Why are we the way we are and not different? What kind of global explanatory principles can we put forward?
3. Why do we feel the way we feel in this world and how do we assess global reality and the role of our species in it?
4. How are we to act and to create in this world? How, in what different ways, can we influence the world and transform it? What are the general principles by which we should organise our actions?
5. What future is open to us and our species in this world? By what criteria are we to select these possible futures?
6. How are we to construct our image of this world in such a way that we can come up with answers to (1), (2), and (3)?
7. What are some of the partial answers that we can propose to these questions?[140]

The questions are designed to intersect, and yet unite to form a whole without necessarily canonising any particular set of answers.

For Apostel and his colleagues, the starting point in any process of actively constructing a worldview is to help people identify those fragments of traditional worldviews that still have currency within their culture and pose the question – *why these fragments and not others?* In other words, they are trying to *reconnect 'the map' to a cultural narrative that gives it significance*. The model clearly seeks to *push out the imaginal horizon within which young people understand the world* in order to see new possibilities and so release the energy that goes with new hopes. In their own way, this project seeks to bring together the worldviews of the age and of culture, seeing them as *sources* that people can use to make more sense of everyday life.

---

140 ibid. 13.

TRADITIONS OF MEANING: IMPLICATIONS FOR A CATHOLIC CURRICULUM

A Catholic curriculum seeks to provide people with a way of interpreting the world capable of standing alongside, and putting questions to, the worldviews that they automatically access in meaning making. The worldview of faith puts questions to the 'commonsense' interpretations of experience that these provide. In turn the worldview of faith must be capable of critical scrutiny itself.

An example of the reflexive nature of the relationship between public worldviews can be drawn from early science. Young people growing up in the 15th century saw the sun rise in the east and set in the west. The commonsense interpretation of this phenomenon was that the sun revolved around the earth. Once they knew that this was not the case, it took a conscious effort to reinterpret what commonsense had told them. Over time this becomes automatic. The point is that *the commonsense interpretation of things is not always right and can change. At the same time these young people were told that what was in the Bible was true.* So they faced a dilemma since people interpreted the Bible as saying the sun revolved around the earth so supporting the commonsense interpretation. So questions had to be put to the Bible as well as commonsense. The basis to resolving this dilemma lay in *respecting the integrity of legitimated methods of enquiry*. This is a basic stance for a Catholic curriculum.

The essential argument of this chapter is that teachers in Catholic schools now operate in a changed context for meaning making and need to understand not only the context but also the process by which meaning is made if they are to educate young people effectively. The project of Apostel and colleagues reflects a secular concern for an issue now well documented by Christian educators – that since the 1970s there has been *a substantial change in people's capacity to interpret their experiences meaningfully*.

Catholic educators are faced with the task of transmitting the most complex of all the traditions of meaning – the worldview of faith. They will have succeeded in this project when their students come to understand that the deepest aspirations of their culture and their age find a home within the worldview of faith.

PRINCIPLE 10: THE PERSONAL MEANING PRINCIPLE

A Catholic curriculum assists students to understand, articulate, and critique what they learn and in the process establish the key elements in a coherent and personally appropriated worldview.

COMMENT

Students acquire a basic interpretive framework in a process that occurs largely 'behind their backs', drawing on sources located in family, peers, the media, etc., which are often appropriated uncritically. The resultant framework is often fragmented and untested and rests on presuppositions that do not stand up to scrutiny. It is in attempting to articulate what this framework is that its strengths weaknesses and biases surface. In our experience, many teachers have had few opportunities to go through this form of personal development and so struggle to articulate what they really believe and value and to examine its coherence. Without such opportunities, implementing this principle can result in the blind leading the blind.

A Catholic curriculum provides opportunities for the types of self-reflection and inter-subjective engagement needed to bring personal meanings to consciousness, to articulate them and critically assess them. While the outcome is often unpredictable, the effort is important. Teachers engaging in this project need to have some awareness of the contours of their own personal worldview.

CONTINUING THE CONVERSATION

10.1 How does the school promote thinking skills within the curriculum?

10.2 What strategies and processes are used to assist students to recognise and adapt biases within their thinking?

10.3 How does the school encourage students to articulate what it is that they really believe? Is this confined to particular areas, and if so why?

10.4 How does the curriculum encourage self-reflection or reflection-on-action among students? In what areas is this most likely to happen? What scope exists to make this an across-the-curriculum issue? What goal should such a curriculum policy seek to achieve?

PRINCIPLE 11: THE HERMENEUTICAL PRINCIPLE

A Catholic curriculum is informed by an explicit theory of meaning making.

COMMENT

In contemporary hermeneutics, there are four principal schools of thought[141]:
- conservative hermeneutics (Hirst) which sees the purpose of education as cultural reproduction and so of reproducing society as it is
- moderate hermeneutics (Gadamer) sees the purpose of education as the critical transmission of the tested traditions on which meaning depends
- critical hermeneutics (Habermas) has much in common with moderate hermeneutics, but critiques the ideologies implicit in traditions and the power interests at work in their interpretation
- radical hermeneutics (Derrida) denies the existence of meaning *per se* and reduces everything to interpretation which can be good or bad depending on the community of interpreters. There is no associated educational theory at this stage.

In this Chapter, we have adopted the moderate hermeneutics model as an explicit theory of meaning making appropriate to a Catholic curriculum.

CONTINUING THE CONVERSATION

11.1 In what specific ways does the curriculum place a premium on the skills of meaning making?

11.2 Does the curriculum, in fact, include a coherent understanding of meaning making? If so, how is it articulated?

11.3 What strategies do teachers customarily use so that students see the whole in terms of the parts and vice versa? Is the hermeneutical circle used as a pedagogical principle in the development of the curriculum?

11.4 What light does the model of moderate hermeneutics throw on the use of these strategies? What changes/alternatives does it suggest?

11.5 Is it possible, or even desirable, for the school to promote a cohesive approach to meaning making? What are the pros and cons associated with such an approach? What impact would such an approach have on the pedagogical practice of the school?

---

141 See Shaun Gallagher for a detailed outline of these four schools of thought.

Part D
THE WORLDVIEW OF THE AGE AS A PUBLIC SOURCE IN MEANING MAKING

Traditions of meaning are the primary interpretive frameworks we appeal to in making sense of the world. They enable us to link our experiences meaningfully to what we know and value so that our understanding of these traditions grows and our personal interpretive framework (worldview) expands.

Traditions of meaning shape what we see as worth learning. Because there is more than one tradition of meaning available to us, we experience these as co-existing either in competition or in co-operation. In our discussion to date we have already encountered three such generic traditions of meaning – *the worldview of the culture in which we live*, *the worldview of the age* and the *worldview of faith*. If young people see these frameworks as existing in competition then they are more or less forced to make a choice for one or the other so that affirming one casts doubt on the other. On the other hand, if these are seen as complementary, then to affirm one is to affirm the other. The understanding we hold about traditions of meaning, therefore, plays an important role in what we see as *valuable knowledge* and so underpins our commitment to learning. This is true for students; it is also true for teachers and school leaders.

The worldview of the age exercises a pervasive influence on all cultures in the region in which it becomes dominant. Since the focus of this study is developments in Western thought, we are dealing with the worldviews that have been dominant there. In the Middle Ages, the medieval worldview shaped the cultures of most of the countries in present-day Europe. It was successor to the Greek and Roman worldviews in this regard. Of course, people living in these periods did not think in terms of 'culture' as we use the term today; rather they spoke of 'civilisation'.

In terms of its influence on cultures, the worldview of faith operates in a similar manner to the worldview of the age. The Christian worldview, for instance, has had a pervasive influence in Western cultures during a timeframe that runs across several ages. So enduring has this influence been that people living in non-Western cultures today see Christianity as 'the religion of the West' despite the fact that Christianity had its origins in the Middle East and is today a dominant influence in Africa, Latin America, Eastern Europe and parts of Asia such as China and Korea. Indeed, the influence exercised by the worldview of Christian faith is greatly diminished in the West today, due in no small part to the influence that the modern worldview, understood in ideological terms, exercises over the knowledge structures of Western cultures. The emergence of this worldview in modernity represents a major shift in the Western intellectual traditions and this is traced in Chapter 10 which follows its development from Descartes to Nietzsche.

The hegemony of the modern worldview is challenged by the postmodern critique and is undergoing serious revision in consequence. It is important that teachers understand the nature of this critique and its impact, since it works in the background shaping curriculum theories through the influence it has in the way knowledge is constructed. This critique runs in two directions. The first is that of 'deconstruction', the attempt by postmodern thinkers to examine why the modern worldview had failed Europe. Prominent thinkers in this direction are the three Frenchmen – Jean-Francois Lyotard, Jacques Derrida and Michel Foucault. Their approach and contribution encapsulate a much wider movement. Their stance is prophetic in the sense that they highlight the 'gap' which exists between what modernity promised and what it delivered in Europe, particularly in the first half of the 20th century. Their thought is framed against the experience of growing up in Europe as it was reconstructed following the Second World War. For them the devastation of war was not only physical, but also intellectual, and moral. We call these the 'prophets of deconstruction' and their critique of modernity is set out in Chapter 11.

There is another group of influential postmodern thinkers who also take a critical view of modernity, but hold that the modern project has not failed, rather it was side-tracked by taking 'an ideological turn' that compromised its best ideals. While they are critical of this ideology and the assumptions on which it is built, they have kept faith with its aspirations and its moral ideals and now seek to retrieve these. These thinkers also highlight the 'gap' that exists between what modernity promised and what it delivers and so their stance is also prophetic. We take social philosophers Jurgen Habermas and Charles Taylor, and more briefly Australian theologian John Thornhill, as representative of the wider groups of 'prophets of reconstruction'. The direction this group gives to postmodern thought, and the issues this raises for a Catholic curriculum, are covered in Chapter 12 which rounds out our treatment of the 'worldview of the age' as a source of public meaning.

10
THE WORLDVIEW OF MODERNITY

The modern worldview has so penetrated the worldview of Western cultures that it serves as a default tradition of meaning to which people, including Catholic school teachers, tend to appeal in making sense of the world. For the majority of people in the West its prescriptions still define what is taken as 'commonsense'. As well as this, *it is important to note that elements of the modern worldview provide the intellectual scaffolding for the disciplines taught both in schools and tertiary institutions.* For a variety of reasons, therefore, a study of the modern worldview, its strengths and limitations, is crucial to any considerations of the contemporary curriculum.

To understand the significance of the modern worldview as an interpretive framework, it is necessary to situate it within the Western intellectual tradition. The modern period, a lengthy era beginning in the 15th century and unfolding across the subsequent five centuries, is a period in which a significant shift occurred in human consciousness. On the positive side, a *growing sense of the self as independent or autonomous* emerged, while on the negative side there was a corresponding *loss of faith in the Christian religious tradition as a tradition of meaning.* As Canadian philosopher Charles Taylor points out, the narrative of modernity is a composite tale, including both *addition stories* and *subtraction stories.*[142] For Taylor, the unique feature of modernity is that, for the first time in the history of the Western cultural tradition, *the final goal of human life was taken as 'human flourishing'*, understood in this-worldly and individualistic terms. He labels this 'exclusive humanism' – 'humanism' because of its interest in human flourishing, 'exclusive' because it excludes consideration of the transcendent in making sense of human life.

---

142 Charles Taylor *A Secular Age* (Cambridge, Massachusetts: Belknap Press of Harvard University Press, 2007), 22.

MODERNITY WITHIN THE WESTERN INTELLECTUAL TRADITION

In discussing modernity, it is helpful to realise that the term 'modern' can be used in two distinct ways. Firstly, it can refer to that *period of history* characterised by an emerging aspiration in the West for greater personal autonomy. In this sense the phrase 'the modern world' is used interchangeably with 'modernity'. 'Modern' can also refer to *a human sensibility* tied to a specific worldview. Used in this way 'modernity' and 'modern' both denote an intellectual movement that has deep roots in the human psyche even today.

In the course of its long development modernity passed through a number of stages. As these unfolded, the modern worldview became progressively more secular in its orientation. The social order of pre-modern societies had left the bulk of people dependent on the will of others. This dependency was understood in moral terms, because the social order was perceived as divinely ordained. Modernity developed as a reaction to this situation as Europe became more settled and more prosperous.

Modernity is characterised by many remarkable achievements. From our present perspective the most notable among these has been the development of modern knowledge systems and the methods of enquiry that underpin them. In his study of modernity, Australian theologian John Thornhill notes that the Western intellectual tradition is built on *shared commitment to accountable intellectual enquiry in the search for excellence.*[143] This tradition had two major thrusts: firstly *developing valid methods of enquiry,* and secondly *testing the truth of propositions* using these methods. Enduring commitment to these two endeavours resulted in the exponential expansion of human knowledge and technology in the modern period.

The Western tradition has been driven by a restless curiosity in three areas: to know about the natural world in order to control it; to explore what it means to be human; and to investigate the mysterious workings of the human mind so that we might come to know what makes enquiry possible and what renders knowledge true. The questions that this curiosity generated have taken different forms in different eras – Greek, Roman, Medieval, etc., – and answers have been arrived at through different methods of enquiry. However, the constant in all these endeavours has been *the commitment of scholars to get at the truth of things.*

Genesis of a tradition

The systematic search for truth was the culture-defining feature of ancient Greece. Among the many geniuses of the era, Socrates, Plato and Aristotle

---

143 John Thornhill *Modernity: Christianity's Estranged Child Reconstructed* (Grand Rapids, Michigan: William. B. Eerdmans, 2000), vii-ix.

introduced the West to *philosophic enquiry* as a way of putting questions to life. Dialectic, as illustrated by Socrates' interrogation of the 'truths of common sense', provided us with a method of *systematic intellectual inquiry*. In dialectic, a statement is proposed as true and questions are put to it to test its internal coherence and external validity. Socrates is credited with establishing dialectic as a *paradigm of enquiry*. Its enduring value is witnessed to by the fact that it has had a perennial place in the education of lawyers and teachers.

The Greeks developed other methods of enquiry which complemented dialectic. The great dramatists of the day, Euripides and Sophocles, made literature an important method of enquiry into the human condition. Herodotus introduced history as a means of enquiry into what makes us human. This multi-dimensional pursuit of 'shared intellectual enquiry' set the pathway for the development of what Richard Tarnas calls *The Passion of the Western Mind*.[144] An intellectual tradition was born in Greece that would shape the cultures of people in the West for millennia.

As the Western tradition developed, new *knowledge systems* were created and with these new frames of reference were developed to make sense of life. With the Romans came law, with the early Middle Ages agriculture, with the Renaissance humanism, economics, and so on. The Western tradition has been alternatively breathtakingly creative, prone to become iconoclastic, and ever open to hubris. 'West is best' has long been its motto. The ideological nature of Western political systems has meant that pluralism in ideas has only relatively recently become one of its distinguishing characteristics.

Late Middle Ages: Dialectic reaches its limits

Thornhill argues persuasively that modernity began as a reaction to the worldview dominant in the late medieval period. The intellectual life of Medieval Europe had been dominated by the Scholastic Movement which began in the 9th century, reached its zenith in the 13th century, and then slowly lost focus. Scholasticism relied heavily on *the method of dialectic* to explore all questions, philosophic, theological and scientific. The movement's initial direction was set by Augustine (354–430) whose thought was dominant in Europe for nearly a millennium.[145] He viewed 'faith as an aid to reason', but also realised that the converse is true – '*reason* is an aid to faith'.[146] In Augustine's view a person had to know what to believe in order to believe.

---

144 Richard Tarnas *The Passion of the Western Mind: Understanding the Ideas that have Shaped Our World View* (New York: Ballantine Books, 1991).
145 Augustine was born in modern Algeria and after a successful career as a teacher in both Carthage and Milan was baptised and returned to his home town in North Africa. The local community requested that he be ordained. He later became the bishop in Hippo (near modern Annaba).
146 Pope John Paul II used these two phrases taken from Augustine as chapter headings in his encyclical letter *Faith and Reason* (1998) Chapter 11 'Credo Ut Intellegam (I believe that I may understand) and Chapter 111 'Intellego Ut Credam' (I understand that I may believe).

Augustine, perhaps more than any other thinker of the Patristic Era (second to the fifth centuries), established theology as *a form of rational enquiry* into religious truth. Augustine formulated Christian theology systematically using the categories of Plato's philosophy.[147] It would not be until the High Middle Ages, when Christian scholars re-gained access to the works of Aristotle, that an alternative base would be developed for theological enquiry. The towering figure in this endeavour was Thomas Aquinas whose synthesis of Christian theology and Aristotelian philosophy set what Catholic Church leaders, even today, see as the standard in theological enquiry.[148] The projects that Augustine and Aquinas initiated shared a common aim – to provide *a rational basis for theological enquiry* that complemented the more mystical and intuitive thinking also alive in the Christian community.

Scholasticism's reliance on the method of dialectic limited its scope as a means of intellectual enquiry, particularly when in the late Middle Ages people were asking new questions about the natural world.[149] Through the so-called Dark Ages, knowledge about agriculture had advanced in leaps and bounds. People, now freed to some extent from the constant struggle for survival, began to ask practical questions about the natural world and about the treatment of common diseases. The time was right for 'the passion of the Western mind' to develop methods of enquiry that could answer these questions.

Church control of knowledge systems

In the late medieval world, the relationship between the academic community, the political community and the Church community was markedly different from what it is today. At that time, the Church controlled the knowledge systems of the day. It legitimated theology, and theology legitimated other knowledge. The Church also licensed teachers and so controlled education. This pattern operated across most of Medieval Europe. Theology's pre-eminence is reflected in its title in medieval times as 'the queen of sciences'– a title that seems quaint to us today because the word 'science' no longer has the meaning it had in the Middle Ages.[150]

In early modernity, the political balance changed and the relationship between the political, academic and religious spheres took on a new

---

147 The works of Aristotle, with the exception of his treatment of logic, were not available in the West as Christianity took shape. They were preserved by Muslim scholars and recovered only in the thirteenth century.
148 ibid. #43.
149 Scholasticism made a resurgence in the late nineteenth and first half of the twentieth centuries driven by the belief that the philosophical thinking of Aristotle embodies a level of truth that cannot be easily ignored. Aristotelian thought, shorn of errors in scientific fact, still represents a valuable philosophical synthesis a perennial philosophy.
150 The word 'science' derives from the Latin word 'scientia' which is translated as 'knowledge'.

configuration. On the theological front, the hegemony of Catholic theology was challenged by the theology of the Reformers (16th century). This split the religious community and brought about new political alignments, so ending the Church's control of education in many countries. Theology lost its status as the primary 'science'. Independently of these developments, Copernicus (1473–1543) proposed a new paradigm in astronomy, one that challenged Ptolemy's earth-centred model of the solar system. Galileo (1564–1642) added to the general discomfort of the time by demonstrating *through direct observation* that the Moon and Venus were not perfect spheres as was required by Aristotelian cosmology.

Rise of the modern academy

So intimately had the natural sciences and theology become entangled, through the dominance of Aristotle's thought, that a challenge to the former, even one based on direct observations, was deemed by Church authorities as heretical. The work of Copernicus was condemned and Galileo, charged with heresy for defending it, lived out the remaining years of his long life under house arrest.

Church leaders were blind to the possibilities which the method of enquiry pioneered by Galileo, and now pursued by others, could open up, and they misread the aspirations for *autonomy in intellectual enquiry* that drove this development. This is understandable if one recalls that culture and faith were so interwoven in the medieval worldview that they could not easily be separated. The idea that there is *a legitimate secular order of knowledge* had still to emerge in practice within the Church even though, as Thornhill points out,[151] it is recognised in Aquinas' teaching. Thus they rejected the new developments. As a consequence, the relationship between the academic community and the Church community was redrawn. As modernity unfolded, the academic community came to take on the role previously held by the Church community in the legitimation and guardianship of knowledge. To these responsibilities a new warrant was added – to oversee *development of the specialised knowledge on which the social systems of modernity depended* – in health, welfare, commerce, education, politics, etc.

The Reformation and the development of methods of enquiry based on the careful observation of nature in the late sixteenth and early seventeenth centuries were the initial steps on modernity's long march to becoming the dominant ideology that it is today. With these taken, the aspiration that would characterise modernity in its later stages and give it moral force, was free to emerge – *desire for personal autonomy*.[152] As the 17th century drew to a close,

---

151 Thornhill, 29.
152 Charles Taylor develops this theme in *The Ethics of Authenticity* (Cambridge, Massachusetts: Harvard University Press, 1991).

this aspiration saw the gradual emergence of a worldview that would recast the social, religious and political systems in European cultures and result in the knowledge structures of those cultures being formulated in secular terms.

Sustaining a 'Shared and accountable enquiry'

By the 18th century, the major contours of the new interpretive framework were in place developed through *the sustained efforts of a succession of creative thinkers*. Figure 10.1 shows the remarkable historical overlap among the key players shaping early modernity. Each made a major contribution to the development of the modern worldview. However, it was the grand synthesis of Newton in physics that generated greatest confidence in the emerging 'scientific' methodology and in the new possibilities this opened up in exploring 'the truths of nature'. People in Newton's day thought that he had discovered the 'truth of things'– had discovered what God knew!

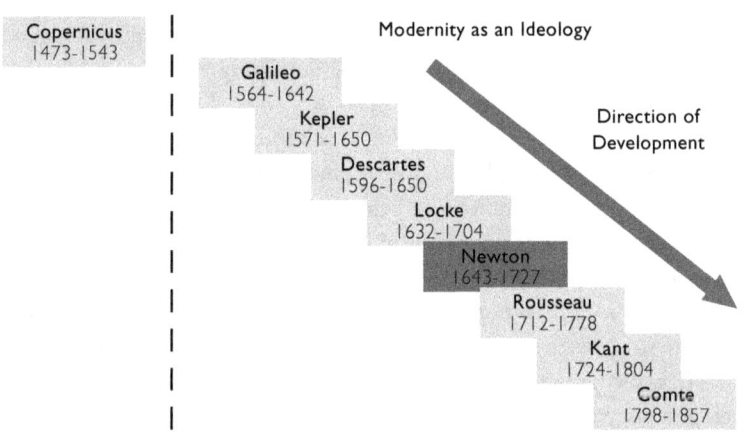

FIGURE 10.1 Prime movers in the creation of the modern ideology

In commenting on early modernity Thornhill makes a valuable observation:

> *What is essential to modernity is a rejection of medievalism, in the name of proper human autonomy, an autonomy that calls the traditionally accepted ways of the Middle Ages to account. It was an accident of history that the project of modernity seized upon this particular methodology as its privileged instrument. Once this choice had been made, however, it was to play a very decisive part in modernity's further development. In the last analysis, however, these developments were an expression of the peculiar genius of our Western cultural tradition: its restless quest for the ideal, and its recognition of reason as essential to the pursuit of this ideal.*[153] (emphasis added)

153 Thornhill, 23

Put in other words, Thornhill's case is this: if many Christians today are unhappy with the rampant secularisation of life that characterises the present age, they should have some sympathy for thinkers in early modernity who were similarly unhappy with the rampant 'sacralisation' that characterised their own age. Their desire was to be free of this, recognising it as a distorted vision of how things should be. As Western history fully illustrates, it is when ideologies are given full rein that their inherent limitations become especially apparent. Something similar is happening with the secularisation of our own age.

MODERNITY TAKES DEFINITE FORM

There is perhaps no character more centrally linked with the rise of modernity than the brilliant French thinker Rene Descartes. His story in many ways highlights the ambiguities inherent in the modern worldview.

Descartes' unintended revolution

Descartes made three major contributions that helped set modernity on its triumphant path. He revolutionised philosophy by re-setting its starting point; he formulated the first philosophy of science; and he provided early science with a vision that would guide its future development. His vision, perhaps more than any other, shaped the modern worldview.[154]

In the pre-modern period, Scripture and Catholic theology provided the foundation of knowledge. However, as a result of the Reformation, multiple understandings of Scripture had arisen, and theological disputes between the Catholic Church and the Reformers resulted in theology losing much of its cultural force. Religion was discredited when the coercive power of civic authorities was invoked to enforce 'orthodox' theological views. This happened on both the Catholic and Protestant sides. As the 16th century unfolded, 'truth' in the theological sense became for many people literally a matter of life and death.

By the start of the 17th century scepticism, which denies the possibility of discovering truth in any objective sense, became fashionable in the intellectual world. It was in this context that Descartes[155] (1596–1650) came to prominence. Descartes was an early physicist[156] and contemporary of

---

154 With the invention of the Cartesian co-ordinate system he also revolutionised mathematics as well.
155 Descartes is credited as the father of modern philosophy, the father of modern mathematics, an early meteorologist, and the first systematic philosopher of science. He remained a devout Catholic all his life and was responsible for converting Christina Queen of Sweden to Catholicism.
156 In Descartes' day physics was explored using the method of dialectic and was a philosophic enterprise. The framework within which this enterprise took place was a tradition which harked back to Aristotle.

Galileo. As a Catholic intellectual, he set out to address the problem posed by growing scepticism. He sought to do this by using doubt, the weapon of the sceptics, to show that the sceptical position was untenable, and in the process put knowledge on a more secure footing. His efforts were to initiate a quantum shift in philosophy.

Descartes began his search for a sure foundation for knowledge by rejecting anything he knew that could be doubted in some way. This was not too difficult. Descartes was familiar with Galileo's work, as he corresponded with him. He was aware of the challenge that Galileo's thinking posed for the science being taught in the universities of his time. He was also well aware of the sceptics' arguments challenging the truths of religion and philosophy. It was relatively easy therefore to call much of what he had been taught into question. However, the one thing that he found he could not doubt was *his consciousness of himself as doubting*. Thus he arrived at the conclusion now famously stated as 'I think, therefore I am'. Since Descartes could not doubt his existence as 'a thinking mind', this provided him with what he saw as the sure foundation on which he could re-build his knowledge. He then set out, starting from this premise, to re-establish all the truths that he had previously known.

In taking the truth of himself as a 'thinking mind' – a *cogito* – as the foundation principle on which knowledge ultimately depended, Descartes set Western philosophy off in a totally new direction. His paradigm starts philosophic enquiry with the question – 'How do I know?' – rather than with the traditional question – 'What is real?'

In both the Christian and Greek traditions,[157] God as Creator provides the reason why things are real. God's existence is therefore the foundation of all knowledge. Truth exists because God exists. In its search for truth humankind gains insight into the mind of the Creator. The search becomes revelatory. Descartes was saying something quite different viz that knowledge is a condition of the human mind and *depends on the knowing subject*. This starting point places *the foundation of knowledge within the natural world*.[158] Knowledge is therefore understood in secular terms without reference to God (and by extension God's representatives). The search for the truth about the natural world is something that can be pursued in its own right. It does not, for example, require a warrant from the Church. Such thinking was to have far-reaching consequences.

---

157 God is understood differently in these traditions. In the religious tradition, God is understood as personal and involved in human history; in the Greek tradition, God is construed in more abstract philosophical terms as the 'prime mover', 'first cause', etc.
158 Because of this achievement Descartes is known as the 'father of modern philosophy'.

Descartes' intended revolution

In Descartes' era, the relationship between religion and science was still being forged. The 'new science', with its emphasis on experiment and measurement, was still in its infancy. Aristotle was still a dominant figure when it came to knowledge of the natural world. Church authorities were concerned because the 'new' science contradicted both the Scriptures and the views of Aristotle. The latter's philosophy, through the influence of Aquinas, now underpinned much of Catholic teaching. In this context it is not difficult to see why Descartes' intervention, although well-intended, was regarded as a threat to faith. Rather wisely, given the sad fate of Galileo at the hands of the Church authorities of his day, Descartes moved from Catholic France to Protestant Holland and thence to Sweden. There his ideas found ready acceptance, particularly among those seeking to explore the 'new' experimental approaches to enquiry in natural science.

In teaching the 'new' science, Descartes argued that truth about the natural world is discovered by measuring the *primary properties* of material bodies. He drew on Aristotle's distinction between the primary properties of a body (mass, length, volume, etc.) that could be measured and which exist *independent of an observer,* and secondary properties (smell, feel, colour, etc.) which *depend on the observer.* Descartes argued that for knowledge to be true, it needs to be independent of the person creating it; it needs to be objective rather than subjective. The challenge facing the 'new' scientist was to discover a way to overcome subjective biases and so reach objective knowledge. This challenge could be met if the primary properties of bodies were measured, as Galileo had proposed. The aim of measurement is to uncover *relationships* between carefully defined variables and, whenever possible, to express these relationships mathematically. By proceeding in this way, the knowledge obtained will be objective and therefore true. In arguing this case, Descartes formulated the first philosophy of science. The myth of science as *the unbiased pursuit of objective knowledge* was born! The notion that objective knowledge could be established through a combination of experiment and inductive reasoning was seen as the most radical aspect of 'Cartesian physics'. Descartes helped establish the idea that *knowledge is legitimated by the method used to create it.* He is a seminal figure in science.

Descartes also contributed to the development of the modern worldview by proposing that Nature be regarded as a giant machine which, like all machines, reflects the design of its maker. As a machine it functions according to the principles inherent in its design. The challenge facing natural science was to discover these principles. What for Descartes was simply a working model became converted, in the hands of later thinkers, into the idea of *Nature, including humankind, as a closed system driven by impersonal, but discoverable laws.* This thinking developed into naturalism which became a dominant ideology in the eighteenth and nineteenth centuries and continues to provide a default element in the worldview of many academic disciplines even today.

Kant and the structure of the human mind

Following Descartes' affirmation of the subjective and objective in human knowing, a number of creative thinkers in England and on the continent, revisited the question of how the mind works. Pre-eminent among these was Immanuel Kant (1724–1804).[159] His radical proposal was that *what we know is the result of the human mind imposing a structure on what is experienced*. In Kant's view, what we know are 'things as they are present to the mind' and this does not necessarily correspond to 'things as they are in themselves'. This view finds support in cognitive psychology. The findings here indicate that the mind filters the information arriving by way of our senses and processes only a small portion of the available data. In this way it structures what we perceive and focuses our attention.

In Kant's analysis, what we know does not necessarily reflect reality since what we know depends on how the mind structures thought – what we know are our ideas. Our knowledge is therefore, at best, partial since we can never attain a 'God's eye view' of reality. We always view reality from within, never from without. Therefore *all knowledge is a human interpretation of reality*. Our interpretive schemes mediate our understanding of things as they really are. Put another way, the mind forces reality into categories with which it can actually deal. Later philosophers would develop this theme further exploring the role that language, understood as a 'structure of the mind', plays in shaping human thought. This was then extended to include the study of how culture influences language and therefore the way the mind works.

Kant proposed that all human minds share the same structure and *that reason is a human universal* which functions the same way in all people, as does conscience. Reason and conscience, as human universals, provide the basis for determining moral issues. They enable us to say 'I ought to… because…' Kant did not recognise culture as a factor determining how the human mind works. However, culture is a factor in how the mind works and people in some cultures negotiate life according to different logics from others. For those living in a Western culture, this finding of anthropology seems initially difficult to comprehend.[160]

---

159 Kant, like Descartes, was a strongly religious person who sought to defend the nature of religious truth. However, his work, particularly in epistemology, was to provide the intellectual basis for modern agnosticism. If ideas exist only in our minds and they are finite, then we cannot know an infinite God. Kant's conclusion was that we can know God only by faith, not by reason.

160 Culture, however, is a factor in how the mind works and people in some cultures negotiate life according to different logics from others. For those living in a Western culture this finding of anthropology seems initially difficult to comprehend. Cf Paul Hiebert *Transforming Worldviews*, 39–44.

Kant exercised a powerful influence over Western thinking particularly on early attempts to explore the *structures of the human mind*. His thinking still has relevance today. *All teachers make assumptions about the structure of the human mind* when planning lessons and deciding on classroom discipline codes. Few ever stop to ask questions about whether these assumptions are valid or how they can be justified. They accept that their assumptions represent 'commonsense'. The work of Edward de Bono and Howard Gardner provide an important challenge to such an unreflective way of thinking.

As modernity reached its 'golden age' in the late 19th and early 20th centuries two competing views of knowledge emerged. The dominant view, following Descartes, held that by following certain methods of enquiry it was possible for science to obtain an *objective knowledge of reality*. The alternative view, following Kant, held that the structure of the human mind is such that objective knowledge in the sense claimed by science is not possible. *In this view, scientific knowledge is not unique but rather, like other forms of knowledge, it provides an interpretation of a more complex reality*. However, the faith people had come to place in science meant that this second voice went largely unheard until the gloss had worn off science and the axioms on which it is based were examined more closely. This happened gradually with the various strands of the postmodern critique beginning to come together in the 1970s.

Classical modernity and instrumentalism

As the 19th century unfolded, most scientists, absorbed by a stunning array of new discoveries and their translation into new technologies, simply lost interest in philosophical questions. The achievements of science seemed to make the worth of scientific knowledge self-evident and rendered its pursuit self-justifying. Science saw itself as largely immune from criticism. In this atmosphere two new developments could occur which impacted on the modern worldview.

Firstly, knowledge was redefined within large sections of the academic community and its meaning became tied to learning achieved using empirical methods of enquiry. Knowledge, in this view, was created through inductive reasoning based on the facts of data. The most ardent advocates of this position were Auguste Comte in France and later Ayers in England. They articulated a theory of knowledge known as positivism which holds that knowledge can be created only by one method of intellectual enquiry – the method of science. Philosophical, historical and literary methods of enquiry do not yield knowledge, only opinion. They provide *interpretations of reality* not an objective understanding of it. The stance of positivism flatly denies that the structure of the mind has a role to play in the generation of knowledge. While fashionable for a time, the narrow base of this epistemology led to its eventual downfall. Echoes of it are still encountered in some 'evidence-based' approaches to school improvement.

A second and more influential development was the rise of instrumentalism. Instrumentalism is concerned with *the utility of knowledge* and has little interest in 'the truth of things' as such. The knowledge accumulated through scientific enquiry is highly valued in this perspective because it *enables people to pursue goals in the most efficient manner*. Under instrumentalism, human interests determine which knowledge is important and which is not. *Knowledge becomes the sum of that which has practical utility.* For instance, if the final goal of human endeavour is human flourishing in this world, then that defines what is worth knowing.

Instrumentalism co-opted science in the mid-20th century as the costs of research rose and became possible only with the financial support of large companies. This development helped undermine the myth of science as the objective pursuit of truth. Science became entangled in the 'spin' business, providing data which was then used to serve the commercial interests of those paying for its production. A blatant example is the cigarette industry's use of science to defend its commercial interests. Less blatant have been attempts to co-opt science on either side of the climate change debate.

Instrumentalism remains a force today and exercises a distorting influence on the attitude of young people, particularly towards the value of particular subjects in the curriculum.

NATURE AS A CLOSED SYSTEM

The process in which Nature came to be regarded as the closed system described by science has been slow, but progressive.

Naturalism becomes the ideology of modernity

Stage 1: God's Two Books

Early scientists such as Descartes, Newton, and even Kant,[161] saw no inherent contradiction between what they believed and what they knew. For them, God had created two books: the book of Nature and the book of the Bible. Each was a guide to the other. Since God was the source of all truth, there could be no contradiction between the truth of God's two books. Any problems that arose were the result of *faulty human understanding*. However, this picture changed as the modern academy developed and as people became more confident in the power of science as a means of enquiry.

---

161 Kant was a noted cosmologist and one of the first to propose that our solar system is part of a spiral galaxy.

Stage 2: Liberal theology and deism

Liberal theologians began to argue that since God is perfect, God is unchangeable. In their thinking this implied that God cannot interfere with the laws that God had created because God, being perfect, does not act in an arbitrary manner. If the Bible contradicted the findings of science then the Bible must be mistaken, since science represents truths that are objective. If the Bible could be mistaken about the natural world then it was open to challenge on other fronts. In particular, its account of miracles had to be challenged. For the liberal theologians miracles were, by definition, impossible, so key elements in the New Testament had to be discounted, including Jesus' resurrection. Christian faith thus loses its core belief, and its meaning. The personal God of the Bible is replaced by the impersonal God of Deism.

Stage 3: The Human Person becomes an Object to be Studied by Science

The attack on faith came from another direction as well. As the scope of science expanded, the human sciences placed the human person *within Nature. The human subject thus became objectified.* If humans can be considered as a part of Nature then science can discover the laws governing human nature. This would make it possible to establish a morality based on science alone and do away with the notion of sin. Using Occam's Razor, a doctrine in science which states that when developing a theory one should use the minimum number of categories, it was now possible to declare faith an unnecessary concept. Thus science could replace religion at the heart of Western culture. The view of Marx, and later Freud, that faith is a form of illusion finds its logical home in such thinking.

Stage 4: Unbelief as normative

The thinking outlined above enabled the yearning for personal autonomy, which had provided modernity with its moral force, to find a new expression – *autonomy from the religious and philosophic traditions of the West.* Theology was excluded from the academy and philosophy fell on hard times. In sociology, secularisation theory took on the guise of dogma.

It is perhaps not surprising that, as the modern worldview was transformed into an aggressive ideology with its roots in naturalism and exclusive humanism, many people lost confidence in the worldview of faith as an interpretive system.[162]

---

162 The treatment here is necessarily brief. A more extended account can be found in D'Orsa and D'Orsa *Explorers, Guides and Meaning Makers.* Charles Taylor provides a still more detailed account in *A Secular Age.*

The world understood as a closed-system: Working model or ideology?

The modern worldview treats the world as a closed system. There are two ways in which this can be viewed.

Closed system as working model

The first understands the closed system as a working model. Viewed in this manner, we take the world as an intelligible system and seek to push the limits of our human understanding ever outwards. The natural world can be construed either as an organic system or as a mechanical system. In each case the working model can guide exploration to uncover successive layers of complexity. Such an approach does not imply that the world is a closed system. It does, however, accept that the closed-system model is an appropriate working model, one that people of faith and no-faith can explore together co-operatively. However, like all working models it has its limits. Exploring experience in the real world using a working model tends to highlight what these limitations actually are.

Closed system as ideology

The second approach, and the one more commonly encountered, interprets the closed-system model ideologically. The answers to all life's questions have to be found within the model since *no other option is possible*. Faith, which puts questions to this model, is dealt with by denying it the right to put questions. This second view is often implicitly incorporated into modern knowledge systems and then transmitted into classrooms through curriculum. This can happen in one of two ways: firstly, in the way the curriculum controls the questions that students may explore, or secondly, by the curriculum's canonisation of some methods of intellectual enquiry to the detriment of others. In the development of the national curriculum in Australia, the design for the proposed History curriculum amply illustrates this dynamic at work. The curriculum presents history as if Christianity had never existed or had any impact on the development of the Western intellectual tradition. The existence of the Catholic school, and other faith-based schools, serves society well in resisting the imperial claims of ideological modernity by questioning the validity of its claims.

BEYOND MODERNITY WHERE?

Modernity represents one of the great eras in the Western intellectual tradition. For two centuries, the level of achievement was such that the limits inherent in its worldview went largely unquestioned. The development of the modern worldview changed all European cultures, and less directly influenced most other cultures on earth. As a tradition of meaning, *its high status has masked the excessive nature of its claims.*

Progress in knowledge has conferred benefits on the few, but these benefits have come at a high cost to the many. This reveals a moral hole in the heart of modernity. Some postmodern commentators, such as Habermas,[163] Taylor and Robert Schreiter,[164] ask how high this cost needs to be before the modern worldview is seriously revised and its limits acknowledged. For them, the project of modernity remains to be completed because the moral ideal of human autonomy has been compromised, and is trivialised when human flourishing is *interpreted only in material terms.* The ideal of personal autonomy, however, remains valid and needs to be reclaimed. The choice is no longer between dependence and independence, but rather between *independence and inter-dependence.* They therefore seek to chart the parameters of a second, less naïve, modernity, one that proceeds on a wisdom tempered by the stories of loss as well as those of gain.

Other critics, like Derrida, Foucault and Lyotard believe that the problem is deeper. They attack the very notion of a worldview. All worldviews are suspect in their eyes, built on presuppositions that do not bear scrutiny, and so are dubious as interpretive frameworks. We take up these themes in the next chapter.

We live and teach in an extraordinary context − at a turning point in the development of the Western intellectual tradition. Obviously, this is not without its challenges. It places a considerable onus on teachers in faith-based schools to think through the issues that shape the curriculum and to check the assumptions they take for granted in teaching. Unless they do so, they may become unsuspecting cheerleaders for a worldview with the potential to seriously undermine the very goals they seek to achieve for students.

---

163 David Smith and Terence Lovat *Curriculum: Action on Reflection* Fourth Edition (South Melbourne: Cengage Learning, 2004) provide an excellent overview of Habermas' commentary.
164 Robert Schreiter 'A New Modernity: Living and Believing in an Unstable World', *New Theology Review* February, May, August, November, 2007.

PRINCIPLE 12: THE WORKING MODEL PRINCIPLE

A Catholic curriculum consistently promotes an understanding of the world as an open system across all disciplines.

COMMENT

While Catholic teaching holds that the world *is* an open system, this is not the perspective of many of the academic disciplines which presume that it is closed. Since it cannot be proved that it is closed, its closed status is a matter of choice and so open to challenge, but not on theological grounds. The challenge is on the grounds that to opt for a closed system reflects a choice of 'working model'. This opens up the possibility of other working models, in which case it is possible to consider, as an alternative 'working model' the world as an open system. The argument is then determined by which model is the more useful. This will depend on the data to be interpreted and the theoretical perspectives with currency in the paradigms that comprise the discipline. The aim here is to *respect the autonomy of the disciplines* without necessarily *taking an unprovable axiom as a statement of reality*.

CONTINUING THE CONVERSATION

12.1 How aware are teachers of the worldview that sits behind the disciplines they teach?

12.2 How do they deal with this in class?

12.3 How aware are teachers that open and closed worldviews constitute working models, and that these permit choices that can be made without compromising the autonomy of the disciplines? If not, how can this issue best be addressed?

12.4 How is this principle suitably dealt with as an across-the-curriculum issue?

11
THE POSTMODERN CRITIQUE: PROPHETS OF DECONSTRUCTION

Our era is often described as 'postmodern'. The critique mounted by postmodern scholars on the philosophical underpinnings and practical manifestations of modernity, the 'postmodern critique', has had a major impact on education, particularly on the design and implementation of curriculum. In this chapter we put the focus on understanding something of this critique in order to open up and clarify its implications for the Catholicity of the curriculum delivered in Catholic schools.

The essential dilemma that we see the Catholic curriculum must address is that of educating in a context in which *the worldview of our particular age is essentially bifurcated, caught between the modern and the postmodern*. In the last chapter we set out the major parameters of the modern worldview and briefly traced the history of its development. We now do the same for the somewhat more precariously based 'postmodern' worldview.

The use of terms such as 'postmodern' and 'postmodernity' can be confusing because they signify quite different things – an era in history, a system of thought or a sensibility.[165] We will address postmodernity firstly as an era of history, then as a sensibility. In our view, it is a misnomer to describe postmodernity as a 'system of thought'. We will, however, include some discussion of key philosophical understandings as proposed by three of the most influential postmodern thinkers, thus providing some entrée into postmodern philosophy particularly its treatment of knowledge.

---

165 Once we have dealt with the distinctions, we will simply use the terms 'postmodern' and 'postmodernity', with context determining whether we are referring to a period, a system of thought, or a sensibility. This is consistent with our treatment of 'modernity'.

MEANINGS OF 'POSTMODERN'

'Postmodern' as an era in history

'Postmodern' can refer to either *the period of history following modernity* (assuming we are in a qualitatively new era) or to *the present stage reached by modernity*. Used in the first sense, the 'postmodern era' begins as the reconstruction of Europe following the Second World War neared completion in the late 1960s. The generation of young people who had grown up through the war now wanted to reconstruct the European intellectual world that had resulted in the physical devastation which they had witnessed at first hand. Paris in the 1960s was the centre of this ferment and the three major thinkers Derrida, Foucault and Lyotard – who have defined the contours of postmodern thought, were part of this environment.

'Postmodern' as a sensibility

Understood as a sensibility, 'postmodern' denotes a worldview – a way of relating to the world that has unique cognitive, evaluative and affective dimensions. This worldview has its own presuppositions, one of which is, ironically, that there is no such thing as a worldview. Delineating the 'postmodern worldview' is difficult because of the particular nature of its claims. Worldviews *underpin commitment* as we have seen earlier, whereas the 'postmodern worldview' *undercuts commitment*. The irony is that the three main protagonists of postmodernity were all very committed people. Irony pervades the postmodern sensibility which is often criticised for being 'self-referentially incoherent' in that it applies criteria to others' positions that it refuses to apply to its own. This is implicit in its denial of worldviews!

Catholic theologian Michael Gallagher[166] provides an insightful treatment of the 'postmodern worldview' which is summarised briefly below. He delineates it, rather tongue in cheek, by setting out its 'ten commandments' as follows:

1. *Thou shalt not worship (instrumental)*[167] *reason.* Modernity's quest for 'objective' truth restricted 'knowledge' to that which can be derived using the method of science. This modern claim about the nature of truth is untenable.

---

166 Michael Paul Gallagher *Clashing Symbols: An Introduction to Faith and Culture* Revised and Expanded Edition (London: Darton, Longman and Todd, 2003), 100–103. The sections in italics are taken directly from Gallagher. The additional content also draws on themes from Charles Taylor's *The Ethics of Authenticity* (Cambridge, Massachusetts: Harvard University Press, 1991) and *A Secular Age* (Cambridge, Massachusetts: The Belknap Press of Harvard University Press, 2007).
167 'Instrumental' is not in the original.

2. *Thou shalt not believe in history.* The modern understanding, that mankind can somehow shape its own history by pursuing its own vision of human flourishing, has proved to be illusory. Its direct consequence is ideological domination.
3. *Thou shalt not hope in progress.* The idea that science can drive human development leading to benefits for all mankind is false. The 'myth of progress' simply entrenches the positions of the 'haves' against the 'have nots'.
4. *Thou shalt not tell meta-stories.* The ideologies of modernity – capitalism, communism, Nazism, etc. – have all been mythologised as 'narratives of human flourishing', which turned out to be little more than illusions. The underlying belief of modernity, that man is the only source of meaning in the universe, is hubristic.
5. *Thou shalt not focus on the self.* Modernity's concern for the human subject has resulted in an interpretation of human flourishing that is materialistic and selfish and which has proved detrimental both to actual human flourishing and to the environment.
6. *Thou shalt not agonise over values.* In modernity human flourishing was understood as increased human autonomy. This gave modernity its moral force and a value-structure. However, the modern construction of human flourishing has been subverted by modern institutions that now impose oppressive constraints on autonomy in the name of the 'public good'. Postmoderns reject this development seeing 'the morality of the public good' as serving only the interests of those in power. In their view, human flourishing can be understood only in immediate terms, in living for the moment, because that is all that a person actually has control over.
7. *Thou shalt not trust institutions.* Institutions were established in modernity to serve the public good but have acquired a life of their own independent of their public mission. They now exist as quasi-independent centres of power that are self-serving.[168]
8. *Thou shalt not bother about God.* Modernity made atheism plausible. Postmodernity takes it as axiomatic. Religion becomes a meaningless concept.
9. *Thou shalt not live for productivity alone.* Modern life saw the pursuit of efficiency as a goal in itself to be pursued without thought of the human consequences. Postmoderns object to the way in which this represses the creative and expressive in human life. It seeks to re-invigorate the expressive as a counter to this dehumanising tendency of modernity.

---

168 In the post-modern critique, the churches exhibit all the features of a modern institution. The Christian Church, by taking on the trappings of modernity in the name of efficiency has, it is claimed, managed to convert itself into what it proclaims it is not!

10. *Thou shalt not seek uniformity.* The impact of modernity on cultures has been to homogenise them, taking North Atlantic cultures as the standard. This reflects the ethnocentric nature of the modern worldview. Postmodern sensibility understands such a stance as a meta-narrative. By way of contrast it *values and celebrates difference* seeing in this a source of emancipation from the oppressive conformity that characterises ideological modernity.

This brief summary illustrates three important features of postmodern sensibility:
- it has developed both as a *critique of and as a reaction* to modernity
- it includes *a range of values* capable of being interpreted both positively and negatively
- its *scope as a tradition of meaning is limited* by the often ironic nature of its claims. It is very much concerned with the 'truth of things' but denies that there can be any such thing as truth!

Gallagher's portrayal of the 'postmodern condition' reflects a number of the attitudes now evident among young people as reported earlier in Chapter 4. Students, along with their parents and teachers, are influenced by the postmodern critique. This critique has a pervasive presence in the media and in the academic world. As a critique of ideological modernity, postmodernity restores some much-needed balance, particularly in its social concern and its commitment to justice. While the postmodern critique is often construed in negative terms because of its inherent ambiguities and negativities, those steeped in the Judeo-Christian tradition will also recognise in it some echoes of the prophetic tradition, and it is to these echoes that we need to attend.

POSTMODERN THINKERS

As an intellectual movement postmodernity takes its name from Jean-Francois Lyotard's book *The Postmodern Condition* published in 1979. However, the critique of modernity began before that. Modernity's promise of progress must have seemed extremely ironic to young people growing up in post-war Europe. Science had been co-opted in the service of war and had shown the full fury of its destructive capacity. The situation was not improved as the realities of the Cold War era unfolded in the 1950s and 1960s. The myth of progress also rang hollow to people living in newly independent nations struggling to extricate themselves from the legacies of colonial rule. In so many areas of human life, there was a large gap between what modernity had promised and what it had delivered. This is the context in which the postmodern scholarly voices began to emerge, and more importantly, to draw significant audiences and exercise widespread influence.

These voices fall into two categories – the *prophets of deconstruction* such as Lyotard, Derrida, and Foucault, all of whom stand in the shadow of Frederick Nietzsche, and the *prophets of renewal*. The prophets of renewal in turn fall into two groups – *secular voices* such as Habermas and Taylor, and specifically *religious voices* such as Schreiter, Thornhill and Gallagher from the Catholic tradition, and Hiebert, Smith and Caputo from the Evangelical and Protestant traditions. The prophets of deconstruction seek to *'deconstruct'* modernity, while the prophets of renewal seek to *revitalise* modernity by reclaiming its *essential moral ideal*. For the prophets of renewal, the essential project of modernity – *the promotion of human autonomy and human flourishing* – has never been fully realised. They hold that it was subverted by being pursued within too narrow an ideology, that of scientism. In consequence, the ideal of human autonomy has been trivialised. Their project is to restore integrity to the worldview of modernity.

In the balance of this chapter we deal only with the postmodern 'prophets' of deconstruction. We have dealt with their thinking in some detail because its influence is so marked in the shaping of contemporary Western cultures. We will listen to the voice of the prophets of renewal in later chapters.

PROPHETS OF DECONSTRUCTION

The shadow of the German philosopher Frederick Nietzsche intrudes into any discussions of postmodernism. Nietzsche lived during the second half of the nineteenth century, at the height of the modern era. His critique of the developing modern worldview was that, while its proponents had adopted a vision of the world as a closed system, they had 'killed God' but were avoiding the full logical consequences of that decision. Put another way, you cannot 'kill God' and still continue to live within the old certainties of truth and morality that depend on the existence of God. Nietzsche set out to explore what the ramifications of 'killing God' actually were, and this came to define his life's work.

Nietzsche: Pushing modern thinking to its logical limits

Frederick Nietzsche (1844–1900) was relatively unknown in his own time, but his insights into what was at stake as modernity took its ideological turn have proved to be much deeper than those of most of his contemporaries. He was a quintessentially modern man in his absolute confidence in reason as the only guide to life.[169] Thornhill acknowledges the inherent logic of Nietzsche's position:

---

169 Biographical details of the various post-modern thinkers have been sourced from articles in the Internet *Encyclopedia of Philosophy* and the Stanford *Encyclopedia of Philosophy* both available on line.

Was not Nietzsche right when he claimed that we should acknowledge the 'death of God' and assume responsibility for the world which must ultimately be shaped by our human will?[170]

Nietzsche's image of the madman

Thornhill captures the essential nature of Nietzsche's critique clearly in the following passage.

> (Nietzsche's) parable of the madman who appeared with the lantern in the market place looking for God shows how profoundly he had grasped the option which confronted the culture of modernity. This famous parable describes a dramatic confrontation between the madman and the people in the marketplace. Because they no longer believe in God they scoff at him and ask ironically where God could have gone to. 'Where has God gone?' shouts the madman turning on them. 'I will tell you. We have slain him – you and I. We are his murderers'. And he confronts them with the stupendous thing they have done in excluding any notion of God from their understanding of their world. 'But how did we do it? How could we drink up the sea? Who gave us the sponge to wipe out the whole horizon? What did we do when we unchained this earth from the sun? ... Do we not now wander through an endless nothingness? Does empty space not breathe upon us? Is it not colder now? Is not the night coming, and even more night? Must we not light lanterns at noon? God is dead. God stays dead. And we have slain him.....'. His hearers can only vaguely grasp the implications of his terrible proclamation, and they gaze at him in shocked silence. 'I am come too early,' the madman declares. 'It is not my time. The monstrous event is still on its way... This deed is still further from men than the remotest stars – and yet they have done it'.[171]

Nietzsche's story

It is hard to understand Nietzsche's thinking outside the context of his life.[172] His early childhood was happy. He had a close relationship with his father who was the local Lutheran pastor. As well as this, his uncle and both grandfathers were Lutheran pastors. Nietzsche's young life was thrown into turmoil when, at age five, his father died a slow and painful death as the consequence of a brain tumour. The following year his younger brother

---

170 John Thornhill *Modernity: Christianity's Estranged Child Reconstructed* (Grand Rapids Michigan: William B. Eerdmans, 2000), 31.
171 ibid. 31–32.
172 Nietzsche's life and thought is very well covered in the 1999 BBC documentary *Human All Too Human* produced to mark the centenary of his death. This is available at video.google.com/videoplay?docid=-184240591461103528#.

also died. The young Nietzsche found it difficult to comprehend why, as he understood it, a loving God could treat one of his ministers and his family in this way. His religious faith was also challenged by the experience of serving as a medical orderly during the Franco–Prussian War and seeing the full horror of the battle at first hand.

Nietzsche had initially sought answers to his questions within his religious tradition and began training as a minister. However, he quickly became disillusioned by the liberal theology of his day and transferred from theology to the classics. An abiding disillusionment with Christianity remained a recurring theme in his writing. His commitment to rationalism led him to dismiss Christian faith as 'the refuge of weak minds'.

Nietzsche was a brilliant, if quite introverted, student. His academic career began with great promise. He was appointed professor in the University of Basel at the age of twenty-four, an unusual honour for one so young. Here he taught philology (literary criticism) for a decade before ill health forced his early retirement. For the next decade, he lived a lonely life. Poor health forced him to alternate between the Swiss Alps in summer, where he liked to hike and formulate this thoughts, and the warmer climate of Italy in the winter. During this period pain was a constant companion.

During his academic career, Nietzsche made something of a name for himself as a writer and cultural critic. He was an amateur composer and became friendly with Richard Wagner who facilitated his entry into German society and was something of a father-figure to him. When the latter became nationalistic and anti-Semitic in his later years, Nietzsche broke with him.[173] Nietzsche always attempted to express his thought with literary flair. Some of his books are written as collections of aphorisms that reflect the style of the Book of Proverbs. God may have been dead for Nietzsche, but religious imagery certainly was not! The main character in his best known book *Thus Spake Zarathustra* seems a conflation of Moses and his image of himself. The monk Zarathustra comes down from the mountains, where he wanders and thinks alone, seeking to bring enlightenment to the people in the valleys below, but they are not ready to hear what he has to say. Nietzsche experienced first-hand the loneliness of the biblical prophets.

Nietzsche and Nazism

Nietzsche attempted to think through the consequences of modernity's 'killing God', in order to work out what truth and morality can be based upon, once God is dead. His conclusion was that both depend on the power of human will. For the older Nietzsche, the will to power was the ultimate

---

[173] This suggests that Nietzsche would have found it very ironic that his thinking would later be adopted by the Third Reich illustrating Derrida's contention that texts can take on a life of their own independent of what their authors intend.

force in human life. He predicted that, through the evolutionary process, a group of people would eventually emerge capable of living in a world devoid of truth and morality as these have been traditionally conceived in Western cultures. However, the people of his time had not reached this point of development. These new people, which he called the 'ubermensch' (English overmen), would be capable of achieving self-transcendence, not on the basis of Christian values, but on the basis of a new understanding of morality. This theme was exploited thirty years after his death by the Nazis who saw themselves as the 'supermen' predicted by Nietzsche, a people charged by destiny to reshape the world and its cultures.

The close association of Nietzsche's philosophy with National Socialism meant that in the post-war years it fell out of favour outside of Germany, only to be revived in the 1970s as postmodernism built up momentum. All three 'founders' of postmodernism – Derrida, Lyotard and Foucault – were influenced by Nietzsche's thought. Each in his own way took up the challenge Nietzsche had posed to define truth and morality in a worldview devoid of the transcendent.

Nietzsche's decline

As the final step in his grand scheme, Nietzsche saw it necessary to find a new basis for Western values – to 'trans-value values', or to determine the parameters within which his 'ubermen' would live. Nietzsche made little progress on this project beyond outlining its scope. In the winter of 1889 he suffered a complete breakdown while living in Italy. The trigger for this was suddenly coming across a horse that had been injured and being overwhelmed by compassion for the suffering animal. His mind, which had been brittle for some time, snapped. He was forty-four. Nietzsche did not respond to treatment and was subsequently pronounced clinically insane. The exact cause of his breakdown remains uncertain.

If Descartes was the 'accidental hero' of modern philosophy, then Nietzsche is its tragic figure. His critique of modernity was, fundamentally, that as a movement it lacked the full courage of its convictions.

Jean-Francois Lyotard and 'Incredulity to meta-narratives'

Jean-Francois Lyotard (1924–1998) was born in Versailles and as a young man once thought of becoming a Dominican priest. On completing his tertiary studies he took up a teaching position in Algeria where he became deeply involved in local politics. He returned to Paris to complete further studies and began his academic career at the University of Paris. Lyotard subsequently taught in a number of universities in the USA. In 1978, the government of Quebec commissioned him to conduct a study of 'knowledge in the computer age' which is reported as *The Postmodern Condition: A Report on Knowledge* (1979). The term 'postmodern' was first coined in this seminal work.[174]

'Be suspicious of meta-narratives'

The main theme in Lyotard's work is well summed up as follows -

> *Postmodernism can be understood as the erosion of confidence in the rational as sole guarantor and deliverer of truth, coupled with a deep suspicion of science – particularly modern science's pretentious claims to an ultimate theory of everything.*[175]

In *The Postmodern Condition,* Lyotard argues that in assessing the state of contemporary knowledge it is necessary to be suspicious of all *'grand recits'* (grand stories). This term, usually translated into English as 'meta-narrative', is not to be confused with 'mega-narrative'. Mega-narratives are 'big stories' which make claims that require *faith in something.* The Bible which requires faith in God, or Star Wars which requires faith in 'the force', are examples of mega-narratives. Meta-narratives are a particular type of narrative, the main claims of which are said to be *demonstrable by reason alone.* For instance, the Enlightenment meta-narrative is that 'history leads inevitably to progress and emancipation'; the Marxist meta-narrative is that 'antagonistic class struggle is the motor of history'; and scientism has a meta-narrative which says that 'given sufficient time science can solve any problem'. Meta-narratives arose in modernity and differ from cultural narratives that are built around myths and are believed rather than demonstrated.

The problem of legitimation

Lyotard argues that the major issue affecting knowledge in the 20th century is *the manner in which it is legitimated.* He construes knowledge as *a transaction* between a sender and a receiver with legitimation acting as a barrier to its acceptance. This is illustrated in the figure below. Whether the information the sender wishes to communicate *as knowledge* is regarded as such by the receiver depends on whether or not it can get through the culturally determined *legitimation barrier.*

---

174 Lyotard had previously labelled this aspect of his thought 'paganism'. By this he meant that just as in pagan times there were many gods rather than one god, in the late modern situation there needed to be many paths to knowledge and not just the one path to knowledge adopted by modernity. In the *Postmodern Condition* he re-badged 'paganism' as 'post-modernism' and the name stuck.
175 James K. Smith *Who's Afraid of Postmodernism? Taking Derrida, Lyotard, and Foucault to Church* (Grand Rapids Michigan: BakerAcademic, 2006), 62.

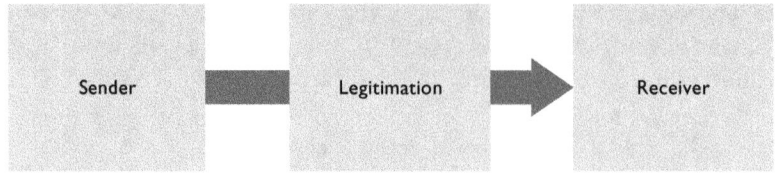

FIGURE 11.1 Communication of knowledge

There are two types of legitimation barriers. The first is *cultural* and the knowledge that passes through this is *narrative knowledge*. The second barrier is imposed by *scientific rationality* and knowledge passing through this barrier is *scientific knowledge*. In both cases, knowledge is related to power. *Whoever controls the legitimation process determines what is knowledge.* As Lyotard puts the matter: 'Knowledge and power can be seen as two sides of the same question: who decides what knowledge is, and who knows what needs to be decided?'[176] These are key questions to be pursued in analysing curriculum statements.

Types of knowledge

Narrative knowledge is held within a culture and requires no explicit legitimation. *Narrative knowledge is local* and to question it would seem totally strange to the locals. For example, people living in Australia know that you drive on the left side of the road. As narrative knowledge, this is passed from one generation to the next. The reasons are unimportant. Narrative knowledge defines the way things are. It is part of 'our' story and so taken on trust, and because it is peculiar to our story, it may not have currency elsewhere, but within our culture it is held to be valuable. In Lyotard's analysis, moral knowledge is deemed to be narrative knowledge. Morality is a product of culture. In saying this, Lyotard acknowledges that he stands in Nietzsche's shadow.

Scientific knowledge on the other hand requires *explicit legitimation*. Power here lies with 'the community of scholars'. In order to qualify as knowledge, proposals must meet criteria set by this community. *Scientific knowledge is held to be universal knowledge* – true for everyone everywhere because it can be accessed by reason and *reason is deemed to be the same everywhere*. It is this claim to universality that Lyotard challenges, because the claim stands on the assumption that scientific knowledge is not narrative in form. His argument is that the way people reason is *context dependent*. What we hold to be rational depends on the context in which we find ourselves.

---

176 Jean Francois Lyotard *The Postmodern Condition: A Report on Knowledge* (Manchester University Press, 1979), 8–9.

For Lyotard, the meta-narratives of modernity are built on assumptions that cannot be justified by reason alone. In his view, the *whole project of science cannot actually lift itself over the legitimation barrier* that it has created for the proposals that constitute scientific knowledge. Science cannot answer questions integral to life outside a certain narrow range; it cannot directly address issues of justice for instance. At heart, it too requires an act of faith in its own axioms. Nor can science be divorced from narrative simply by appeal to reason. Science needs to acknowledge the narrative ground on which it stands; scientific knowledge is a product of culture and cannot claim to be independent of it by appealing to the nature of human reason. In his view, this is an appeal to an abstraction which does not exist in reality. Far from being narrative-free, science has always relied on an epic story to help legitimate its claims viz that of the dedicated scientist impartially searching for the truth of things. However, as Thornhill and Tarnas have pointed out, *the dedicated pursuit of the truth has been integral to the Western intellectual narrative from its inception*, and cannot now be co-opted by science alone, so reducing other chapters in this mega-narrative to the status of fables.

The Commodification of knowledge

The success of science has, however, created a major imbalance with other forms of knowledge and this now distorts learning. Scientific knowledge has been 'commodified' and treated as a new form of product to be traded. Narrative knowledge is also now being treated in the same way. The result is that education's role in the promotion of 'human flourishing' is diminished and is being recast as *just another means of production*. This dehumanises learning and changes relationships central to learning. Smith sums up Lyotard's critique colourfully in observing:

> While in modernity science was the emperor who set the rules for what counted as truth and castigated faith as fable, post-modernity has shown us the emperor's nudity. As such, we no longer need to apologize for faith...[177]

He goes on to note that while ideological modernity renounced faith, it never fully escaped from it – which is Nietzsche's critique. *Postmodernity asks modernity to own up to what it puts its faith in.* As this happens, a new space opens up, one that makes dialogue possible with people of other 'faiths', including secular faiths. Smith concludes somewhat hopefully -

---

177 James Smith, 71.

The exclusion of faith from the public square is a modern agenda; post-modernity should signal new openings and opportunities for Christian witness (that is for mission) in the broad marketplace for ideas.[178]

Teachers have a new responsibility in Catholic schools to help students understand and negotiate this market place.

Jacques Derrida and the birth of 'deconstruction'

Jacques Derrida (1930–2004) was born of Jewish parents in Algiers. As a young student his studies were interrupted when laws against Jews passed by the French Vichy government were enacted. This was to have an impact on Derrida so that throughout his life he was concerned for 'the marginal voice'. On graduating from high school, Derrida moved to Paris where he completed his studies in the intellectual ferment that was Paris in the 1960s. He subsequently held a variety of academic positions in Paris and also in the USA, principally at UCLA. Derrida belongs to a group of contemporary thinkers who study how human experience is present to the conscious mind.[179]

Issues in interpreting texts

Derrida's unique approach can be illustrated through his analysis of the act of reading. Reading is a conscious act in which we assume that when we read we understand what the author meant to convey, that as a reader we have direct access to his or her ideas and what they mean. We see 'through the text' to the meaning that lies 'behind the text'. We assume that meaning is conveyed by the text, but exists in another realm. This process is summarised in the diagram below. There are a number of assumptions that sit behind this model:
- that the author's use of language conveys the author's meaning
- that the way in which the author uses language corresponds to the way in which the reader understands language
- that meaning exists in a realm independent of language.

---

178 ibid. 73. Words in brackets not in the original.
179 The study of conscious experience is known as phenomenology the study of things as they appear in consciousness, as phenomena. It is a form of modern philosophy initiated by Edmund Husserl at the beginning of the 20th century. Derrida belongs to the 'post-structuralist' school of thought which challenged the view that language structures thought.

The postmodern critique: Prophets of deconstruction

FIGURE 11.2 Reading and meaning: Two configurations

Derrida questions this model, holding that meaning cannot be separated from the language in which it is represented. Meaning is embedded in language. The user employs his or her understanding of language to interpret what the author's language conveys. Since people use language in different ways and with different fluency and sophistication, there is never just one interpretation. An author can mean more than the text conveys, and the text can be interpreted as saying more than the author intends. We have already encountered this phenomenon in the way Nazis read Nietzsche's work. Texts can take on a life of their own if the ideas they contain have interpretive power. The author's meaning is not privileged. This is the stance of what Gallagher calls 'radical hermeneutics'.[180]

Life as 'reading' and interpretation.

For Derrida, meaning is always mediated by language and exists as an interpretation. Language can therefore distort meaning. It is not as transparent as we often assume. In Derrida's thinking 'reading' is not confined to what we find in books or on our computers. We continuously 'read' the 'events' that make up our lives. Life has a quality of 'textuality'. We use language to interpret the significance of what we encounter. Since all that we know comes to us *in the form of interpretations shaped by language,* our capacity to make sense of things is constrained or augmented by the power of language.

We have seen this in the use of the words 'culture' and 'worldview' which are neologisms coined during modernity. Does this mean that culture and worldviews did not exist before the modern period? Obviously not! What was missing was our capacity to access language with the explanatory power these words now give us. Our interpretive capacity was constrained by language. This broader picture is represented in Figure 11.3 which is itself another form of 'text'.

---

180 Gallagher 10–11.

FIGURE 11.3 'Reading' as interpreting an 'event'

'There is nothing outside the text'

A much-quoted line from Derrida is that 'there is nothing outside the text' by which he means that knowledge comes in the form of interpretations made in context. Words, however, can signify multiple things and carry their history with them, so they are rarely neutral. They can both denote and connote. We see this with words such as 'gay' and 'duck'. Contexts shape meaning. If 'everything is an interpretation' does this mean that our knowledge is merely subjective and relative?

Can interpretations ever be true?

James Smith suggests that, while this is a common interpretation of Derrida, it is not true to what he is saying.[181] Derrida holds that interpretations can be true or false. The criteria which determine this are set by the 'community of interpreters' and reflect the worldview of that community. Meaning is culturally determined. Interpretation is not something done in total isolation; it requires justification. In particular, the criteria developed depend on the worldview of 'the community of interpreters'. Derrida's main point is that too often the 'community of interpreters' seeks to claim that their particular interpretation is universal, the only way to read an event. However, this is the case *only if the worldview of the community is accepted*. All worldviews, as we have seen, are based on presuppositions that are axiomatic and therefore not able to be proved. 'Deconstruction' is a process by which these dominant interpretations can be challenged by revealing the way they depend on unstated axioms.[182] Here Derrida joins forces with Lyotard.

---

181 James Smith, 37–38. For an extended treatment of the possible relationship between Derrida's radical hermeneutics and the Church, see John D. Caputo *What Would Jesus Deconstruct?: The Good News of Post-modernism for the Church* (Grand Rapids, Michigan: Baker Academic, 2007).
182 Lyotard, in challenging the distinction between scientific knowledge and narrative knowledge, provides a good illustration of how Jacques Derrida's approach to deconstruction works in practice. Derrida's contention is that the major categories of Western philosophy, since Plato, have been formulated in terms of dualisms immanent/transcendent, life/death, light/darkness, essence/existence and so on. He further contends that in these pairs one term is privileged at the expense of the other, without any justification being given. For instance, to return to Lyotard, in the pair scientific knowledge/narrative knowledge modernity privileges the first at the expense of the second. Derrida demands that this bias be justified. This is the essence of his form of deconstruction.

Speaking to this issue Smith sums up the position well.

Deconstruction's recognition that everything is interpretation opens a space for questioning – a space to call into question the received and dominant interpretations that often claim not to be interpretations at all. As such, deconstruction is interested in interpretations that have been marginalized and sidelined activating voices that have been silenced. This is the constructive, yea prophetic, aspect of Derrida's deconstruction: a concern for justice by being concerned about dominant, status quo interpretations that silence those who see differently. Thus, from its inception, deconstruction has been, at root, ethical –concerned for the paradigmatic marginalized described by the Old Testament as 'the widow, the orphan, and the stranger'.[183]

Deconstruction can move in two directions

Taken in one direction, it provides a technique that seeks to address the challenge posed by Nietzsche – how to live in a world in which truth is only a human construct. However, it can take another direction: *it can lead to renewal*. Deconstruction, certainly as practised by Derrida, insists that marginalised voices be heard because their interpretation of events can be correct. Social justice often demands that this be the case in public life.

Michel Foucault: 'Power is knowledge'

Michel Foucault (1926–1984) is certainly the most complex of our 'prophets' of deconstruction. As a lad he grew up in Poitiers where he attended the local Jesuit college. His home life was problematic and as a tertiary student he had difficulty in accepting his sexuality. This led to bouts of depression and an attempted suicide. He recovered, however, and went on to graduate in psychology. He practised and taught psychology for a short time in Paris (where Derrida was one of his students) before taking up a post in Tunis. He returned to Paris in the politically charged aftermath of the 1968 student riots. Although he disavowed Marxism, Foucault was always a political radical.

Smith, and independently John Caputo,[184] suggest that there is considerable scope for deconstruction in advancing the mission of a Church that often claims to speak for the marginalised but, in doing so, invokes *its own interpretation of what 'marginalised' means*. It can, for example, easily ignore the marginalised voices in its own community. The development of contextual theology has often given marginalised groups a voice. These evangelical scholars make common cause with recent popes in their call

---

183 James K. Smith, 51.
184 John Caputo *What Would Jesus Deconstruct? The Good News of Post-modernism for the Church* (Grand Rapids, Michigan: Baker Academic, 2007).

for the Church to be continually renewed.[185] In the Christian context, deconstruction entails asking – 'who are the marginalised voices that we need to listen to?', and then listening to them. It can serve a prophetic function. As we have seen previously, Derrida's early experience of being one of these marginalised voices shaped his thinking. As he maintained, context always shapes interpretation.

Historical case studies of modern institutions

Foucault developed an interest in the history and philosophy of science, particularly as this unfolded in the medical and human sciences. In a number of studies carried out in the late 1960s and 1970s, he endeavoured to trace how modern institutions developed by tracing the interconnected roles of knowledge and power as these played out in prisons, hospitals and schools. For example, his first major study was the treatment of madness. During the Enlightenment, rationality was held in such high regard that madness was interpreted as a 'flight from reason' and people so afflicted were locked out of sight. However, by late modernity madness had been 'pathologised' and understood as a 'mental illness' capable of treatment. Foucault explored the changes in society that made this shift in perspective possible. He made similar studies of medical clinics, penal institutions and at the time of his death was doing a study of human sexuality. Foucault used a form of 'grounded' social philosophy in which he held a mirror up to society saying – 'This is the way you are' and then posing the question – 'Is this the way you want to be?'

Foucault developed a form of enquiry that looked at changes that had occurred in society across time and posed the questions – what had happened in society that made such changes possible, and what did this tell us about how society functions? His studies were multi-disciplinary and resulted in a social philosophy. He did not seek to establish cause and effect relationships, but rather highlighted *how the convergence of attitudes and events could produce their own effects*. The methodology underpins his deconstruction of attitudes and practices in the operation of modern institutions which he saw as the real sources of power in society.

---

185 For example 'The proclamation of the Word has Christian conversion as its aim: a complete and sincere adherence to Christ and his Gospel through faith' (Pope John Paul II *Redemptoris Missio* #46). See also James K. Smith's 'Applied Radical Orthodoxy' in *Who's Afraid of Post-modernism?*, 109–146.

Masked power–knowledge relationships

Based on a number of these detailed historical case studies, Foucault built up his analysis of the relationship between knowledge and power in modern institutions. His major conclusion was that the relationship is far more complex than modernity's dictum that 'knowledge is power'. What society counts as *knowledge is rarely neutral* but *reflects dominant beliefs about how power should be used* to achieve social, economic and political goals. The specialised knowledge that characterises the operation of modern institutions, such as hospitals, prisons and schools, is developed and maintained to support power relationships that often operate out of sight, and so go unacknowledged. Foucault sought to bring these into the open, 'to uncover the secret submerged biases and prejudices that go into shaping what is called the truth'.[186] He was concerned with the underlying issues of justice that these power relationships mask.

Suspicion of modern institutions

If Lyotard was suspicious of modern meta-narratives because of their unsustainable claims on truth, Foucault was equally suspicious of the way in which knowledge claims were used to mask power claims. In contemporary institutions, the acquisition of power enables those in power to shape what is deemed to be worthwhile knowledge and so form people to live in society according to norms predetermined by those in power. This erodes human freedom. Schools are inevitably caught up in this dynamic as is the school's curriculum.

Through his case studies, Foucault sought to show how this dynamic works out in practice by highlighting the power–knowledge relationships at work. As Smith notes of his method:

> *Like a genealogist whose patient documentation of a family tree shows the family's complicity in the evils of slavery, so Foucault's genealogy (of institutions) intends to show that modernity's claims to scientific objectivity or moral truth are fruits of a poisoned tree of power relationships.*[187]

Foucault is not saying that power is bad; rather he is saying that one needs to be suspicious of the way in which modern institutions use knowledge to mask power relationships which, if unacknowledged, are dehumanising in their effects. The churches have taken on many of the trappings of modern institutions and are now caught up in the 'suspicion of institutions' highlighted by Foucault. Smith sees it as imperative that they now employ his form of deconstruction in order to renew themselves and revitalise their

---

186 Smith, 86.
187 ibid. 87 (words in brackets not in the original).

mission. In education, this 'suspicion of institutions' should lead us to ask questions such as:
- who determines what decisions need to be made about the curriculum?
- how are these decisions made?
- how does the curriculum seek to form students: implicitly and explicitly?

so that power is exercised in such a way as to truly reflect the mission of the school, and curriculum is not some opaque agenda driven by other interests.

POSTMODERNITY'S OPTIONS: UNDERSTANDING THE WORLD AS AN OPEN SYSTEM

The postmodern critique, in its deconstructive guise, may be interpreted from two perspectives. From one point of view the prophets of deconstruction take Nietzsche's project further by suggesting that, with God off the scene, the issues of truth and morality are determined by power interests. This is achieved by exercising power over knowledge through controlling the interpretive community (Derrida), or through control over what constitutes knowledge (Lyotard and Foucault). In this perspective, truth and morality have no objective reference points, and so are relative. Meaning becomes problematic and this opens the door to nihilism. From another point of view, the prophets of deconstruction can be interpreted as saying that Nietzsche's project has failed because the assumption that the world is a closed system narrows human life down to what is permitted by power interests, with catastrophic results. As a description of reality it is inadequate, and even as a 'working model' the world as a closed system is highly problematic. If this axiom fails, then the logical solution lies in exploring human experience on the basis of an alternative axiom – the world as an open system. While this does not, of itself, imply that 'God is alive', it does not close this option off as Nietzsche and his followers have tried to do. 'God' becomes an open question.

Our second group of postmodern thinkers –Habermas, Taylor and Thornhill, the 'prophets of reconstruction' – stand within this alternative framework. In addition, all three analyse and seek to retain what they judge to be the significant achievements of modernity, seeing these as important contributions to human wellbeing. Their work helps frame an understanding of the world as an open system and explores the place of knowledge within that system. It is to these postmodern thinkers that we now turn.

PRINCIPLE 13: THE DECONSTRUCTION PRINCIPLE

A Catholic curriculum acknowledges the value and autonomy of the academic disciplines that stand behind the public curriculum, but takes a critical stance towards the worldview they often implicitly contain.

COMMENT

The basis of this critique is that the disciplines often fail to recognise either the axiomatic structure on which they are built, or their inherent limits. The academic disciplines are the 'jewel in the crown' of Western cultures and underpin the drive for excellence in academic endeavour that characterises them. All humankind have benefitted from their development. However, as currently constituted, they often operate from axioms that have acquired taken-for-granted status as 'the way things are' and the very power of the disciplines puts these limitations beyond critique.

Academic disciplines have four characteristic components:
1. a knowledge base
2. methods of enquiry
3. a language of discourse and a community of scholars who determine what can be included in the knowledge base
4. what are legitimate methods of enquiry and what problems can be legitimately pursued within the discipline.

The disciplines have legitimate autonomy in all these matters.

A Catholic curriculum recognises that the disciplines are important cultural constructs, but that they have their limits. As knowledge has become more specialised, there is a growing tendency for reductionist accounts of the human condition to appear. While some academics try to push out the range of explanation beyond the limits of their discipline, others attempt to bring everything within the range of their discipline. Students need to know that the genius of the Western tradition does not lie in reductionist accounts, but in the ability of scholars *to bring the disciplines together to make sense of a complex problem with each throwing its own light on some aspect of it until the whole problem is understood and a solution devised.* The interdisciplinary approach used in medicine provides the paradigm here.

CONTINUING THE CONVERSATION

13.1 Is the structure of the academic disciplines and their strengths and limits as sources of meaning, addressed as an issue within the curriculum? If so, where and how?

13.2 How is the autonomy of academic enquiry addressed? Are teachers aware of the Church's teaching on this matter?

13.3 What approach does the curriculum presently take to interdisciplinary enquiry? Is this adequate to a Catholic curriculum?

13.4 How is the 'structure of knowledge' presented as a topic within the curriculum? Is the treatment consistent across the curriculum. If not, why not?

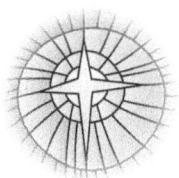

12
POSTMODERN CRITIQUE: PROPHETS OF RECONSTRUCTION

Our three 'prophets of reconstruction' –Habermas, Taylor and Thornhill – share a common goal to reconstruct the essential project of modernity. In this sense they have an optimism that distinguishes them from the 'prophets of deconstruction'. It is this optimism that needs to inform the Catholic curriculum in a secular age.

Modernity put organised religion on the defensive. It came to interpret its successes in terms of the classic 'subtraction story'[188] which we can put in equation form as follows:

modern life = human life – religion.

The impact of this narrative seems to have produced a stultification of the religious imagination both within and outside the Church. Charles Taylor decries the tendency for people to interpret the modern age in terms of such a story, a tale of what has been lost. He sees the rise of secularity as an 'addition story', a hard-won human achievement whose significance needs to be appreciated, particularly by people of faith. For him the postmodern equation reads:

secular public square + many worldviews = modern life (reconstructed).

Because worldviews underpin commitment, they act as engines. The secular public square enables the power of different engines to be combined in the interest of the common good. Noted Rabbi Jonathan Sacks changes the metaphor, but speaks to the same idea, with his notion of civil society as 'the home we build together'.[189]

In this chapter we consider three prophets of reconstruction as a balance to the three prophets of deconstruction featured in Chapter 9. In doing so we complete our survey of postmodern thought. Our three prophets of reconstruction all construe the human condition within the world understood *as an open system*. This shapes their understanding of what it means to be human, their understanding of knowledge and their understanding of society. Each of these scholars holds that these three

---

188 Charles Taylor *A Secular Age* (Cambridge, Massachusetts: The Belknap Press, 2007), 26 etc.
189 Jonathan Sacks *The Home We Build Together: Recreating Society* (London: Continuum, 2007).

elements in human thinking are related. They hold that *anthropology* (our understanding of what it means to be human) *shapes our understanding of all else*. In this they argue that the modern worldview is deficient, and that Descartes needs to be called to account!

All three explore the relationships that give contemporary society its shape, and are interested in how individuals find a home in that society. They explore how religion can and should function in the new 'public square' created by the postmodern condition. Their analyses share a common theme viz that *how we understand the human person shapes our theory of knowledge* and *theories of knowledge influence how people understand society*.

Finally, all three prophets of reconstruction use a method of enquiry pioneered by Foucault. They look at how people's attitudes have changed over time and then ask – *what has changed in society that has made such a change possible?* For instance, in exploring secularisation, Taylor asks – 'why is it so hard to believe in God ... (in) the modern West, while in 1500 it was impossible not to?'[190] This method of enquiry is often described as 'genealogical' in that it traces the history of developments *in thought and practices* with respect to the topic under review. It does not seek to establish 'cause and effect' relationships, as happens in science, but rather *to look for convergences in thought and practice that bring about an effect* which may have *no single cause*. This method of enquiry seems unique to postmodern thought. The approach is multi-disciplinary weaving history together with the social and human sciences to build *a social philosophy*.

JURGEN HABERMAS: KNOWING INTER-SUBJECTIVELY

Jurgen Habermas (1928–) grew up in Germany as it recovered from the Second World War. The Nuremberg trials made a significant impression on the young Habermas and left him puzzled as to how German intellectual life had become so manifestly flawed that its key intellectuals could sympathise with Nazi objectives. Habermas' name is closely associated with critical theory which developed at Frankfurt University early in the 20th century using Marxist forms of social analysis. He is widely regarded as one of the most influential social philosophers alive today.

In Chapter 2, we examined the 'critical theory approach' to curriculum which stands behind the work of Australian curriculum theorists such as Smith and Lovat (2004) and Grundy (1998). These scholars draw inspiration

---

190 Charles Taylor *A Secular Age*, 439. While the question may seem simple, it takes Taylor almost eight hundred pages to answer! Habermas has made a similar study noting the changed way in which people in the West have come to think about 'public life'. Jurgen Habermas *The Structural Transformation of the Public Sphere: An Enquiry into a Category of Bourgeois Society* (Cambridge, Massachusetts: MIT Press, 1991).

from Habermas' *Knowledge and Human Interests* (1980). In this book, he proposed that people's human (subjective) interest in seeking knowledge centred on three needs: to control, to find meaning, and to escape from oppression. While this thesis has a certain face validity, Habermas abandoned it in the 1980s as his thinking about the nature of knowledge developed. His emphasis moved from what motivates people to learn to the two basic modes in which we acquire knowledge.

Modes of knowing: Subject to object

In the first mode, the knower *as subject* studies something *as an object*, either because *it is an object* (as in the case of the exact sciences) or because it *can be 'objectified' in some way* (as is often the case in medical science). Habermas realised that this model breaks down when applied to the study of people, as occurs in the social and human sciences. Here attempts to 'objectify' commonly backfire, because people change once they know that they are being observed. This undermines the possibility of 'objective' assessment. To take an example, when an organisation undergoes a review, the minute the word 'review' is uttered, people change; they seek to control the flow of information to the review so that it reflects best on them. Because people change when they know they are being measured in some way, the 'objectification' process is only ever partial. This weakens the strength of conclusions that can be drawn from such studies – a particular problem in educational research.

Habermas understands people *as active agents* who do not cease to be active agents when they are being observed. *Their subjectivity precludes their study as objects*. In his view *it is simply not possible to establish a subject–object relationship with another subject*.

Modes of knowing: Subject to subject

Anthropologists adopt an alternative approach to knowledge when studying cultures. They identify *emic* views (what the insider sees) and *etic* views (what the observers sees). Knowledge of the culture then emerges *in a process of dialogue*. Here two subjects seek to identify a common object – culture – by bringing their subjective understandings of it together. Neither the emic nor the etic view is, of itself, ever fully determinative of the situation. Habermas calls knowledge developed in this way *communicative*. It is communicative in that it can be generated only through *rational discourse between subjects studying a common object with the aim of developing consensus within agreed rules*. Communicative knowledge is *inter-subjective* the relationship involved is *subject to subject* not *subject to object*. The human sciences and social sciences increasingly operate from the *inter-subjective paradigm of knowledge*.

Communicative reason/communicative action

When reason is used in knowledge-discourse it is said to be *communicative reason* and the process by which *consensus is sought within agreed rules* is called *communicative action*. Habermas juxtaposes the communicative use of reason against its *instrumental use* in science. Instrumental reason seeks to know in order to *efficiently achieve a predetermined goal*, as now happens with most research. Habermas contends that much of the knowledge embedded in the wisdom of a culture is arrived at using communicative reason, rather than instrumental reason. For him the malaise for which modernity needs to be treated is the dominance of instrumental reason over communicative reason.

He challenges what he sees as the overuse of instrumental reason in examining the questions life poses and asks – what has been happening in society that enabled this 'colonisation of reason' to occur? It is in answering this question that Habermas develops his theory of democratic society and suggests that without greater stress on the development and use of communicative reason, the essential problems of society cannot be understood, let alone addressed. The clear implication of his thinking is that, in a complex society, *education must help young people develop communicative reason*. In other words, it must help *young people acquire the skills and perspectives necessary to engage in communicative action*. In practice this means employing inter-subjective modes of learning.

Habermas' theory of society has been criticised for the archaic way in which he treats the role of religion as a source of order in society. However, in recent years he has revised his views considerably. This has occurred in notable dialogues with Cardinal Ratzinger[191] (now Pope Benedict XVI) and later with Charles Taylor.[192] His more recent thought has focused on the place of religion in a pluralist society.[193] Here his views have much in common with those of Taylor. He argues that, as currently configured, religion (meaning Christianity) has been excluded from the public square and public discourse. This means that problems essential to society (for example as caused by the multi-faith nature of Western societies) remain unresolved because there is no adequate forum or framework within which they can be addressed in public discourse as long as this discourse remains secular. He argues for an expanded understanding of the public square, one in which people of all 'faiths' religious and secular can engage in the forms of inter-subjective learning needed to address issues now facing society. In this context he speaks of a coming 'post-secular' age.

191 Jurgen Habermas and Joseph Ratzinger *The Dialectics of Secularization: On Reason and Religion* (San Francisco: Ignatius Press, 2006).
192 Judith Butler, Jürgen Habermas, Charles Taylor and Cornel West *The Power of Religion in the Public Sphere* (New York: Columbia University Press, 2011).
193 Jurgen Habermas *An Awareness of What is Missing: Faith and Reason in a Post-secular Age* (Cambridge: Polity Press, 2010).

Reconstructing modernity

For our purposes, however, Habermas' main contributions in negotiating a way through the morass created by the postmodern condition lie in three directions:

- his affirmation of *the human person as agent, and his exploration of the inter-subjective nature of human learning*
- his acknowledgement that creating knowledge is something human agents *do. We learn by engaging actively.* The discourse through which we acquire most of what we know demands *subject–subject interaction.* Learning is seriously undermined when it is pursued passively. An important implication of this understanding relates to theological discourse. As a knowledge-discourse, theology is something *people must learn to do*, otherwise it ceases to be communicative action.

  This represents a new perspective on theological learning for many people and leaves them with the question – what does it mean 'to do theology'?[194]
- *his proposal that we need to achieve a better balance in education between subject–object learning and inter-subjective learning.* Since most of what we learn about *living in right relationships* comes through inter-subjective learning, this form of learning needs to be more highly valued.

The inter-subjective nature of all learning was a matter close to the heart of John Paul II in his reflections on the nature of learning. We will return to this theme in a later chapter.

CHARLES TAYLOR: THE SELF AND THE SEARCH FOR AUTHENTICITY IN A SECULAR AGE

Those familiar with the work of Canadian philosopher Charles Taylor (1931–) will recognise the influence his thinking has had in formulating the major themes of this book. Taylor[195] grew up in Quebec, the French-speaking part of Canada. The experience of living between two cultures and two languages had a profound influence on his understanding of what it means to be human which provides the pivot around which his thinking turns. His experiences as a French-speaking boy with an English-sounding name attending an English-speaking school, highlighted early for him the important relationship that exists between culture and language.

---

194 We take this matter up in some depth in *Explorers, Guides and Meaning Makers.*
195 In 2010 Taylor was interviewed over the period of a week by David Cayley for CBC for its Ideas Series. An edited version of these interviews subsequently formed the basis of five one-hour programs broadcast in 2011 entitled *The Malaise of Modernity.* The material that follows in drawn from Taylor's own reflections on his life and thoughts as presented in these broadcasts. See www.cbc.ca/ideas/episodes/2011/04/11/the-malaise-of-modernity-part-1---5/

Taylor's critique of modernity moves in three directions modernity's *theory of knowledge* is inadequate, its *notion of freedom is flawed*, and its *moral ideal*, while valid, has been co-opted and trivialised.

Critique of Descartes' theory of knowledge

Put simply, Taylor argues that Descartes 'got it wrong' by taking a theory of knowledge as the starting point for philosophy. In doing so, he (inadvertently) set modern philosophy off on a wild-goose chase from which many of its adherents have yet to return. As a Rhodes scholar studying philosophy at Oxford in the 1950s, Taylor rejected the basic tenets of the analytic philosophy then in vogue which held, following Descartes, that what we know is present as 'ideas in the mind', with the implication that human beings can be thought of as 'minds on legs'.

According to Taylor, Descartes imagined the world as a giant machine which the human mind could observe 'from the outside' and, by understanding it from this perspective, could control it. The human mind could gain this God-like view because the methods of science could achieve 'objective' knowledge of what was viewed. To Descartes' imagination, 'things out there' corresponded to 'ideas in the mind'. The immediate problem with this picture, as Taylor points out, is that it invites scepticism. If our 'ideas in the mind' do not correspond to 'things out there' how would we ever know? The wild-goose chase began as philosophers sought to address this problem! Descartes' mistake here was fundamental. In his flawed anthropology, humans are construed as 'disengaged minds', or 'minds on legs', who can somehow know the world from without. However, there is no such vantage point.

Taylor argues that if a person's understanding of what it means to be human is flawed, then their understanding of what knowledge is and how society works is also likely to prove problematic. Anthropology provides the starting point in philosophy.[196]

---

[196] In this he differs from Sire, discussed earlier, whose position is essentially Aristotelian. While Taylor claims to be 'anti-epistemological' his thought is based in critical realism. That is, the real world exists and we can know it, but our knowledge of it is provisional and so is often flawed.

Understanding of the human person

In Taylor's anthropology, human beings are understood as *embodied, social and interpreters*. As *embodied* we think, feel and act *as a person existing in a real world*. As *social*, we are born into an existing society which shapes us *through the agency of culture*. Not only are we unique, but so too is our culture. As *interpreters*, we search for meaning *through our use of language. Culture provides us with a language, and language provides us with a culture.* Culture and language play a mutually reinforcing role in shaping who we are. For English-speakers, language is a means of communication it is *functional*. For French-speakers, language is who they are it is *constitutive*.

Understanding knowledge

Knowledge does not exist as 'ideas in the mind'. It is *created when we engage with the world through language*. Taylor's understanding of knowledge parallels that of Habermas. In the exact sciences, *a subject studies an object*. Inter-subjective knowledge is created when subjects engage in forms of enquiry that require discourse. He adds, however, that these two modes of knowing are not mutually exclusive. There is an area of overlap, which we see demonstrated in the case of mental illness. Here chemical treatment is an option, so too is growth in self-understanding through the intervention of a therapist. The question that produces all the headaches is this – *how do we get the balance right when our knowledge base provides options?*

It is this search for balance-points that characterises much of Taylor's thought. Like Habermas, Taylor places considerable emphasis on the inter-subjective nature of knowledge, and the need to get a better balance between this and instrumental knowledge if the major problems facing the human world are to be solved.[197] Instrumental solutions tend to rely on the coercive use of power. Communicative solutions rely on discourse. Problems which are essentially cultural in nature *can be solved only through discourse*.

Understanding society

The arrival of modernity brought about a change in human consciousness that had profound impacts on the way society is structured. In pre-modern times people had what Taylor describes as a 'porous identity'. They believed strongly that things outside themselves could take control. We find this in their belief about evil possession. This belief meant that magic and curses carried an aura of fear. In Christian times, relics took on this power as well. However, as more control was gained over nature, people became less fearful

---

[197] Taylor defines the instrumental use of reason as follows: 'Instrumental reason is the kind of rationality we draw on when we calculate the most economical application of means to a given end. Maximum efficiency, the best cost-output ratio, is its measure of success'. See Taylor *The Ethics of Authenticity*, 5.

of these arbitrary forces. They developed into what Taylor calls 'buffered selves' as their world became 'disenchanted'.

The Reformation fed this development particularly through the way in which the reformers 'secularised' time. The main reformers opposed the view common in the Middle Ages that life had 'higher times', generally associated with the 'festive' in human life. They saw time as *a commodity not to be wasted*. To avoid wasting time, people needed to exercise self-discipline. The need for personal discipline became an important part of the *modern moral order*. This proved so productive in human terms that it was seen as self-justifying. As societies became more disciplined, benefits accrued: it was possible to impose quarantine regimes and so resist plague; better discipline led to new forms of military organisation resulting in more successful armies; it also resulted in new forms of educational provision; and, eventually, to the formation of a civil service.

However, the disciplining of society brought about *an expressivist reaction* known as the Romantic movement. It was from this strand of modernity, and not the scientific strand, that the moral ideal of authenticity emerged.

Against the tendency to control and homogenise people, the Romantics affirmed *the uniqueness of each individual*. In this development, Taylor finds the roots of modern individualism which he defines descriptively as follows -

> *We live in a world where people have a right to choose for themselves their own pattern of life, to decide in conscience what convictions to espouse, to determine the shape of their lives in a whole host of ways that their ancestors couldn't control. And these rights are generally defended by our legal systems. In principle, people are no longer sacrificed to the demands of supposedly sacred orders that transcend them.*[198]

Commenting on this definition he notes that very few people want to undo this achievement of modernity even while thinking it is incomplete.

However, an important insight was lost with the development of individualism – that life has a heroic dimension, a higher purpose, something worth committing oneself to. Instead, people began to focus on their individual lives, which resulted in a 'narrowing of life'. People have lost important markers in making sense of their lives and are less concerned for the welfare of others and of society. The 'me generation' emerges as an example of what Taylor calls the 'individualism of self-absorption':

> *everyone has a right to develop their own form of life grounded on their own sense of what is really important or of value. People are called upon to be true to themselves and to seek their own self-fulfilment. What this consists of, each must, in the last instance, determine for him or herself. No one else can or should try to dictate its content.*[199]

---
198 Charles Taylor *The Ethics of Authenticity*, 2.
199 ibid. 14.

Authenticity as the moral ideal of modernity

Authenticity as a powerful moral ideal

Taylor suggests that when people focus on the negative consequences of this self-absorption, evident in Gallagher's ten precepts of the 'postmodern sensibility' cited previously, they lose sight of *the powerful moral ideal that it contains*. This ideal developed in modernity and has resulted in the postmodern 'culture of authenticity'.

Taylor defines a moral ideal as follows:

> *a picture of what a better or higher mode of life would be, where 'better' or 'higher' are defined not in terms of what we happen to desire or need, but offer a standard of what we ought to desire.*[200]

Moral ideals play an important role in how we think about, and engage in, the relationships that define our life-world.[201] Authenticity *being in contact with one's inner self and being true to oneself* was the moral ideal that emerged in modernity and gave it moral force.

The genesis of this ideal, which has strong roots in the religious tradition, can be traced back to the Romantic notion that human beings are endowed with a moral sense an intuitive sense of what is right and what is wrong. In this perspective, morality is not a matter of calculation; it is a voice within. Being moral is a matter of being in contact with our moral feelings, of coming into contact with our inner depth. In other words, there is not only an *external world* to be understood and in a sense conquered, but there is also an *inner world* to know as well *the world of the subjective*. Modernity is characterised by this 'massive subjective turn... a new form of inwardness, in which we come to think of ourselves as beings with inner depths'.[202]

Rousseau was perhaps the first to understand and articulate this change as it emerged in modern culture. He advocated the need to recover *authentic moral contact with ourselves*, which he saw as masked by the imposed moral standards of the disciplined society. He advocated a new understanding of freedom self-determining freedom by which he meant 'I am free when I decide for myself what concerns me, rather than being shaped by external influences'. Here we see the beginnings of a movement towards the 'constructed self'.

These two ideals authenticity and self-determining freedom both arose in modernity and are often confused with each other. They are two complementary facets of the modern sensibility that sit well with the notion

---

200 ibid. 16.
201 In Hughes' model this higher order is provided either by the ethical framework of culture or the spiritual framework sourced in a conception of human destiny that transcends culture.
202 ibid. 26.

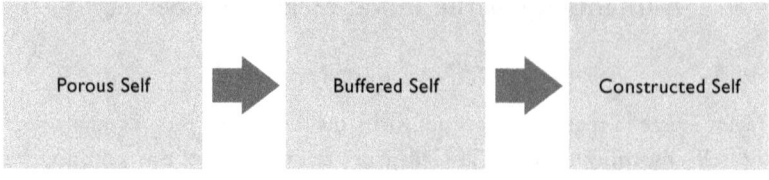

FIGURE 12.1 Developments in the idea of the self as modernity advanced

that *each of us has an original way of being human*.[203] According to Taylor, this idea entered very deeply into human consciousness in modernity.

The change in human understanding of the self in modernity is a movement in three parts.

Each step is associated with a greater sense of the power of human agency in structuring personal identity.

The conception that there is a certain way of being human that is my way – that I am called on to live my life in this way and not in imitation of anyone else's was a new idea in modernity and immortalised in postmodern times by Frank Sinatra's hit song *I Did it My Way*.

Authenticity and self-fulfilment

Taylor points out that the understanding can be taken further:

> Not only should I not fit my life to the demands of external conformity; I can't even find the model to live by outside myself. I can find it only within.
>
> Being true to myself means being true to my own originality and that is something only I can articulate and discover. In articulating it, I am also defining myself. I am realising a potentiality that is properly my own.[204]

Authenticity comes to be couched in terms of the goals of self-fulfilment and self-realisation. This understanding sits well with the notion *that our commitments are guided by a personal worldview anchored in a tradition of meaning*. While the ideal of authenticity can be trivialised into 'doing your own thing', *it contains within it an important understanding about what it means to be human* – what it means to be a human agent.

Authenticity and personal identity

Taylor poses an important question. If we accept that the moral ideal of authenticity is expressed through self-fulfilment and self-realisation, how can this ideal be best realised in human life? What does the ideal call for?

---

203 ibid. 29.
204 ibid. 29. Taylor draws on and acknowledges the work of Herder.

His response points to *the dialogical nature of human life* which demands that we transcend the individualism of self-absorption.

We become full human agents capable of understanding ourselves (our inner depths) only through the acquisition of the languages of human expression the languages of culture. Our acquisition of these languages, which we need to define ourselves, is mediated by others, in particular the 'significant others' in our lives those who matter to us. Thus, *we acquire the means of expressing our uniqueness and identity in a process that is dialogical. We do not create ourselves*; rather we come to define our identity inter-subjectively. As Taylor observes:

> *We define this always in dialogue with, sometimes in struggle against, the identities our significant others want to recognise in us. And even when we outgrow some of the latter our parents, for instance and they disappear from our lives, the conversation with them continues within us as long as we live.*[205]

Our concept of what is 'a good life' is defined by what we have shared with those we love this is how what is 'good' is made accessible to us. In this sense, *our identity is formed by those we love*. The relationship between 'me' and 'family and friends' is determinative of who I am as a person. We would argue that the love of God has also to be factored in.

Transcendent dimension of identity

Taylor takes the argument further. If authenticity involves discovering the 'inner self', then it involves finding that which makes me different from others. This can be done only against a background that includes some sense of *what we see as significant and able to stand up to criticism*. I can define my identity only against *the background of things that matter*. Authenticity then assumes that there are demands that exist beyond the self. This opens up the notion of quest and with it the transcendent.

In any expression of authentic individualism, authenticity has to include some view of *how individuals live together*. It requires a social doctrine. Taylor suggests that this now takes two characteristic directions:

- *soft relativism* which holds that everyone should have the right and capacity to be themselves. Thus no one has a right to criticise other people's views. What is required is *procedural justice* which prevents discrimination. This is a universal right.
- *affirmation of ordinary life* which holds that *some relationships are inherently more important to self-fulfilment than others*. These need to be privileged because it is through them that *our identity is established and recognised*.

---

205 ibid. 33.

Reconstructing modernity: Authentic education

Taylor's insights are put into practical effect by American educator Robert Starratt[206] who offers a valuable educational interpretation of the ethic of authenticity. He proposes that the starting point in education is building a student's self-esteem by helping the student discover his or her talents. Education implies a process of self-discovery – not only of our inner wealth – 'I am the one with these talents', but also in terms of future possibility – 'what do I have to offer others, if I can develop and use my talents?'. This implies *an ethical understanding of talent*, both on the part of the individual, and of society. Schools have an ethical obligation to help young people develop their talents as an expression of the ideal of authenticity.

Secondly, Starratt suggests that talents are developed in a community context and students need to be encouraged *to put their talents at the service of the community*. Through the process of inter-subjective learning they begin to discover new depths to their identity. Education also nurtures a level of self-transcendence by helping young people develop *a sense of the heroic* which enables them to interpret life as a quest.

Finally, in advancing down this path, students come to understand that *authenticity requires self-discipline* without which it is impossible to develop the inner self or be true to oneself, either as a person or as a member of a community. For Starratt the above program defines the essential *ethical dimension of schooling*. He converts Taylor's insights on restructuring modernity into an educational program that is highly relevant to the Catholic curriculum.

JOHN THORNHILL: RE-LAUNCHING MODERNITY AS A MOVEMENT

John Thornhill is a noted Australian theologian and a former member of the International Theological Commission to which he was appointed by John Paul II. One of his significant theological studies has been into the nature of modernity.[207] We have found his study to be a helpful Catholic source in reframing the idea of a Catholic curriculum, in particular his contention that modernity's project is valuable but remains unfinished and needs to be taken up again.

---

206 Robert Starratt's thinking is set out for a secular audience in *Building an Ethical School: A Practical Response to the Moral Crisis in Schools* (London: The Falmer Press, 1994). The best treatment for a religious audience is found in an address to Catholic School Superintendents in 1984, entitled *The Religious Development of The Catholic School Teacher*. In our view, this treatment has not been surpassed in his later writings. The section above combines ideas from both these sources.
207 John Thornhill *Modernity: Catholicism's Estranged Child Reconstructed*.

Modernity: From movement to ideology

Thornhill argues that, in the course of its 500-year history, modernity, which began as a movement with its roots deep in Christian charity, that in seeking to gain greater control over nature in the cause of human flourishing, became identified with an ideology – scientific naturalism. This ideology was, and remains, too limited to carry forward the great hopes held by modernity's founders. Under the impact of science's obvious achievements, modernity converted from a humanistic movement into an ideology serving the interests of the powerful who benefited from the resultant narrowing of life as experienced by the bulk of humankind. This occurred because the tenets of the ideology, particularly through their acceptance by academia, became a taken-for-granted part of modern cultures and so resistant to critique. This has had disastrous consequences which have become more and more obvious with the passage of time and are now experienced in both the developed world, and with especially serious consequences in the developing world.

Modernity's quest for autonomy

The founders of modernity sought to free human beings to engage in legitimate human enquiry into the developing secular order. This meant freeing this order from existing ecclesiastical–political–social controls. It also aimed to advance the notion of human autonomy that was a separate, but related project, which also required the refashioning of the existing ecclesiastical-political-social structures. Much of the analysis of modernity focuses on a subtraction story in which religion features negatively and politics features positively. This narrative ignores the very significant work done by religions to adapt to the new secular order, particularly in the second half of the twentieth century. Religion in the 21st century cannot be represented by a caricature based on its response in early modernity any more than contemporary politics can be portrayed as Machiavellian!

Restructuring modernity: Re-launching the modern movement

The capacity to take a step backwards and recognise just how great was the vision of modernity, has allowed contemporary scholars to re-affirm the value of the original project. It has then enabled them to consider how it may still be carried forward, and why it is very important to do so. All our 'prophets of reconstruction' concur in this view.

Thornhill acknowledges the validity of the early modern need to free the emerging secular order from the authority of an all-encompassing tradition, and the great opportunities that the achievement of this autonomy has offered and continues to offer for the West. He sees this as consistent with the Western notion of excellence as 'shared human intellectual achievement'. Having explored a range of American and European scholars, Thornhill argues that *modernity is coming to the end of its ideological phase and is now ripe for a broadening of its intellectual base.* He notes an emerging consensus which both seeks *an enlarged paradigm of knowledge* and *a renewed commitment to the accountability* which comes with any genuinely shared intellectual inquiry.

Thornhill completes his study by looking at the role 'catholicism' might play in a renewed modernity. For him, 'catholicism' is an element of the Christian Church that is found in the Roman Catholic communion, but which also transcends that communion.[208] In speaking of catholicism as a historical phenomenon, Thornhill emphasises two things: a wholeness which is *hospitable to all* that is life-giving before God and a *realism* which owns unhesitatingly *the truth of God* manifested in Christ. In his view, it is these characteristics which allow the Catholic Church to provide hospitality to other Christian denominations, other religions, and indeed all persons of good will, in such a way as to promote the dialogues that foster unity at the human and religious levels. Thornhill also argues that the Christian churches can in our time also provide a unique witness, and make a major contribution in the public square where, within the emerging paradigm of knowledge, they have a legitimate voice.

While postmodern thought is often characterised as pessimistic, this is only one side of the coin. There is an optimistic side as well. In this chapter we have endeavoured to demonstrate this as an important element when the topic is 'a Catholic curriculum'.

---

208 The need for Christian religions to reclaim their catholic roots is also a theme developed by John Smith in *Whose Afraid of Post-Modernism? Taking Derrida, Lyotard, and Foucault to Church.*

PRINCIPLE 14: THE PROPHETIC PRINCIPLE

A Catholic curriculum defends the existence of objective standards of truth and moral values as important constructs in the Western intellectual tradition. In doing so it highlights the gap that exists between what ideological relativism promises and what it delivers.

COMMENT

Ideological pluralism is based on the assumption that the human community and it alone is the source of all meaning, so it determines what is true and moral. Since different groups go about this task in different ways, and reach different conclusions, truth and morality are relative concepts. This being the case, there are no objective standards and it is wrong to criticise those who see the world differently from you. This argument has now crept into 'the common stock of everyday knowledge' and so has a taken-for-granted status for many people. While the case against this form of relativism can be readily made on theological grounds, that is not the import of this principle. The case needs to be made on rational grounds, and students need to leave Catholic schools knowing what it is, otherwise all attempts to help them make meaning in their lives runs the risk of being frustrated. The case made needs to be capable of holding its own in the public square since so much depends on it. In choosing to challenge ideological pluralism, a Catholic curriculum raises its prophetic voice.

CONTINUING THE CONVERSATION

14.1 How does the curriculum address the difference in perspective that people bring to the consideration of issues because of their different cultural backgrounds and the different histories that determine these backgrounds?

14.2 How does it address the legitimate differences that arise, even within the one culture, because of differences in class and gender?

14.3 How does it account for difference in religious outlook and the way in which this influences what people hold to be true:
- within Catholicism?
- across Christian denominations?
- between faiths?

14.4 Given the legitimately different ways of viewing the world, what concept of truth and moral values does the curriculum convey to students? Is the portrayal cohesive? Do students understand it as cohesive?

14.5 What understanding of 'tolerance' is developed within the curriculum? Is this consistent with the affirmation of truth as objectively determinable?

PRINCIPLE 15: THE PUBLIC SQUARE PRINCIPLE

A Catholic curriculum helps students understand the tensions that exist in their society in its presentation of 'the public square' and its recognition of the important place the public square holds in a democratic society.

COMMENT

The public square is the metaphorical forum for discourse in a democratic society where issues of importance to the culture are discussed and potential solutions to tensions proposed. It is the place where public meaning is developed. Public meaning proceeds on the basis of discourse and is informed by scholarly interventions as well as by political ideologies. This discourse in the West has to date been conducted on a secular basis. The reasons for this are historical and particular to Western cultures. Advocates of a 'post-secular' public square hold that issues of public importance now arise that have religious dimensions which often cannot be resolved within a discourse that is secular. This is because many people living in Western societies, including those from Islamic countries, do not share the history which led to the secular construction of the public square. Secondly, the problem that the present construction of the public square set out to address has itself faded into history. In consequence, the public square as currently constituted has come to privilege the secularist position which is itself a form of faith that now seeks to stereotype all people of religious faith as 'conservative', 'the religious right', 'fundamentalist' etc., in order to advance its own position. In accusing people of religious faith of being 'intolerant', secularists fail to admit their own intolerance towards people of faith. Students need to understand what is going on here, and what is at stake, as this problem is imported into their homes nightly on the media. It is not only an important religious issue; it is an issue for the culture and society as well.

CONTINUING THE CONVERSATION

15.1 Does the school have its own equivalent of the 'public square' in which issues of importance in school life for students can be raised debated and resolved? If not, why not?

15.2 What level of self-governance by students is encouraged within school life?

15.3 How does the curriculum develop its understanding of the 'public square' and the place in civic life this has in a democratic society?

15.4 In what ways does the curriculum identify, and then develop, the skills and attitudes students need to participate effectively in the 'public square'?

15.5 Does the curriculum address the issues that stand behind contemporary debate about a 'post-secular public square'?

PRINCIPLE 16: THE NATURE OF LEARNING PRINCIPLE

A Catholic curriculum respects knowledge developed through science with its subject–object form of knowing. It also respects knowledge developed inter-subjectively, holding that most of what is learned in schools happens in this mode.

COMMENT

The methods of enquiry used in the empirical sciences depend on the ability to treat what is being studied as an object to 'objectify' it. This process has its limits and beyond these, empirical methods are invalid. Empirical methods are often invalid when what is being studied in another 'subject' such as happens in much of the social sciences and the human sciences. Here knowledge has to be generated inter-subjectively respecting the subject–subject relationship involved, and this requires a degree of trust between subjects.

Education, as John Paul II pointed out well in *Faith and Reason,* proceeds on the basis of a 'hermeneutics of trust', since much of what we learn has to be taken on trust as we do not have either the time or the resources to test out all that we need to learn. We have to put our trust in traditions and the people who convey them. This places the relationship between the teacher and the learner at the centre of learning. The inter-subjective nature of learning has important implications for a Catholic curriculum since a 'hermeneutics of trust' depends ultimately, as the Pope points out, on the 'truth of the human person', on whether or not he or she is seen as authentic. If a 'hermeneutics of trust' is a theme in learning, then the counter-theme is a 'hermeneutics of suspicion' with the balance point between these two continually being re-negotiated. With the 'postmodern turn' it moved decisively to towards suspicion which undermines the value of inter-subjective learning. A Catholic curriculum re-affirms the value of learning inter-subjectively.

CONTINUING THE CONVERSATION

16.1 How does the curriculum address the pedagogical challenges that arise when learning is defined in inter-subjective terms?

16.2 In what specific ways does the pedagogy of the school seek to balance the hermeneutics of trust with the hermeneutics of suspicion? Or is this simply left to chance?

16.3 When the relational environment of the school is examined, in what ways are students treated as objects? As subjects? Is there a balance point here, and if so how is it determined?

16.4 How does the analysis implied in the above questions influence the learning environment of the school and the curriculum theory of the school as these operate in practice?

16.5 Is this influence consistent with, or counter-productive of, the school's stated mission?

Part E

THE WORLDVIEW OF FAITH AS A PUBLIC SOURCE IN MEANING MAKING

The worldview of faith in its many forms constitutes a tradition of meaning for the majority of the people on the planet today, as it has for most of human history. The majority of people hold that the world is an open system although they differ substantially in how they think of this system.

In Part E, we explore the worldview of faith from a Christian perspective as it bears on the issue of meaning. We make the point that within the worldview of Christian faith there is a core the constants that need to be interpreted in different settings the contexts. The Christian worldview developed originally within local contexts, growing in the process to take on a discernibly universal form which now has to be continually re-interpreted in local contexts. There is an ongoing interplay between the local and the global that drives the development of the Christian worldview. This worldview underpins the commitments of local people in responding to the Gospel challenge to mission in particular settings. One of these is your school or educational setting.

The worldview of Christian faith has its roots firmly set in the Hebrew tradition which provided Jesus with his tradition of meaning. In Chapter 13, we look at three important aspects of this tradition, which we are in the process of rediscovering today. The first is the way in which the development of the community and the development of the tradition went hand in hand with the scriptural text, providing a guide to authentic development. Secondly, we look at the way in which the Hebrew community has been able to maintain its identity through nearly 4000 years and what can be learned from this. Finally, we look at the critique that the Hebrew construction of knowledge offers its Western counterpart and the important value this tradition places on difference and diversity.

Chapter 14 explores the five constitutive elements of the Christian worldview the person Jesus Christ, his message, his community, its mission, and the ethos that should guide it in mission. These five elements are present in all authentic articulations of the Christian worldview and so constitute a point of unity among Christians. We then go on to look at how, within this tradition, the Catholic worldview is articulated contrasting two interpretations of this worldview, one by Richard Rohr widely used in Rite of Christian Initiation of Adults (RCIA) programs in the USA and one by Australian Bishop David Walker. Both these articulations of the Catholic worldview have been employed in major curriculum projects in Australia that sought to implement a Catholic curriculum at school system level. The two approaches throw into relief some of the issues that have to be taken into account in assessing articulations of 'the Catholic worldview' as a public source in meaning making.

In Part D we traced, in some detail, developments in the academic world that resulted in the two major forms of postmodern critique deconstructive and reconstructive. In Chapter 15 we offer a comparable account of developments in Catholic thinking (and the Catholic worldview) in response to living in 'the postmodern condition'. In 1974, ten years after the Second Vatican Council, Paul VI called a general synod of the Church to review progress since the Council. Following this synod he published *Evangelii Nuntiandi* which marks something of a watershed in the development of Catholic thinking and practice in addressing the challenges facing the Church in carrying forward the mission of Jesus.

For Paul VI, the mission of the Catholic Church is encompassed by the term 'evangelisation'. There is still a general lack of clarity about the meaning of this term among Catholics, which is amplified by its use in the expression 'new evangelisation' which came to figure prominently in the thinking of John Paul II. In Chapter 15 we set out to clarify the meaning of both terms with reference to official Church teaching on the theology of mission.

The bottom line consideration here is that the Church has undergone something of a quantum shift in its self-understanding with consequences for how it now construes its mission. Developments since 1974 have implications for how we now articulate the Catholic worldview as a public source of meaning.

We argue that one important consequence of this shift is that all Catholics now need to develop the skills required to 'do theology'. The need, seen as a response to living in the postmodern condition', now has to be part of any conversation about Catholic curriculum. 'Doing theology' must become an essential element in the experience of 'being a postmodern Catholic' if Catholics are to overcome their learned passivity towards mission. As a field of study, theology has both a knowledge base and methods of enquiry. 'Doing theology' is a method of enquiry that teachers in Catholic schools need to master and pass on to their students if they are to make sense of their own lives. Their experience of 'being Catholic' is going to be quite different as the newer understandings of mission bed down. All this is encompassed in John Paul II's use of the term 'new evangelisation'. Catholic schools can play a major role in helping students negotiate the changes envisioned by a 'new evangelisation'. Understanding why this is so, and how teachers can participate, are now important elements in any conversation about Catholic curriculum.

13
THE WORLDVIEW OF FAITH

The worldview of a faith is a *source of meaning* held by a community and is usually a principal marker of identity within that community. As such, it is a complex reality, capable of multiple expressions even within the one faith community. Despite the range of ways in which this worldview is understood and expressed, these expressions have one thing in common – they take the existence of the transcendent in human life as axiomatic, that is they interpret the world as an open system. The great world religions are expressions of the worldview of faith. One way of representing this complexity is set out below.

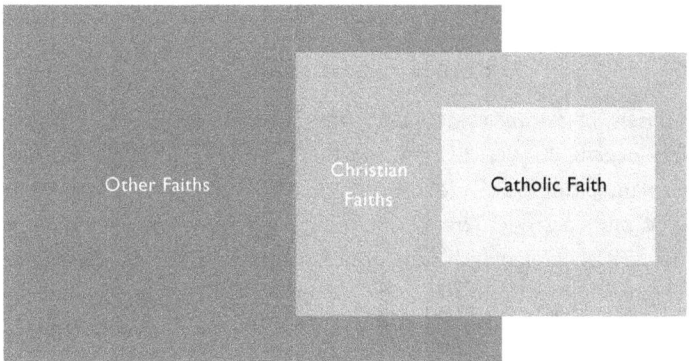

FIGURE 13.1 Being Catholic as a way of being human

The diagram indicates that the Catholic worldview is a specific form of the more general Christian worldview. However, there is also considerable overlap between the values and goals pursued by Christians and those pursued by people of other faiths. The increasing willingness of people who take the worldview of faith as a source in meaning making to work together has made inter-religious dialogue a feature of the postmodern situation, one for which John Paul II must take considerable credit.

In this chapter, we explore a number of themes critical to reframing the conversation about the Catholic curriculum. In the first instance, we look at why the worldview of faith is important in making sense of experience. We then examine the important role played by the Hebrew worldview in shaping the worldview of faith as it is understood within the Western tradition. This raises a number of issues which are foundational to the Catholic worldview, in particular, the way in which knowledge is understood in this worldview.

THE WORLDVIEW OF FAITH AS A TRADITION OF MEANING

The worldview of faith as expressed in a faith community provides an important *tradition of meaning* for members of that faith community. That is it stands as *a coherent frame of reference to which people appeal in making sense of life*. For Catholics this worldview can be expressed only through culture. It is therefore integrally related to culture and *complements and seeks to transform* the worldview of the cultures in which it is expressed. Both faith and culture provide coherent frames of reference in making sense of life. Each enables us to interpret important aspects of our personal and collective experiences, which is why Catholic schools strive to bring about an *integration of faith and culture*.

Contemporary tensions

The worldview of culture is *historically determined* and in Western cultures carries resonances of its origins, particularly its Christian origins. These resonances are built into the narratives through which culture is conveyed. While many understand cultural narratives as illustrating the complementarity between faith and culture, secularists in recent years have sought to provide a revisionist account which seeks to interpret 'religion' as *a stage of cultural development that people in the West have now passed through*. On the basis of this revisionist account, they challenge the legitimacy of the worldview of faith as a tradition of meaning and its place in education. Therefore, how we understand and value the worldview of faith, considered across many faiths as a source of meaning, *plays an important role in how we understand and critique the worldview of our culture*.

As people of other faiths enter Western societies, their narrative comes to be interpreted in terms of the national narrative. It is a dynamic in which the new arrivals begin to discover, buried within the national narrative, values and beliefs with which they can identify. A process known in sociology as *acculturation* occurs whereby part of 'their plan for living' becomes part of 'our plan'; part of 'their story' becomes conflated with 'our story' and vice versa.

We see this very obviously in the area of cuisine, but the process goes deeper than that. At its most fruitful, people learn that they have something to offer the host culture in the ongoing development of the local 'plan for living' and this realisation enables them to contribute successfully to it. However, this capacity to contribute in the public square is diminished when the worldview of faith is denied legitimacy, as happens in secular societies. Cultures such as that of Australia, which have been successful in integrating people from diverse religious backgrounds, are able to do so because the local cultural narratives are *sufficiently 'catholic' to embrace the worldview of faith in its many manifestations*. In this sense, as we indicated in Chapter 11, drawing on the thought of Habermas and Taylor, the creation of a 'secular public square' has represented a significant political achievement. However, if the plan for living in modern multi-faith, multi-cultural communities is going to be 'more or less successful', the public square will have to take on its 'post-secular' configuration in which the worldview of faith is recognised as a source in meaning making. The public square is an area where the themes and counter-themes alive in our culture have to be brought into a new balance. This implies that the secularist colonisation of the public square will have to be wound back. This is now a major tension point in postmodern life.

Integrating the worldviews of faith, culture and the age

As we saw in Part C, the worldview of culture is strongly influenced by the worldview of the age. As persons-within-culture, our worldview is shaped by the hopes and possibilities, as well as by the particular demands and constraints, of the historical context in which we live – a world in which modern and postmodern sensibilities compete in providing cultural norms.

The way we look at the world today is shaped by the *three sources* that stand as worldviews and are accessed as traditions of meaning when we try to make sense of the unfamiliar in life. Each of these three worldviews is able to throw some light on new situations without ever being able to offer a definitive explanation of it. They exist in creative tension with each other. The task for the individual is knowing *how to discern which is most appropriate in making sense of particular situations*. This task is made difficult because:

- all three are evolving as a consequence of ongoing interaction with each other
- the worldviews proceed on the basis of contradictory axioms and while they can complement each other, they often offer alternative explanations of new situations
- the communities that sponsor the worldviews are often in conflict with each other because of imbalances in power relationships between them
- all three worldviews are evolving in response to the pressures created by globalisation.

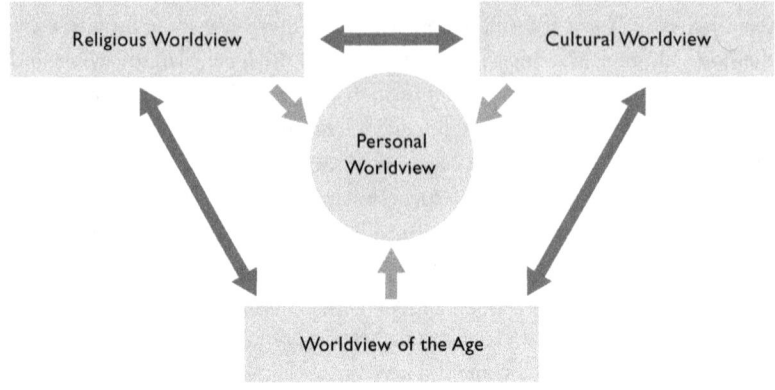

FIGURE 13.2 The postmodern context for meaning making

People today make sense of life within the situation summed up in the diagram above.

In the balance of Part E we want to look at the way in which the worldview of faith acts as a source in meaning making and trace some of the implications this has for curriculum in Catholic schools. We begin by examining the Hebrew worldview of the Old Testament. This is both the foundation on which the Christian worldview is built and an important source in its own right, shaping the development of the Western tradition even though it is not Western in its formulation.

GENESIS OF THE CHRISTIAN WORLDVIEW: HEBREW FOUNDATIONS

The worldview of faith in its Christian formulation builds on the significant foundations laid by the Hebrew peoples of Old Testament times. As Christians, we often fall into the trap of taking this foundation for granted, and so fail to appreciate its uniqueness. The Hebrew worldview is a tradition of meaning anchored by the Hebrew Bible.[209] This worldview was the principal tradition of meaning within which Jesus and the first Christians made sense of their world. Secondly, the worldview illustrates important dynamics in how a faith community develops, guards and nurtures the worldview of faith as eras change and as culture changes. Thirdly, the Hebrew worldview stands behind the oldest religious tradition to have shaped the West. The community of Israel is unique in its longevity. This

---

209 The Hebrew Bible is based on those books of the Bible originally written in Hebrew. The Christian Old Testament is based on the Septuagint version of the Old Testament that was written in Greek. Both acknowledge the central place of the Torah and Prophets but differ on what is accepted as the Writings.

indicates the power of this worldview in maintaining the identity of its sponsoring community and the commitments that sustain this identity. The ongoing existence of the now multi-cultural faith community, which today identifies itself as 'Israel'[210], is taken by its members as living proof of God's faithfulness to the covenant made with Moses.

THE HEBREW WORLDVIEW: THREE THEMES

In exploring the Hebrew worldview we focus, in the limited space available, on three major issues:
- the *substance* of the worldview – what Israel knew
- the *dynamics* by which the worldview came into being and by which it is sustained
- the *critique the worldview makes of the Western construction of knowledge*.

The Hebrew worldview shaped Jesus' worldview. It provided him with a language, categories of thought, cultural narratives, a means of worshipping God, and the symbols he called on to express his message, including the Kingdom of God. Hence, in exploring the worldview of faith from a Christian perspective, the starting point is the Hebrew worldview. The Hebrew worldview was formulated outside Western thought patterns. It has its own view of knowledge which provides a critique of Western thought and thus affords some helpful insights into the postmodern situation.

THE HEBREW WORLDVIEW IN OUTLINE: A TRADITION OF HOPE WITHIN HISTORY

Israel's worldview developed over a period of almost two millennia, in the cut and thrust of an often tragic history, and involved a dynamic interplay of beliefs, feelings and values all interpreted *through the medium of story*. Bearing in mind that this worldview developed in stages, we can delineate it with reference to four of its *constitutive elements*:
1 Israel's place among the nations
2 Israel's sense of history and of hope within history
3 Israel's worship of the God who liberates
4 Israel's God as the God who does justice.

Israel's place among the nations

Throughout much of its history, Israel wrestled with God's purpose for them among the nations.[211] While aware of themselves as called to be a *special people*, over time the consciousness grew that their God was the

---

210 Not to be confused with the country of Israel.
211 This theme plays out in a different register in contemporary Christian theology which wrestles with the special place of the Christian religion vis-à-vis the other world religions.

God of all peoples. While they attempted to connect these two realities, and determine what it meant for them, the issue remained unresolved in Jesus' time. The Hebrew worldview was not missionary, at least not in the sense which came to apply in the Christian community, but was most certainly missional in a broader and deeper sense.[212] Indeed, the whole of the Bible is a witness to *God's mission* – how God effects this mission within history and what God calls people to be and invites them to do.

Israel's God as the God of history

Israel's worldview was shaped by extraordinary leaders who were the meaning-makers within society both in times of turbulence, when events were out of Israel's control, and during more settled times when the actions of kings and religious leaders betrayed the terms of the sacred covenant between the people and God. The king and the prophet often played overlapping roles in the developing of the Hebrew worldview.

Christians inherit from the Hebrew narrative their understanding that *God reveals Godself within human history.* The most distinctive feature of the Jewish people is their sense of history, over-riding diversity in theology, culture and racial characteristics.[213] The Old Testament is witness to a religion in which *theological narrative* plays a central role. The culture of Israel is built around its unique theological narratives preserved as sacred text.

Israel worships the God who liberates

Israel was a community bound together by *shared experiences* which, as Anderson points out, are more important even than blood or soil. At the heart of Israel's narrative was a pivotal event, the people's delivery from Egypt. This provides *the paradigm of liberation* which is repeated again and again in the narrative, so shaping Israel's identity. Israel's sense both of history, and of hope within history, developed from God's action in *repeatedly liberating his people.* In the enculturation of each generation, this narrative was told, not as a past event, but *as something that is continually happening.*

Embedded in the *Book of Deuteronomy* is a quote from a much older source, probably an excerpt from an ancient liturgy, reminding us that Israel always placed the memory of its deliverance at the heart of its worship.[214]

> *My father was a wandering Aramean who went down to Egypt with a small household and lived there as an alien. But there he became a nation great, strong and numerous. When the Egyptians maltreated*

---

212 See James Chukwuma Okoye *Israel and the Nations: A Mission Theology of the Old Testament* (Maryknoll, New York: Orbis, 2006).
213 Bernhard W. Anderson *The Living World of the Old Testament* (Harlow, Essex: Longman, 1978), 2.
214 ibid., 11.

and oppressed us, imposing hard labour upon us, we cried to the Lord, the God of our father and he heard our cry and saw our affliction, our toil and oppression. He brought us out of Egypt with his strong hand and outstretched arm, with terrifying power, and with signs and wonders; and bringing us into this country he gave us this land flowing with milk and honey. Therefore, I have now brought you the first fruits of the products of the soil which you, O Lord, have given me (Deuteronomy 26: 5–10).

It is very clear from this passage that, while the ancestors are mentioned, *the core experience is that of the Exodus*. It is the source of their enduring hope and it is this hope that is celebrated in Israel's worship. As Old Testament scholar Walter Brueggemann puts it –

Jews…are a people of hope, but they can be a people of hope only if they are not alienated from and ignorant of their tradition. Therefore, it is important to identify the shape and substance of that hope.[215]

The writer of the 1 Peter will remind Christians to 'always be ready to offer an account of the hope that is in you' (1 Peter 3:15). In the teaching of Paul VI, this call to account for the hope we carry within will feature in Catholic mission theology as 'proclamation', the primary mode of Christian mission.

The Hebrew worldview has at its heart a *transforming hope* which points to a better human arrangement beyond the status quo. Israel's hope was not hope in the historical process; rather *it was a hope nurtured and sustained, despite all the evidence that there was no hope.*[216] *A tradition built on hope will have a place for imagination.* In the Hebrew case the genius of the people lay in the imaginative nature of its story-telling, its oral tradition and its literature.

When the biblical writers came to finalise their theology of human beginnings in *Genesis*, they did so by setting it down as narratives of hope. Against a background of God's creativity, the *Genesis* narratives of Abraham, Isaac and Jacob provide the basis for hope *the God who makes promises, keeps them*. In imagining a better future, the prophetic texts also strike a strong note of hope. The major prophetic themes *bring together God's vision and Israel's hopes* for a social order different from that of other nations, an order which will embody peace, justice, freedom, equity and wellbeing.[217] Jesus takes up the theme of hope within history (but also beyond history) in his interpretation of the Kingdom of God.

---

215 Walter Brueggemann *Hope within History* (Atlanta: John Knox Press, 1987), 73.
216 ibid. 73–80 provides a discussion of elements of the hope literature of the Old Testament.
217 ibid. 75.

Israel's God is a God who does justice

Exodus tells the story of deliverance leading to the covenant between God and the motley group of slaves that had fled Egypt. It is a story of a righteous God who sided with, and supported, a rag-tag group of people who had been badly oppressed. *Within the Hebrew worldview, God's action is then interpreted as setting the pattern for how they are to treat each other.* Justice, or righteousness, in the Hebrew understanding is a broad term. The great prophets Hosea, Jeremiah and Isaiah located God's justice within the covenant relationship, and declared that failure to exercise *compassionate justice towards the most marginalised* was breaking this covenant. At times they pointed out that injustice even negates the worship of God (e.g. Amos 5:21,24; Isaiah 58:6–7).

> *A people cannot be just before the covenant God, they cannot know or worship him, when they do not heed his call to take the cause and defend the rights of the poor and oppressed in the community.*[218]

In essence, justice implies fidelity to the demands of a relationship. The just person, in the biblical account, is one who *lives in right relationship with God, fellow humans and with God's creation*. Justice covers all the relationships that define the human life-world. We will return to this theme later in dealing with the Catholic curriculum.

BETWEEN TEXT AND COMMUNITY: DYNAMIC BY WHICH THE TRADITION WAS CREATED

The Hebrew tradition developed through a *unique process*. It is a tradition that combines two dimensions a *written* dimension and an *oral* dimension. The written tradition now has a definitive form the Hebrew Bible.[219] The oral tradition developed alongside this written tradition and provides an *ongoing* qualification of it as times and circumstances change. This second strand is often called *the rabbinical tradition* and was still in the process of formation in Jesus' life time. It took on a more definitive character and grew in importance after the fall of Jerusalem in 70 AD. This cataclysmic event which led to the destruction of the Temple, ended temple worship as

---

218 John R. Donahue 'Biblical Perspectives on Justice' in John C. Haughey *The Faith That Does Justice: Examining the Christian Sources for Social Change* (New York: Paulist Press, 1977), 77.
219 This is not the same as the Christian Old Testament. The Hebrew Bible is made up of Torah, Prophets and 'the Writings'. The Christian canon also includes the Torah and Prophets, but includes additional books when considering the 'Writings'. To make the matter even more complex Catholics and Protestants disagree on which of these additional books should be in the biblical canon.

a defining characteristic of the Jewish faith. The rabbinical tradition became, and remains, the means of interpreting the community's understanding of its authoritative texts. This interpretive process was already present in the Wisdom texts. These sought to interpret the Torah and Prophets in the post-exilic period as the Jewish religion became disconnected from its ethnic roots and became the religion of a *diaspora* that is, of peoples now scattered among and increasingly drawn from many different cultures.

In the biblical tradition, *the community creates the text and the text creates the community*. One cannot be understood without the other. It is this *reciprocal interaction* between text and community that results in the text becoming *the authoritative expression of the faith of the community*.

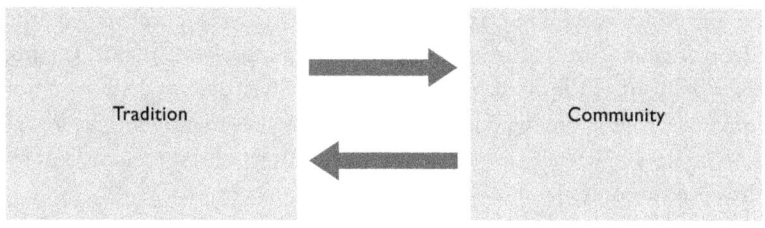

FIGURE 13.3 Tradition and community

The dynamic outlined in Figure 13.3 establishes the paradigm within which the Christian Scriptures will be created.[220] The tradition is interpreted by the community and so the community grows in its understanding of the text. A *hermeneutical circle* is established in which understanding of the text expands as the experience of the community expands.

DYNAMIC BY WHICH THE TRADITION IS SUSTAINED

The worldview of Hebrew faith underpins Jewish identity, which has proved remarkably resilient. Walter Brueggemann advances an important thesis as to why this is the case. He argues that for any culture to survive, it needs to develop three capabilities *to conserve, to adapt, and to educate the next generation*. In his view, Israel has been able to do this because it has nurtured *three kinds of consciousness* within the community, or what we might more properly describe as three 'voices', reflected in the three major elements of the Hebrew text Torah, Prophets and Wisdom.[221]

---

220 This theme is developed in canonical criticism. See for instance Donn Morgan *Between Text and Community* (Minneapolis: Fortress Press, 2007) or James Sanders *Canon and Community: A Guide to Canonical Criticism* (Eugene Oregon: Wipf and Stock Press, 2000).
221 The third section of the Hebrew text is the 'Writings' which includes the Wisdom literature. This section of the text can be understood as an ongoing attempt to interpret the first two sections in the post-exilic period.

The Torah voice

This voice is concerned with preserving *what is authoritative in the tradition what God has disclosed*. It stands behind the first five books of the biblical text, the Torah, making them the most authoritative elements in the tradition. Its major concern is *to conserve and to pass on what is central to the tradition*. The regard for Torah in the biblical community reflects Israel's concern that there be *an authoritative voice* in its tradition.

The voice of the prophet

Israel's narrative records that its authoritative voice was often *co-opted by those in power*, the king and the priests. While the early leaders of Israel are identified as speaking on behalf of God – as God's 'prophets' – as the Hebrew people evolved politically and the nation broke up into kingdoms, the notion of the leader as prophet diminished. A new understanding of 'prophet' arose, as one who lacked public position but who brought '*a word from the Lord*', generally on behalf of those who had been marginalised by the decisions of leaders.

The major concern of these later prophets was *the gap* that had opened up in the life of the people between *what God had promised them* and *what the leaders were delivering*. God had promised his people liberation and the leaders often adopted courses of action that resulted in their experiencing new forms of oppression. When faced with impending doom, not infrequently as the result of poor political decisions, Israel waited on this 'word from the Lord' delivered by the Lord's charismatic prophets. *The prophets also sought to conserve what was best in the tradition, in the face of its abuse by those in authority*. Theirs was a call for renewal in the life for the community. From the perspective of those in power, the voice of the prophets was seen as radical in its demand for justice, and several attempts were made to co-opt it in the interests of those in power. This gives us the notion of false prophet.

The Wisdom voice

As the history of Israel unfolded in the post-exilic period, it became necessary to *interpret its written tradition*, at that time the Torah and the Prophets, *for a new time*. The 'Writings', which were composed in this period represent the emergence of a third voice the Wisdom voice. Here the concern is *to make sense of the tradition in the new historical and cultural contexts*, when Israel was no longer simply an ethnic people, but a religious community drawn from many nations whose worldview was now exposed to the cultures of Greece and Rome. In Palestine itself, the religious worldview portrayed in the Torah and Prophets was under threat due to a policy of cultural colonisation pursued by its Hellenic overlords. Tensions between faith and culture rose to the surface in community life and had to be resolved. As the composition of Israel changed, it became necessary to adapt the tradition, but to do so in a way that was faithful to what was core to it. This required *practical wisdom*. The third voice emerged in response to this need.

Sustaining identity

Brueggemann contends that the reason the community of Israel has survived is that *it has been able to both make a place for, and nurture, all three 'voices', and not only to do this, but also to hold them in creative tension as well*. He holds this to be of profound significance for the preservation of identity in all faith communities. The Hebrew experience is that *the faith community begins to fall apart when one of these voices becomes too dominant and excludes the others*. A willingness to hear all three voices and live with the creative tension this generates, gives the faith community the capacity to both *conserve* what God has disclosed and to *adapt* to new cultural and historical circumstances. Brueggemann's very practical conclusion is that *any faith community that wishes to survive must design its education initiatives to nurture all three forms of consciousness*. There is obviously a message for the Catholic curriculum in this contention.

Catholic theologian Michael Gallagher makes a similar point in noting the tensions in Catholic theology between *liberation theology* (the prophetic voice), *dialogue theology* (the wisdom voice) and what he calls 'revelation theology' (the Torah or authoritative voice). The first does theology from the *perspective of the marginalised*, the second from a *perspective grounded in human experience*, and so in culture, while the third does *theology 'from above'*, relying on the authority of Scripture as God's final word in Jesus Christ. As he notes:

> *the liberation school offers a radical critique of culture as embodying assumptions of irresponsible escapism. The dialogue model prefers to listen for the deeper desires of the culture in its various levels. The revelation approach wants to recreate culture into Christian forms, to convert human attitudes to the unique light of the gospel.*[222]

Gallagher highlights *the need for convergence* among these three strands of thought in creating a spirituality capable of sustaining people living in the postmodern condition.

Understanding the plural nature of the biblical tradition has important implications for education in all schools drawing on it, including Catholic schools. It raises the practical question – how do we nurture the different

---

222 Michael Gallagher *Clashing Symbols: An Introduction to Faith and Culture*, 164–5.

voices within the Catholic community needed to sustain identity, and what implications does this have for the shape of the Catholic curriculum?[223]

BIBLICAL CRITIQUE OF THE WESTERN CONSTRUCTION OF KNOWLEDGE

In 2003, Jonathan Sacks, Chief Rabbi of the UK, and a much respected commentator on religion and society, set out some important insights for contemporary cultures, drawing on the Hebrew worldview as his source.[224] In the course of this he sought to address what he sees as a significant imbalance in the way knowledge is constructed within the Western intellectual tradition and which has been devastating in its recent consequences. In this he joins the growing list of postmodern prophets of reconstruction.

Sacks argues that the great strengths of the Western tradition are its methods of enquiry. These seek to draw *general conclusions from the study of particular events, cases etc.,* and so generate knowledge that is universal. This feature of the Western construction of knowledge the search for what is universal he traces back to Plato.

His critique of Plato is that the latter, in over-emphasising the commonalities in human experience, disregards the important place that difference has in that experience. This sets a pattern that has now become entrenched in the psyche of the West. However, in 'the postmodern condition', cultures are being forced *to adapt to difference on an unprecedented scale* and this is now having a counter-impact on human consciousness in many Western countries, particular in the UK. This means, according to Sacks that we, in the West, have to *relearn the importance and value of difference.*

Sacks calls for a paradigm shift in the Western construction of knowledge that permits us to acknowledge both *the importance of commonality* and the *importance of difference*. However, he suspects that 'the enchantment of Plato's ghost' haunts the Western imagination and inhibits the emergence of such a paradigm. For Sacks, Plato's single most powerful idea was that *truth is universal*. If something is true, it is true for everyone, at all times and everywhere. The implication is that there is only *one truth about the essentials of the human condition*. This leads to an attitude commonly encountered today which he articulates as follows:

---

223 The implication is that the biblical tradition, and those that depend on it, are plural by nature. That is, they do not have one definitive form. The plural nature of the Christian tradition is something that has drawn the attention of both Catholic and Protestant scholars. See, for instance, Bevans and Schroeder *Constants in Context* (Maryknoll, New York: Orbis, 2004) and Justo Gonzales *Christian Thought Revisited* (Maryknoll, New York: Orbis, 2003).
224 Jonathan Sacks *Dignity of Difference: How to Avoid the Clash of Civilizations* Revised edition (London: Continuum, 2003).

> *If I am right, you are wrong. If what I believe is the truth, then your belief, which differs from mine, must be an error from which you must be converted, cured and saved.*[225]

The Hebrew Bible provides a counter-position. The biblical narrative *does not begin with the particular*. The first eleven chapters of *Genesis* deals with the human universal before focusing in on the story of the particular, beginning with Abraham. The *Book of Genesis* is significant in the Western tradition, according to Sacks, as its *'great anti-Platonic text'*, and so has much to say to a postmodern age with its emphasis on 'the dignity of difference'.

In dealing with the essentials of the human condition, the narrative of Genesis rejects all attempts to impose 'an artificial unity on divinely created diversity'. A major theme of Judaism emerges from this, that *there is one God, but not one path to salvation*. As Sacks puts the matter, the God of Israel is the God of all humankind, but the demands made on the Israelites are not asked of all humankind. The significance of this statement is that:

> *God, the creator of all humanity, having made a covenant with all humanity (in the person of Noah) then turns to one people and commands it to be different, teaching humanity to make space for difference (because) God may be found in the human other, the one not like us.*[226]

He goes on to comment that:

> *The essential message of the Hebrew bible is that universality… is only the context of and prelude to the irreducible multiplicity of cultures, those systems of meaning by which human beings have sought to understand their relationship to one another, the world and the source of being. Plato's assertion of the universality of truth is valid when applied to science and the description of what is. It is invalid when applied to ethics, spirituality, and our sense of what ought to be.*[227]

Reflecting the major themes of postmodern thought Sacks concludes his reflection on the significance of the Hebrew worldview for the contemporary world by noting:

> *There is no way we speak, communicate or even think without placing ourselves within the constraints of a particular language whose contours were shaped by hundreds of generations of speakers, storytellers, artists and visionaries who came before us, whose legacy we inherit and of whose story we become part. Within any language we can say something new. No language is fixed unalterable, complete. What we cannot do is place*

---

225 ibid. 50.
226 ibid. 53.
227 ibid. 54.

ourselves outside of the particularities of language to arrive at a truth, a way of understanding and responding to the world that applies to everyone at all times. This is not the essence of humanity, but an attempt to escape from humanity.[228]

In this, he is in agreement with comments by Derrida noted earlier.

Within the understanding of Judaism, the fact that God makes a covenant with a particular people does not exclude other possibilities. *God is both the author of diversity and is the unifying presence within diversity.* We therefore need to respect *the dignity of difference*. Sacks concludes:

If we are to live in close proximity to difference, as in a global age we do, we will need more than a code of rights, even more than mere tolerance. We will need to understand that just as the natural environment depends on biodiversity, so the human environment depends on cultural diversity, because no civilization encompasses all the spiritual, ethical and artistic expressions of mankind.[229]

In outlining these core themes in the Hebrew worldview, Sacks is following contours lines found in contemporary Catholic thinking about dialogue *as a fundamental mode of mission*.

It is salutary to reflect on the fact that the Hebrew worldview, as it was understood at the beginning of the Common Era, provided the tradition of meaning that shaped not only Jesus' outlook on the world, but also that of the first generation of his followers whose faith is articulated in the New Testament Scriptures as we have them today. The Hebrew worldview placed particular emphasis on *the value of justice*, understood as *living in right relationships within our life-world* (that is with God, family and friends, society, the faith community, and the natural environment). That *a relational understanding of the human condition* becomes central to Christian anthropology is therefore not surprising.

The Hebrew worldview has its own integrity. God's covenant with Israel has never been revoked and, as Sacks' contribution indicates, still provides important insights. His provocative interpretation of the Hebrew worldview provides an important critique of what we, in the West, have come to take for granted in the construction of knowledge. He provides us with a *biblical rationale from re-valuing difference* which, as we noted in outlining the human context of curriculum, is very much on teachers' minds. In doing this, he makes a valuable contribution to any conversation about the nature of a Catholic curriculum. He also illustrates at a very practical level how a tradition of meaning functions in making sense of experience.

---

228 ibid. 54–55.
229 ibid. 62.

PRINCIPLE 17: THE DIGNITY OF DIFFERENCE PRINCIPLE

A Catholic curriculum promotes a particular understanding of the human person both as a 'self' and as a 'person-in-community'.

COMMENT

The two poles in this principle exist as theme and counter-theme in the life of a Catholic school. Taken too far one way, the result is individualism, taken too far the other way results in institutionalisation and a repression of individuality. The construction of personal meaning implies being in contact with oneself and being true to oneself. This is the touchstone of authenticity and identity. Many influences are at work shaping personal identity with rational choice being a major factor both in constructing the self and 'deconstructing' other influences. The notion that *students are subjects and not objects* is an important one in Catholic education. As a self, each individual has a unique dignity, and with this the 'dignity of difference' comes into play. Personal dignity is respected when young people are encouraged to discover what about them is unique, particularly with respect to their talents and their story. A Catholic curriculum has to be expansive enough to permit such explorations.

The counter-theme requires that young people work through issues associated with *why they have the talents that they do* and how they might best be put to use. This raises the issue of purpose and the Christian ideal of putting one's talents at the service of others which enhances the relationships that define our life-world. This also has curriculum implications. The school curriculum is deficient when it fails to provide adequate opportunities for students to put their talents at the service of the community. Several constructions of 'community' can be brought into play here, reflecting the various communities to which students belong and the mission interests that a Catholic curriculum can serve.

CONTINUING THE CONVERSATION

17.1 How does the school set about promoting a healthy self-esteem among students? What are the curriculum implications in pursuing this goal? How are these addressed across the curriculum?

17.2 What is the school's central message to students about developing their talents? Is this presented in ethical/moral terms? When the overall curriculum design is taken into account, how well do 'message' and 'practice' align?

17.3 Who are the 'marginalised' in the school? How is this determined? What provisions are made to overcome the 'gap' between what the school promises all students and what it delivers to these students? Where is this prophetic voice located within the school community and how well is it listened to?

PRINCIPLE 18: THE AUTHENTICITY PRINCIPLE

The school curriculum is the principal means by which most students encounter the worldview of faith *as a worldview*, so within a Catholic curriculum the presentation needs to be authentic to Catholic faith, but also authentic in its acknowledgement of the life-world in which young people live.

COMMENT

The worldview of faith is often presented as an ideal in human living which is eschatological in its orientation and construed in ahistorical and acultural terms. Such a development is almost unavoidable in a tradition 2000 years in the making. However, to be meaningful to young people this worldview has to 'land' in a particular age and a particular cultural context. *Faith always needs to be recontextualised as ages change.* This requires a certain humility on the part of the presenters in acknowledging that the worldview of faith itself has limits and that the role God's Spirit plays is important in how the community of faith comes to transcend these limits. False certainty is inauthentic to a Gospel that tells us to 'read the signs of the times' and respond. It will be hard to recontextualise the worldview of faith if the local culture is ignored as a source of values and its worldview ignored. In these circumstances, faith can move outside 'the common stock of knowledge' and become irrelevant in explaining and throwing light on the life-world of young people. The recontexualisation of faith needs to occur within a broad concept of mission as God's mission in which *all* are invited to participate, not just Catholics. Such a concept of mission *recontextualises all the relationships that define the human life-world* giving each purpose and clarifying what 'living in right relationship' can mean in fairly concrete terms. The Church has a special mandate to proclaim God's mission as taught and exemplified by Jesus and this is effected through a Catholic curriculum.

CONTINUING THE CONVERSATION

18.1 How adequately is the worldview of Catholic faith presented as a source of public meaning within the curriculum?

18.2 How well are the cognitive, evaluative and affective dimensions of the Catholic worldview presented?

18.3 How is the question – 'What does it feel like to be Catholic today?' raised, explored and addressed with teachers and students? What are the curriculum implications of raising this question?

18.4 How is the narrative structure of the Catholic worldview presented? How are the heroes and heroines given emphasis in this presentation? On what basis are they chosen and how are the commitments that characterised their lives related to their understanding of the worldview of faith? How is a balance effected between living witnesses and historical characters?

18.5 How is the mission dimension of the Catholic worldview addressed as an across-the-curriculum theme with relevance to the four sets of relationships that define the life-world of young people? What implication does the understanding of mission have for 'living in right relationships' in these four areas of life?

18.6 How are the connections between the worldview of Catholic faith and the worldview of Australian culture drawn together within the curriculum?

14
THE CHRISTIAN WORLDVIEW

In this chapter we look at a particular version of the worldview of faith, that is of the world understood as an open system – the Christian worldview. We focus firstly on its constituent elements, then at the different interpretations of the link between tradition and community found in the Christian churches, before dealing more specifically with the Catholic worldview.

The Christian worldview presents a particular vision of what it means to be human *that is always linked to the environment in which human life is lived out.* The Christian vision is a constant challenge to the human imagination and is always carried by a community living in a particular environment. The community of faith has the responsibility to:
- *interpret the vision* which necessarily occurs within the imaginal horizon of the times in which they live
- *formulate a response* to the needs of the times in a way that is faithful to the vision.

The churches and individual Christians have often failed to meet this responsibility preferring instead to canonise a specific interpretation of the vision that characterised a particular age or culture. This was certainly true of the Catholic Church in the modern period. The understanding of the Church as the 'pilgrim people of God' journeying towards the Kingdom proclaimed by Jesus, represents not only a change in understanding, but stands as a permanent challenge to the temptation to 'settle down' in any one interpretation of the Christian vision. The challenges inherent in the Christian worldview are to:
- *discern* what is happening in the environment
- *expand the collective imagination of the community* so that the possibilities implicit in the Christian vision can emerge
- *articulate the hopes* that flow from an enlarged vision
- *formulate a response* capable of realising these hopes.

Christians believe that God is at work in such efforts.

What sociologists of religion, and even many Christians, often fail to grasp is the capacity of religion, in our case the Christian religion, to rise to these challenges. Adaptation to the new global reality is currently centre stage in such diverse events, and their accompanying processes, as the 2011 Edinburgh Conference of the World Council of Churches, the 2011 Global Buddhists' Gathering in Bangkok, and the 2012 Catholic General Synod on the New Evangelization (in preparation at the time of writing).

CONSTITUTIVE ELEMENTS IN THE CHRISTIAN WORLDVIEW

The Christian worldview *provides a concrete understanding of the world as an open system*. It is a specific elaboration of the matrix model discussed in Chapter 5 (Figure 5.3). In the model 'God' is no longer an abstract entity, because in the Christian worldview 'God' takes on a particular form in Jesus. Our model is revised in Figure 14.1 to take this into account.

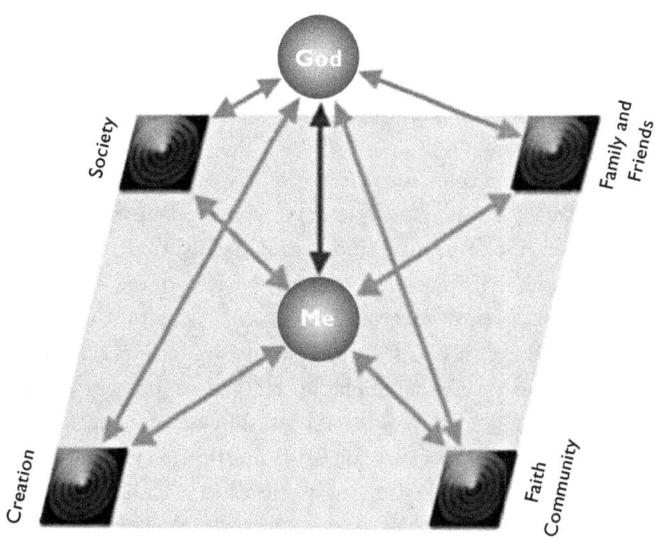

FIGURE 14.1 Conceptualising the worldview of faith

The Christian worldview has five constituent elements:
1 *relationship to the person Jesus*
2 *a message* which covers all the relationships that define the human life-world
3 *a community* which celebrates who Jesus is, and carries his message into the world
4 *a mission,* that of the community of faith, to continue God's project initiated by Jesus
5 *an ethos* that spells out values for living in that life-world.

It is impossible to speak of Christianity adequately without holding its five constituent dimensions *person, message, community, mission and ethos* together.

The Gospel sets a direction along which the Christian churches in their local and global manifestations have negotiated a path through changes in the political, economic and social arrangements that have characterised cultures for more than two millennia. Jesus' message and example sets out the *hopes and values* that shape all the relationships that define the subjective life-world as present in the diagram above: Me–Society, Me–Family and Friends, Me–Faith Community, Me–Creation. It therefore offers a vision of what 'human flourishing' can mean. This vision was spelt out originally in the context of a particular culture and age and requires *constant reinterpretation and re-articulation* as cultures and ages change. This challenge is something that the major Christian churches have had to struggle with and each has evolved its own particular way of balancing *the need to conserve* what is best in their developing tradition with *the need to adapt* the tradition to embrace the challenges that arise as contexts change. Christian history is replete with examples of both false 'canonisations' and graced moments when new insights have become powerful influences in the transmission of faith.

The central axis in the Christian worldview, and the source of its power, is the Me–Jesus relationship. People develop this relationship both directly through the study of Scripture, and through worship and prayer, but also indirectly through their involvement in the mission of the faith community, particularly in the area of social transformation, which includes education. A frequent challenge of Christian educational leadership is to help people with a less specific, or what might be termed indirect or unrecognised relationship with Jesus, formed through mission-oriented activities focused on justice, reconciliation, or care for God's creation, to recognise the nature of the relationship and make it more specific and personal.

THE CHRISTIAN WORLDVIEW: PERSON, MESSAGE, COMMUNITY, MISSION AND ETHOS

As a historical person, Jesus lived and died two millennia ago. The defining belief of Christians is that Jesus is unique in that God raised him from the dead and that he lives and can be known inter-subjectively. Jesus is not someone who was, but someone who is. Christian life is experienced subjectively in developing a relationship with the *Jesus who is*.

Knowing Jesus: Between text and tradition

When the authors of the Gospels set out to explain to their communities the significance of Jesus' life, they did so within the traditions of meaning then accessible to them. The authors of Mark and Matthew sourced their tradition of meaning predominantly in the Hebrew worldview. For the author of Luke this worldview was moderated by his focus on Christianity as a religion for the whole world, and the obvious advantages of the imperium of Rome in actually achieving this. The author of John explains the significance of Jesus using ideas drawn from Hellenic culture.

The Gospels, taken together, provide us with *four theological interpretations* of who Jesus is drawn from *multiple interpretive traditions*. These interpretations were accepted by the early Christian communities as *authentic expressions of the faith of the community* traceable back to Jesus, the foundation on which the new religious tradition rested. As with the Hebrew community in Old Testament times, there is *a symbiotic relationship between the emerging tradition and the community, underpinned by a written text* that was understood as containing God's definitive communication with humankind. This text is not the same as the tradition which continues to unfold along the trajectory set by the text, with the text remaining its constant reference point. As Catholic educators, we are caught up in this unfolding.

The message

In the Gospels, Jesus' teaching is dealt with thematically by the authors who reconstruct both his message and his deeds from authentic sources available to them. Christian tradition traces these sources to Jesus' immediate followers, because the major driving force behind the development of the Gospels was to tell the Jesus story and point out its significance at a time when the generation who knew Jesus and his disciples was passing away. The authors of the four Gospels each had a theological framework which shaped both the sources they used and the order in which they set out their accounts. Their choices were determined by the situation of their communities,[230] that is, their motivation and their selection of material was driven primarily *by pastoral concerns* that were being thrown into sharp relief by the context of the community. Their presentation of Jesus and his message needs to be understood from this perspective.

Modern biblical scholarship provides considerable insight into what Jesus' message actually was. There seems little doubt that the core of his message, and a constant reference point in Christian faith, was his teaching about *the compassionate love of God for all of God's creation and the coming of God's Kingdom within that creation.* As taught by Jesus, the Kingdom or reign of

---

230 Donald Senior and Caroll Stuhlmueller *The Biblical Foundations for Mission* (London: S.C.M. Press, 1983), 112.

God is a reality that begins in time and extends beyond time. This aspect of his message is the central theme to the prayer he taught his disciples, which we know as the *Our Father*. This is a prayer that addresses the human condition acknowledging human frailty and our need for support, forgiveness, reconciliation and salvation.

The Gospels, understood in their proper context, provide a major starting point in knowing the person of Jesus inter-subjectively. And it is here that a further dimension of Jesus' message begins to unfold for the Christian. *To be drawn into this inter-subjective relationship is to be drawn into the mystery that is God*, and in being so drawn to encounter more fully what it means to be a human person. For the Jesus who is, is God, and exists as a *person-in-community*, the community of the Trinity. The *Trinity-as-community* shares a common mission, God's mission, and it is into this mission that the Christian is ultimately drawn, in communion with others. This is the pattern of God's action which reflects the reality of who God is. When this understanding is combined with the Hebrew Bible's notion that man is made 'in the image of God' we arrive at the Christian conclusion that *to be fully human is to be a person-in-community*. This stands in stark contrast to modern individualism.

The community

From the sociological perspective, we know that what makes a group of people a community is having shared values, common goals and mutual commitments that, taken together, define the group's mission or purpose. As recorded in the Gospels, Jesus begins his ministry by calling together a group of people who go on to become his disciples. The group includes men and women. The particular focus within the Gospels on the twelve is deeply symbolic, representing the twelve tribes that originally comprised the people of Israel. It also indicates that the Christian community is the 'New Israel' to be gathered from the ends of the earth. This community becomes the group to which the risen Jesus commends the mission to make known God's grace and intention for all humankind. It is to this community that Jesus entrusts the Eucharist as a centre of unity.

The early New Testament writings tell the story of this community as it grows, and in the process create *the myth* (narrative symbol) *of the Christian community* which becomes an integral part of the culture of Christian churches. There seems little doubt that the presentation of the Christian community in *Acts*, for example, is idealised particularly when compared with the community dynamics evident in the authentic letters of Paul. However, vision always rests upon ideals, and so narrative combines elements of fact combined with ideals the best aspirations of the community.

Over hundreds of years of Christian history, the growth of the Christian community led to its becoming an institution with the accompanying institutionalisation of its works in mission. Jesus' mission then became the preserve of professional people working within the career structures that characterise professional life. This has become true of both lay and clerical professionals. The consequence has been the disempowering of ordinary Catholics in mission to the point that they meet their mission responsibilities largely by funding and praying for the success of the work of the professionals. Their own call to mission, a responsibility of all the baptised, has become significantly suppressed. This is a most serious state of affairs since, Jesus' mission needs to be carried out in homes, workplaces, and in the 'public square', that is in a variety of settings in which institutional professionals do not operate. This development reflects the influence that modernity has had on the Church, and its negative impact on local faith communities.

The success in mission of a global Church depends on *the vibrancy of local communities* and it is the lack of vibrancy of these communities in the West that gives rise to talk about the new evangelisation, a theme to which we will return in a later section. At the core of this problem is *the failure of the local communities to engage in mission outreach of the type that brings about the spiritual (personal and communal) and material (social and cultural) transformation* essential to Jesus' message of the Kingdom. It is little wonder then that Church leaders such as Australian Bishop Michael Putney suggest that Jesus' teaching about the Kingdom must be placed at the core of the curriculum in Catholic schools.[231]

The mission

The mission of the faith community, as Jesus explained it, is to make present God's loving reign within history and to be witnesses to its presence. To his hearers, Jesus' message drew a sharp distinction between God's Kingdom and what they were experiencing. It appealed to what was best in the ideal of the Kingdom which had a deep provenance in their religious tradition. The coming of God's Kingdom would require both a reversal of values and a change of heart – by which Jesus meant a change in worldview. In essence, his message provided an *alternative worldview* that fully encompasses aspirations implicit in the Hebrew worldview.

Jesus' message of the Kingdom is at the level of vision, and it has been subject to a variety of interpretations resulting in many different understandings across the history of Christian mission. The missionary mandate to preach the Gospel to the whole of creation (Mark 16:15–16) does not include within it a claim to power over humanity or the natural world, but rather a claim to be at their service, a service which includes first and foremost making the Gospel available as *good news* for humanity. This humble approach to mission

---

[231] Michael Putney 'Do Jesus and His Church have a Curriculum?' *Journal of Catholic School Studies* (Vol. 80, Issue No. 1, May/June 2008), 4–35.

characterises thinking in contemporary missiology and mission practice among most Christian denominations.[232]

The response to Jesus' vision of the Kingdom was equivocal even in his own day and in the years following his death. Some Christian communities pursued that vision and in the process became 'Church'.[233] Others did not take up the missional challenge, and remained inward-looking. They maintained fidelity to their Jewish roots, but lacked a sense of missional responsibility to the wider world, and thus eventually died out. All this illustrates a simple fact – *changing the traditions of meaning by which people make sense of their lives is difficult to accomplish in practice.* This is a reason for the importance of Christian education.

Jesus' understanding of God set a new direction for the faith community's relationship with society, with family and friends, and with the natural world. It implied an ethos for inter-personal relationships as well. Jesus' understanding that to be human is to be a person-in-community led him to entrust the future of his mission to a community.

The ethos

Clearly, Jesus was not naïve in making this choice. He established his community of disciples with a particular ethos and this for a number of reasons. Firstly, he was aware of the sad history of leadership among his own people when it came to living out its covenant with God. Secondly, throughout his recorded ministry he was a vigorous critic of the contemporary Jewish leadership. Thirdly, he had to address the politics that were emerging even within his immediate disciples. It was against this background that he set down the ethos of Christian discipleship as the *compassionate care of and service to others*. God, as reflected in the parable of the Prodigal Son, provides the model of this ethos. Jesus provided his own witness to this ethos in his treatment of his immediate community.

The Christian tradition has been constructed around a person, a message, a community, a mission and an ethos. History shows that the tradition fractured in the 12th century when the Latin and Eastern Churches separated. The Latin Church then fractured again in the 15th century with the Reformation. In consequence, today the Christian worldview has multiple expressions and the faith community multiple institutional forms.

The Catholic Church remains unique among the Christian churches both in its organisational structure and the claims it makes with respect to the tradition. Among the great world religions, the Catholic Church is the only

---

232 Missiology, the study of Christian mission history, thought and practice in cross-cultural and inter-cultural settings, is probably the most ecumenically oriented branch of contemporary theology.
233 Stephen B. Bevans and Roger P. Schroeder *Constants in Context: A Theology of Mission for Today*, 10–31.

one with *a clearly defined teaching authority respected by all members.* Even when they may disagree with elements of what is being taught, Catholics do not disagree with the right of the Church to teach authoritatively. The Catholic Church does not define its beliefs from within a 'community of argument'.[234] It holds that, in regard to core beliefs, its interpretation of the Christian tradition is definitive. However, in asserting this, it does not generally deal with alternative interpretations in terms of right–wrong/true–false, but acknowledges that alternative expressions of the tradition have a certain claim to legitimacy, and so it searches for common ground. All churches are bound in communion, which exists at various levels and in varying degrees, in pursuit of a common mission – *to proclaim and live the Gospel as the condition of bringing God's Kingdom into being in time.* In this context what unites the churches – the realisation of God's Kingdom – is always more important than what divides them.

The Christian churches have a unique capacity and expertise to bring people together. Church leaders have provided leadership in promoting dialogue among various religious groups in order to broker peace and negotiate reconciliation in healing wounded societies and cultures. This has become part of a shared mission to make the Kingdom of God present in places where it is clearly absent. In arriving at this point, the churches have had to reinterpret Jesus' vision for a new time and place, and this has led to significant developments in both theology and the understanding of mission particularly in the last two decades. The churches now see dialogue with each other and with people of other faiths as not only essential to mission, but indeed constitutive of it. To enter into dialogue is to accept 'the other' as a dialogue partner which means *acknowledging the other as a co-seeker of the truth and a holder of truth.* Dialogue involves risk in that it can point up limitations that exist in a church's understanding of Jesus' vision of the Kingdom. Only a truly catholic church is willing to take those risks in the interests of its mission.

THE CATHOLIC WORLDVIEW: TWO INTERPRETATIONS

Across its history, there have been a number of portrayals of the Catholic worldview each of which reflect the dominant theological perspectives of the time and the contexts in which those perspectives were developed. This aspect of the Catholic story is well traced by Catholic theologians Stephen Bevans and Roger Schroeder in the first section of their book *Constants in*

---

[234] This expression is used by University of Chicago theologian Kathryn Tanner to describe the Protestant approach to doctrine. Kathryn Tanner Chapter 6 'Commonalities in Christian Practice' in *Theories of Culture: A New Agenda for Theology* (Minneapolis: Augsburg Fortress, 1997), 120–155.

Context.[235] Here they trace the interplay of the three 'voices' – authoritative, prophetic and wisdom – noted earlier in the work of Brueggemann, in the development of Catholic theology and the influences these have had on the understanding and practice of mission within the Catholic Church.

Constants in Context

Any articulation of the Catholic worldview, as a tradition of meaning, has to make sense in a particular context. There are no context-free articulations of the Catholic worldview. This is not to say that across contexts there are not constants. We have referred above to certain constants as constitutive elements in the vision of Jesus that have to be grounded in particular historical and cultural contexts if his mission is to be achieved. The two guides providing this grounding are the Church's official teaching as an expression of its teaching authority (*magisterium*) and the Church's *sensus fidelium,* that is what the Catholic community over the long haul accepts as authentic expressions of its faith. These two elements provide the guard rails, so to speak, within which the Catholic worldview continues to evolve.

In attempting to delineate the Catholic worldview it is necessary to keep in mind:
- that constants always have to be interpreted in a context
- that people representing each of the 'voices' within the Church – authoritative, wisdom and prophetic – understand this worldview in a legitimately different way. Thus dialogue among them is central in clarifying the meaning of the Catholic worldview as it continues to evolve as a public source of meaning.

This means that a number of factors tend to shape articulations of the Catholic worldview as a public worldview and so there is need to establish the touchstones in such articulations. The five constants – the proclamation of Jesus, his message, his mission, his community and his ethos – provide such touchstones.

Challenges in articulating the Catholic worldview

Three variables seem to influence how the Catholic worldview is articulated by scholars and Church leaders and, in reviewing different interpretations, it is well to consider how these come into play. The **first variable** is *context*. Statements can be contextualised, made appropriate to particular audiences, taking into account their situation and stage of development. Such statements tend to have a *pastoral orientation.* The **second variable** is *position in the Church.* Theologians tend to articulate the Catholic worldview in terms of belief statements, generally drawn from systematic theology,

---

235 Bevans and Schroeder, 35–72.

and often expressed in non-contextual terms.[236] Such statements have a decidedly *theological orientation*. The **third variable** is how the writer actually understands the term 'worldview'. Different understandings here result in different articulations of 'the Catholic worldview'. For instance, if 'worldview' is understood in philosophic terms, the articulation is generally cognitive, stressing the Catholic worldview as 'a coherent set of beliefs'. If in cultural anthropological terms, the articulation embodies cognitive, affective and evaluative dimensions.

If the understanding is more anthropological, then the articulation takes in, not only the cognitive dimension, but also the affective and evaluative dimensions as well. The worldview is expressed in terms of commitments, particularly emphasising commitment to 'mission' or 'discipleship'. These are not mutually exclusive positions. A bishop, for instance, articulates the Catholic worldview as a theologian, from within his immediate pastoral context, and his interpretation of his mission within that context. If he thinks of 'worldview' only in the philosophic sense then he will articulate 'the Catholic worldview' in that sense.

There is thus a range of ways in which 'the Catholic worldview' can be articulated. Some treatments we have found helpful are those of Richard Rohr and Joseph Martos,[237] Thomas Groome[238] and Lawrence Cunningham.[239] To make our discussion more concrete, we now focus on two articulations which illustrate the different approaches. Both share a common feature in that they have been used to underpin major Australian curriculum projects that set out to assist schools implement a Catholic curriculum using values integration as an over-riding strategy. The approach illustrates a pastoral understanding while the second is more theological in its orientations. Both can be assessed in terms of how well they address the five constants noted in the first part of this chapter.

The Catholic worldview: Rohr and Martos

Rohr and Martos frame their articulation of the Catholic worldview by posing a very postmodern question which can be restated as follows. In the 1950s, the Catholic worldview was the sole tradition of meaning for most Catholics in the U.S. Being Catholic was 'a condition of existence', like being black. By the 1990s, the Catholic worldview had lost its privileged place for

---

236 E.g. Richard McBrien *Catholicism* (San Francisco: HarperSanFrancisco, 1994), 9–17 and Laurence S. Cunningham *An Introduction to Catholicism* (Cambridge: Cambridge University Press, 2009).
237 Richard Rohr with Joseph Martos *Why Be Catholic? Understanding Our Experience and Tradition* (Cincinnati: St Anthony Messenger Press, 1990).
238 Thomas Groome *Educating For Life: A Spiritual Vision for Every Teacher and Parent* (Allen Texas: Thomas More, 1998).
239 Lawrence S. Cunningham *An Introduction to Catholicism* (New York: Cambridge University Press, 2009).

most Catholics. How should Catholics understand the Catholic worldview in this new context?

The Rohr and Martos articulation of the Catholic worldview was widely used in RCIA programs in the USA in the 1990s[240] and provided the framework within which the Australian curriculum project, *A Sense of the Sacred*, a well-resourced and widely used attempt to implement a Catholic curriculum, was developed.[241]

Rohr and Martos articulated the Catholic worldview by identifying eight distinguishing features. The Catholic worldview at the start of the 21st century is characterised by:

- *an optimistic view of creation*
  Creation is good and God's gifts are intended for our enjoyment when used wisely. God's gifts are signs of God's goodness to us since God shines through all of creation. God's gifts therefore fit naturally into Catholic worship. The distinguishing thing about Catholicism is its understanding of the sacramentality of all creation. This takes a particular form in the seven sacraments of the Church which provide the means by which the life of the Catholic community is nurtured and sustained.

- *a universal vision*
  The Catholic vision speaks across history, geography, race, and culture and by doing so has the capacity to bring people together. This vision addresses God's dream for humankind as humankind can understand it. Since human understanding is involved, the Christian vision reveals itself progressively.

- *a holistic outlook*
  God's vision for humankind centres on the concept of wholeness and authenticity. Wholeness means engaging fully in the relationships that define our lives, demanding as this may be. Sin is the enemy of wholeness. Holiness, as a form of wholeness, demands personal transformation of mind and heart towards the ideal set out in the Gospel. This is made possible through the life, death and resurrection of Jesus.

- *personal growth*
  Christian life is a journey, a process of ongoing growth towards an eschatological ideal. It touches the heart and requires perseverance, hope and trust in God's sustaining help. The effort required on our part is to

---

240 'Eight Good Reasons for Being Catholic' was published in the popular *Catholic Update* series distributed within Catholic parishes across the USA (CU 0888, Cincinnati: St. Anthony Messenger Press, 1988).
241 For a summary of Australian system-level attempts to implement a Catholic curriculum see Therese D'Orsa 'In the second modernity it takes the whole curriculum to teach the whole Gospel' *Journal of Catholic School Studies* (Vol. 80, No. 1, 2008), 36–52.

build a relationship with God to the point when we can listen to God and let God's power act through us. This feels scary for most of us because it involves the experience of not being in control, one from which we normally draw back. To grow, we have to trust in God's promises.

- *social transformation*

  The mission of the Church is to make the Kingdom of God, which is central in Jesus' message, a reality in the context in which we live. The mission of the Church will always remain unrealised as long as people remain marginalised and oppressed.[242] The Church has an advocacy role and a healing role to play in addressing the plight of the marginalised.

- *a communal spirit*

  The Church exists as a community of communities committed to the mission of Jesus. The institutional nature of the Church, and the institutional nature of its worship, generate a dynamic which can mask people's experience of Church as being 'part of a community'. The presence of communities of religious within the Church today provides a countervailing dynamic, as do efforts to revitalise parishes as 'living communities'.[243]

- *a profound sense of history*

  The Catholic Church has survived intact for twenty centuries which gives it a unique perspective on the human condition and the human heart derived from living within many forms of political, social and cultural and economic organisation. The Gospel vision can be lived in any place and at any time.

- *a respect for human knowledge*

  The Catholic vision respects reason and promotes understanding. While in different historical periods this aspect of the Catholic vision has sometimes been suppressed, the Church's intellectual life has always re-emerged with renewed vigor. It has played a major role in the development of the Western tradition. As a consequence, it does not feel threatened by the advance of knowledge, because it believes that all truth has its source in God and so there must always be a point of reconciliation when truths, as we know them, appear to be in competition.

---

[242] As the former superior general of the Jesuits, Fr Pedro Arrupe, famously put the matter 'This rediscovery of what might be called the "social dimension" of the Eucharist is of tremendous significance today. In the Eucharist we receive not only Christ, the Head of the Body, but its members as well Wherever there is suffering in the body, wherever members of it are in want or oppressed, we, because we have received the same body and are part of it, must be directly involved. We cannot properly receive the Bread of Life without sharing bread for life with those in want'. 'The Eucharist and Hunger' in *Justice with Faith Today* (St. Louis: Jesuit Resources, 1980).

[243] The extraordinary growth of lay communities in our time should be noted as a manifestation of the Church as community of communities.

This articulation illustrates the *pastoral orientation*. The outline[244] is helpful in highlighting the fact that the Catholic worldview is not only 'a thing of the mind' but also 'a thing of the heart' and 'a thing of the imagination'. The presentation of Martos and Rohr also highlights how the Catholic worldview centres *on a person, a message, a community, a mission and an ethos*. While hopeful and optimistic, we believe this articulation underplays the shadow side of human life suffering and sin – which are definitely part of Jesus' message and of the Catholic worldview.

The Catholic worldview: Bishop David Walker

The second interpretation of the Catholic worldview is that offered by Bishop David Walker, an Australian Bishop with a keen interest in Catholic education and its direction in his diocese. His articulation of the Catholic worldview is integral to a curriculum project seeking to implement Catholic curriculum. Named *Our Vision Our Values*, this project is ambitious in scope, seeking to integrate within a single project the Catholic worldview and the *Values Education in Australian Schools* project sponsored by the federal government. The design of the project integrates faith values based on the bishop's articulation of the Catholic worldview with values seen as central to Australian culture. The aim of the project was to incorporate the resultant values set into regular lesson planning at the local school level using values-integration strategies across the curriculum.

The articulation of the Catholic worldview used in this project reads as follows:

> *The Catholic Worldview is a comprehensive perception of the universe, revealed to us in Jesus, that provides insights into the meaning of life and how to live it.*
>
> *The Catholic Worldview is experiencing life through the eyes of our Catholic faith.*
>
> *The Catholic worldview perceives:*
> 1. *God as Trinity, a communion of Persons who love us and invite us to share in their divine life for all eternity;*
> 2. *the action of the Spirit in the world, inviting and empowering all people to respond to the divine love;*
> 3. *Jesus as God's Son, who saved us through his life, death and resurrection and through whom we enter into the life of God;*
> 4. *the meaning and purpose of life as grounded in God's love for us and our response as disciples of Jesus;*

---

244 The above account sets out an idealised version of the Catholic worldview. Rohr and Martos also point out that the Church has not always lived up to this ideal and that this too constitutes part of its historical understanding. Its institutional leaders are aware of the need for the Church to be aware of its own fallibility and need for renewal. This is now understood as an integral part of its mission.

5. *the Church as the communion of disciples that makes present to the world the mystery of Jesus and, through its sacramental life, makes us part of that mystery;*
6. *the presence of God in our daily life, in the Eucharist, in the Sacred Scriptures and in the living tradition of the Church;*
7. *the cross of Jesus in the struggles and hardships of life, and approaches them as Jesus did his cross, with trust and confidence in God;*
8. *each human being as a unique person created in the image of God, having an inalienable dignity that is always to be respected;*
9. *an imperative to proclaim to others the love we receive from Jesus, by loving them as Jesus loves us;*
10. *an obligation to work to create social conditions in which the unique dignity of each person is respected and all human rights protected.*[245]

This statement is set out in doctrinal terms, using the language of Church discourse and so is more formal than the previous interpretation. Its emphasis on discipleship reflects a major priority of the diocese as presented in its mission statement. Jesus' teaching about the Kingdom of God is muted, and mission is addressed somewhat indirectly. What is unique in this project is its attempt to explicitly *connect the mission of the diocese making disciples with efforts to promote the values of Australian culture within the school curriculum.* This is a practical way to pursue the global Church's mission goal of 'evangelising cultures' in a way that makes sense to both teachers and students.

The two statements of the Catholic worldview illustrate two quite different ways in which this public worldview can be articulated. While both identify the *constants, as with other similar statements, they do so with different emphases.* The statements illustrate well how articulations of the Catholic worldview can change as contexts change, as locations within the Church change, as the understanding of 'worldview' changes, and as the language used changes.

The point for teachers to remember is that the Catholic worldview can be expressed in a number of ways. The important issue is how, in any particular articulation, the constants and the context are brought together.

---

245 Catholic School Office, Diocese of Broken Bay *Our Vision Our Values: Support material for K–12 Schools in the Diocese of Broken Bay*, 2008, 16–17.

PRINCIPLE 19: THE SACRAMENTAL PRINCIPLE

The Catholic community is distinctive in being an intensely sacramental people. A Catholic curriculum, therefore, introduces students to the central role language, the symbolic, and ritual play in the cultural and religious dimensions of life.

COMMENT

Sacramentality as a principle is central to any understanding of Catholicism. Richard McBrien defines this as 'the fundamentally Catholic notion that all of reality is potentially and in fact the bearer of God's presence and the instrument of God's action on our behalf'.[246] This understanding is captured in St Ignatius of Loyola's famous saying about the importance of 'finding God in all things'. The sacramentality principle takes on particular shape in the seven formal sacraments of the Church. God becomes present to us through the sacraments, but they do not set a boundary to God's presence. The particular genius of Catholicism is its use of material things to symbolically reveal God's action occurring in the different dimensions of meaning. This happens both in the popular piety of ordinary people and in the great spiritual traditions of Catholicism. Catholics have 'a sacramental imagination' that needs to be nurtured. In the context of the school, culture and faith need to be brought together *aesthetically* in the life of the school. All schools have a symbol–ritual system. At issue here is *how well this is developed and how intentionally it is used* in the service of meaning making. This is an important issue in a Catholic curriculum.

CONTINUING THE CONVERSATION

19.1 What are the major rituals of school life and how are these used to establish meaning? What meanings are these rituals meant to convey? How effective are they in achieving their goal?

19.2 How well does the school utilise the array of talent at its disposal to convey meaning intentionally through the use of the expressive and performing arts?

19.3 How effective are school liturgies in building a sense of community among students? What meanings do students draw from their liturgical experiences? Are these productive or counter-productive?

19.4 How well-developed is the symbol system of the school? How rich are its symbols and how dynamically are they developed? In what ways is the symbol system tied to the school's narrative system in conveying meaning by highlighting the students' immersion in a shared story?

---

246 McBrien, 1250.

PRINCIPLE 20: THE KINGDOM PRINCIPLE

A Catholic curriculum is open to the worldview of faith in all its variety. Conscious of its own identity and mission, the Catholic community seeks to engage with people of goodwill in building the Kingdom of God.

COMMENT

In a multi-faith society it is important that there be exchange and co-operative action across faiths and within faiths. It is similarly important to *consolidating faith in the home* which must be a project of high priority in building God's Kingdom. The task is not helped by the baggage of history that exists between denominations and faiths. Catholics share the theology of the Kingdom with other Christian denominations and this serves as a framework for co-operative action. Benedict XVI speaks of the need for a 'Courtyard of the Gentiles'[247] among people of faith. The reference here is to the Jewish temple, and the way in which the Jewish people gave effect to their belief that God was the God of all peoples. The Courtyard of the Gentiles was an area in the temple where non-Jewish and Jewish people could meet, mix, discuss and pray together a sort of 'religious public square'. It was the commercialisation of this space that drew Jesus' ire, led him to drive the merchants out, and initiated the events that led to his death. The Catholic Church is the only world religion with the organisational capacity to provide a 'Courtyard of the Gentiles' for people of faith, so it falls to it to provide leadership in this matter. This is a new development in the mission of the Church and is clearly relevant to Catholic curriculum. Secondly, students need to understand that the worldview of faith provides a coherent tradition for people of other faiths. This is often linked to their culture which, if non-Western, will operate on different presuppositions to Christian faith since it has different beliefs and a different history.

CONTINUING THE CONVERSATION

20.1 What sources do staff draw on in determining their aspirations for students and what the school can achieve for them? What process is involved in articulating these aspirations and what level of consensus exists about what they are? How are these aspirations currently articulated?

20.2 Is there a 'Kingdom of God' theme implicit or explicit in these aspirations? If so, what is it and how is it translated into curriculum and pedagogical practices?

---

[247] Pope Benedict XVI as quoted in the *Lineamenta* 'The New Evangelization for the Transmission of the Christian Faith' #19.

20.3 Do students understand the meaning that teachers are trying to convey in their witness to the coming of God's Kingdom in the way school life functions, or do they see school life more in functional/transactional terms?

20.4 How can school life best be reframed in transformative terms and what are the curriculum implications of school renewal framed in these terms?

20.5 In what ways does the school seek to assist parents become more effective agents in the faith development of their children, particularly in multi-denominational and multi-faith homes?

PRINCIPLE 1: THE PIVOT PRINCIPLE

A Catholic curriculum places Jesus, his message, his mission, his community and his ethos, at the centre of all learning, whether dealing with public meaning (teaching about public worldviews) or personal meaning (helping students develop a personal worldview).

COMMENT

This fundamental principle underpins all the considerations in this book, as was asserted in its *Introduction*.

The two aspects of meaning – public and personal – are often confused in Catholic schools. The first requires *a systematic presentation of knowledge, practices and values*. The second requires reflection which respects the students as subjects and their attempts to articulate their understanding of the world which may or may not agree with the formal account. As noted previously, our experience has been that even teachers find this difficult. Many seem to have negotiated many years of Catholic education without ever having to articulate what they actually believe. Faith, like culture, seems to have a 'stock of everyday knowledge' that enables people to avoid this, that is until some form of crisis arises, and by then it is often too late. The result is that people may *know a lot about faith*, without it having a great deal of practical influence on what they actually believe or how they live their lives. *The fact that faith has a core eludes them.*

A Catholic curriculum seeks to retrieve this core, a process which begins with the ability to pray which is not easily learned at school, if it is not first learned at home. This is the project par excellence that requires home–school co-operation and support. Prayer is based around a simple idea Jesus is not a person *who was;* he is a person *who is* and therefore it is possible to enter into the inter-subjective relationship with him that we call prayer. This is the axis on which all else turns and ultimately the pivot around which all the relationships that define the human life-world turn. It is only when this relationship is established that the worldview of faith begins to make personal sense. Then the message, mission, community and ethos get into the game of life.

CONTINUING THE CONVERSATION

1.1 What opportunities does the school provide so that students learn how to pray? How are these structured into the life of the school?

1.2 What is the school's essential message about Jesus and how is this secured within school life?

1.3 What is the connection between the Gospel values witnessed to in school life and the mission directions pursued by the school in its strategic planning? What are the curriculum implications of such a connection?

1.4 In what ways does the school use its symbol system and narrative to identify with, articulate and celebrate those Gospel values alive in the ongoing life of the school? Which particular values have currency as the charism of the school and how does the school make this determination?

1.5 If the charism of the school is located within the great spiritual traditions of Catholicism which have their source in religious orders, how is it translated into language and symbols that have meaning for people whose connection with the narrative of these traditions is indirect? How well is the translation process accomplished in your school? How does it influence the school's curriculum and pedagogical practices?

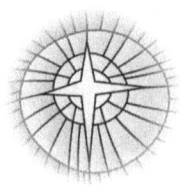

15
THE CATHOLIC WORLDVIEW: DEVELOPMENTS IN POSTMODERN TIMES

The Catholic worldview underpins the Church's commitment to its mission. As Asian American theologian Peter Phan explains the matter:

> It is a truism in contemporary ecclesiology that the nature of the Church is defined by its mission. The Church is what it does. But what it does, designated by the umbrella term *mission*, is complex and multiple: witness, proclamation, catechesis, worship, inculturation, interreligious dialogue, liberation, to name only the most obvious activities the Church performs. These activities are carried out not in the abstract, above space and time, but in concrete situations, at a specific time, in a particular place, with and for determinate groups of people in their own socio-political, economic, cultural and religious settings.[248]

If the Catholic worldview is to be held as a tradition of meaning, then it must enable people to *make sense of their setting and events occurring in that setting*. It therefore has to be articulated in such a way that it makes sense in the postmodern context, for it is here that the contemporary challenges of mission arise. This is where Jesus' vision of the Kingdom, and the hope it offers, need to take concrete form and be realised – within a local community and a local Church.

MISSION DEFINES THE CHURCH

The Catholic worldview encompasses how Catholics *understand* Jesus' vision, what they *do to advance it in practice*, and what it *feels like to be Catholic* today. Major changes in the way in which Catholics think about mission therefore have a profound effect on the way the Catholic worldview is articulated, the commitments that it underpins, and how Catholics feel about their faith.

---

248 Peter C. Phan *In Our Own Tongues: Perspectives from Asia on Mission and Inculturation* (Maryknoll, New York: Orbis, 2003), 3.

Concerns about the mission of the Catholic Church

A major concern of recent popes has been that local churches in the West have lost the missionary dynamism that once characterised them. This concern motivated the choice of topic for the 1974 general synod on *Evangelization in the Modern World*[249] and is again a concern motivating the choice of the 2012 synod *The New Evangelization and the Transmission of the Christian Faith*.

The need for a 'new evangelisation' was first raised *as a local issue* by John Paul II when he visited Poland in 1979. He raised it, again as a local issue, in discussion with the Bishops of Latin America in 1983. It became a theme for universal Church consideration in 1990 when he raised it in his encyclical on mission, *Redemptoris Missio*, and remained firmly on his agenda for the balance of his life.

'Evangelisation' and 'new evangelisation': The problem of meaning

The concepts of 'evangelisation' and 'new evangelisation' have proved problematic because of the lack of conceptual clarity which surrounds them. In Church teaching evangelisation refers to *the mission of the Church in all its forms*. The mission of the disciple of Jesus is to evangelise, that is to bring the Good News to people, societies, cultures, and to the whole of creation, in whatever way is appropriate in particular circumstances. Evangelisation defined in this way denotes the *what* of mission.

The 'new' in the term 'new evangelisation' does not indicate a 'new' mission; rather it refers to *the how* of mission, the need to go about things in a new way, with a new vigour, etc. These two conceptions are, however, related because *how you do something* is related to *what it is you want to do*.

However, even here, there is a problem because since the Second Vatican Council the *what of mission* has expanded considerably. Mission is now seen as including new forms such as inter-religious dialogue, reconciliation, care for the earth, pastoral ministry, work for human development, peace and justice, etc. This development leads to a confusing situation in that an older, and much narrower, construction of mission is now promoted by new modes, and so lays claim to the title 'new evangelisation'. As a consequence, the term 'New Evangelization' is now used to cover a confusing array of approaches.

---

249 Pope Paul VI expressed this concern in opening his apostolic exhortation *Evangelii Nuntiandi* (1975) written to draw together and interpret the various strands of discussion at the 1974 synod on evangelisation.

In attempting to reduce this confusion, the 2012 *Lineamenta* document[250] notes:

The New Evangelization is *a frame of mind, a courageous manner of acting* and Christianity's *capacity to know how to read and interpret* the new situations in human history which, in recent decades, have become the places to proclaim and witness to the Gospel… the new evangelization is seen as a needed impetus for weary and worn-out communities to help them rediscover the joy of the Christian experience… (#6).

In the next section the document comments more specifically:

> A 'new evangelization' means, then, to work in our local churches to devise a plan for evaluating the previously mentioned phenomena in such a manner as to transmit the Gospel of hope in a practical way. In the process, the Church builds herself up by accepting these challenges and becoming more and more the artisan of the civilization of love.
>
> A 'new evangelization' also means to have the boldness to raise the question of God in the context of these problems, thereby fulfilling the specific character of the Church's mission and showing how the Christian perspective enlightens, in an unprecedented way, the great problems of history (#7).

This theme is then further expanded:

> A new evangelization is synonymous with mission requiring the capacity to set out anew, to go beyond boundaries and broaden horizons. The new evangelization is the opposite of self-sufficiency, a withdrawal into oneself, a status quo mentality and the idea that pastoral programs are simply to proceed as they did in the past. Today a 'business as usual' attitude can no longer be the case' (#10).

However, to move beyond the 'business as usual' attitude demands new skills and these have yet to be developed. One of the skills most in need of development to promote a new way of doing mission, and the one most relevant to any discussion about a Catholic curriculum, is that of being able to 'do theology', a point to which we will return in a later section. *It is commitment to developing such generic skills* that distinguishes the new evangelisation from 'business as usual' masquerading as something 'new'.

CHURCH MISSION AND CHURCH IDENTITY

Uncertainty about the *what* of mission often results in uncertainty, or at least a lack of confidence, in the *how* of mission. For instance, if a school is confused about its basic mission, then this confusion will be reflected in

---

250 *Lineamenta* for the 2012 Synod 'The New Evangelization for the Transmission of the Christian Faith'.

its various major structures – curriculum design, management structures, pedagogy etc. – because *mission brings cohesion to all these elements*. The same applies to the Church. Confusion about the direction of mission often results in confusion about structures, deployment of personnel, and even the appropriate exercise of authority within those structures.

Need for a 'new evangelisation'

As we have noted above, the major concern underlying the 'new evangelisation' is that in local Church life a 'business as usual approach' is no longer getting the job done! While there are still people coming through the front door of the local parish, their numbers hardly seem to offset those leaving via the back and side doors! A sharp decline among Mass-going Catholics has focused the minds of Church leaders and is slowly forcing a serious re-evaluation of Church life. In particular, it has led to major efforts to discern *why things are the way they are* so that an effective response can be made, rather than simply allocating blame.

This process of discernment began in earnest at the Second Vatican Council (which for most people in schools today is ancient history as it happened before they were born). It was the subject of continental synods in the lead up to the Jubilee Year of 2000 and has continued, generally at the national level, to the present. Such gatherings of Church leaders have provided the major forums in which the teaching of Vatican II has been translated into the local situations.

A Church 'Missionary by its Very Nature'

A key statement in the Church's teaching on mission found in the documents of Vatican II is that the '*Church by its very nature is missionary*' (*Ad Gentes* 2). This has been interpreted to mean that *the focus of Church life lies beyond itself.* It lies in carrying forward the mission of Jesus *which has a much broader scope than a narrow focus on the internal life of the Church.*

The basic understanding at play here is that *God's relationship with God's creation is fundamentally a mystery*. While we gain some insight into this mystery through Jesus, and reflection on how God is at work in local cultures, much still remains out of sight and in need of discernment.

Jesus' message is that God engages actively with the world. Jesus conveys this truth by appeal to the Jewish notion of 'God's loving reign', or as more commonly translated, 'God's Kingdom'. By this, he meant that people *in history* are called on *to live in right relationship* with each other, with God and with the natural world. Living together in this way pre-figures, or is a sign of, their life together *beyond history*. In Jesus' teaching, the Kingdom has both a *now* and a *beyond now* dimension. Jesus' message of the Kingdom, which disappeared from Catholic consciousness in the period when the Church understood itself as the embodiment of God's Kingdom on earth, has been reclaimed in post-Vatican II theology.

God's Kingdom reaches beyond the Church

Jesus established a community to be a witness to his vision of the Kingdom. As a consequence, the Church has as its particular mission:
- to *proclaim* the Gospel
- to be *witness* to the Gospel
- to *work with others* to make God's Kingdom a reality.

This commission is lived out not only in the life of the Christian community, but also in the life of society more generally, since the life of the faith community is integrally related to the life of the wider society. Catholicism has to be 'catholic' in the sense that it cannot retreat in on itself, as it did in modernity, and still be true to its fundamental mission.

This means, in practice, that Christians have to be willing to *enter into dialogue with others,* since the building of God's Kingdom involves a collaborative effort, one involving *all peoples*. Rabbi Jonathan Sacks' notion of intercultural exchange set out in his book *The Home We Build Together* provides a useful image that captures much of the Christian notion of the Kingdom.[251] *The building of God's Kingdom is therefore not something that Catholics do by themselves or for themselves.* The Kingdom is God's gift and promise *to us all*. There must be a place for everyone in building it, religious and non-religious alike. It is a project that has the capacity *to bring people together*, and in the context of the Catholic school, this is often what happens. It is therefore an important concept for leaders in Catholic schools to get across to *all members of the school community*, students, staff and parents and clergy.

Modes and forms of the Church's mission

This brings us to an important distinction. The Church's mission has two *constitutive modes*:
Mode 1. *proclaiming* the Gospel, by word and by witness
Mode 2. *dialogue*[252] with others which enables Jesus' vision of God's
   Kingdom to realised.

---

251 See Jonathan Sacks *The Home We Build Together: Recreating Society* (London: Continuum, 2007).
252 Dialogue in the Church's understanding means more than talking. In Pope John Paul II's understanding *dialogue happens as distinct levels*: living together peacefully; working together on common projects; seeking to understand the worldview of the other and the ways in which this challenges one's own worldview; worshipping/praying together where this is appropriate; seeking to understand why respective worldviews are the way they are and how differences can be reconciled. (See *Redemptoris Missio* ##56–57.)

The various *forms of mission* outlined by Phan earlier are pursued within these two modes. For instance, as teachers the most common form of evangelisation we encounter is in Catholic schools which are part of the pastoral ministry of the Church. Here the Gospel is proclaimed and lived out in daily life. In the context of various classes, students and teachers enter into a dialogue about issues that cover the whole life of the school. Proclamation, witness and dialogue are integral to what is happening.

The various forms of mission take on a different emphasis in different social, political and cultural settings, depending on the needs and opportunities that exist in those settings. The forms may change over time in the one setting as needs change. Issues surrounding justice, for instance, are different for people in this country depending on whether they are Indigenous or non-Indigenous employed or unemployed, etc. Responses to them include raising awareness, prayer, direct action, advocacy, fund-raising to support other forms of action, and so on. People find their own level of missional response. Who needs to be engaged in dialogue and how this might best be done depends on which group is the mission focus. When justice issues are addressed by practical action (a form of mission), this has a *witness* value, and may provide the opportunity to let people know *why we do what we do* (*proclamation*). It almost always requires that we enter into *dialogue* with others, including those we wish to help, to achieve an outcome.

Evangelisation embraces the various forms of mission and uses them as *the means through which the local Church provides a witness to the Gospel, proclaims the Gospel, and enters into dialogue with others to bring about social transformation consistent with the Gospel* in a particular context. This is how God's Kingdom comes.

GOD'S KINGDOM AS THE CENTRAL FOCUS OF MISSION

A major change in the Church's understanding of its own identity occurred at Vatican II with the realisation that *the building of God's Kingdom was not the sole responsibility of the Church*. This change is summed up well by Phan in observing that prior to the Second Vatican Council the understanding was that 'God's Church had a mission'; as a result of the Council and its analysis of the contemporary situation, a new understanding has emerged, viz 'God's mission has a Church'.[253] While the Church carries responsibility for its specific mission, God achieves God's mission beyond the boundaries of the Church. God is somehow at work in all peoples, and in their cultures and religions, and while this calls for discernment, it

---

253 Peter Phan 'Proclamation of the Reign of God as the Mission of the Church' in *In Our Own Tongues: Perspectives from Asia on Mission and Inculturation*, 32–44.

also provides the basis for ongoing dialogue with others which can take a number of forms living together, working together, praying together, and exploring each other's traditions.

Resolving the issues around *how God acts in the world* in cultures and other religions now constitutes one of the frontiers faced by Catholic theology, particularly how this can be aligned with the Catholic belief in Jesus as universal saviour. While there are questions to be resolved, the basic issue that lies behind them in no longer questioned: people do find their salvation through means other than the Church. The call to build God's Kingdom is universal, even though it happens in local contexts. No one is excluded from participation in this project.

Identity and mission are always strongly related. *A change in identity has implications for mission* and vice versa. The change in the Catholic understanding of its mission both in terms of what and how – outlined above has implications *for all the relationships involving the faith community*. We are talking here of *changes on a massive scale for Christians* particularly those whose understanding of the Catholic worldview is premised on the presupposition that *change is not needed, because we have the truth*.

The growth in the Church's understanding of its identity and mission means that Catholics are called to *a substantial personal conversion*, and to *a fundamental reworking* of what it means to be a Catholic faith community. In this context, it is easy to see why 'business as usual' is not getting the job done.

A horizon beyond the parish as spiritual service station[254]

'Business as usual' connotes *an institutional approach to religion* which can be traced back to the influence of the modern worldview and the secularisation of modern institutions including the Church. The contemporary Church is now highly institutionalised and thus open to the critiques leveled at modern institutions by postmodern thinkers such as Foucault. Of course the Church is more than an institution, but is cannot escape sociological reality. The Church as institution relates to other institutions, including government, and is more or less forced to follow the paradigms for institutional life. The issue for it is how to balance institutional life with communal life.

In the modern period, the various *forms* the Church's mission takes – social welfare, health, community development, aged care, advocacy, education, etc. – were institutionalised. As a consequence of modern secularisation, the agencies of mission joined other non-government organisations (NGOs) as a part of civil society. Local mission responsibilities were then taken over by Church agencies such as Centacare, Caritas, St Vincent de Paul Society,

---

[254] For Catholic theologian Stephen Bevans' outline of 'the missionary parish' see 'A Missionary Parish: Beyond the Spiritual Service Station' in *New Theology Review* (Vol. 24, Number 2, May 2011).

Catholic Mission, Catholic Family Welfare, Catholic Health, Catholic Aged Care. While this development has given the Church an important and much-needed presence in the public square, it has also *displaced important mission responsibilities at the local level.*

Reclaiming the mission orientation of the local parish

The role of ordinary Catholics in mission moved from active to passive – to supporting the Church's agencies through their prayers, and especially by helping to fund them. Stripped of these mission functions, the parish became a kind of *spiritual service station* that Catholics visited once a week for a spiritual 'top up'. Across the modern period, a regime was put in place under which Catholics could effectively *pay their way out of any responsibility for mission in their local context.* This was, of course not the intention, but it was an outcome of the structures put in place.

The unfortunate consequence was that, at the local parish level, mission became remote – *something others did.* Few parishioners, even today, think of their local Church as *having a mission.* To ask: 'What is the mission of this parish?' too often draws a blank look. So ingrained has the service station model become that *'spiritual topping-up' is taken to be the mission of the parish.* This is a long way from the vision of the Gospel.

The lack of any articulation of *the mission of the parish,* or any process by which this can be defined, often puts the parish at odds with the local Catholic school. Thirty years ago, few Catholic schools had any clear sense of what their mission was. That is no longer the case. A difficulty for many schools now lies in being paired with a parish that has little sense of its own identity because it has little sense of its mission.

As Phan has pointed out, mission is defined by 'what the Church does'. There is great need for the local Church and the local school to be working, not only on the basis of the same understandings, but on the understandings reflected in the teaching of the Church when it comes to mission.

FROM MAINTENANCE TO MISSION

It is perhaps little wonder then, that Church leaders see the need to re-invigorate Christians *by changing the parameters of parish pastoral ministry from the present focus on 'maintenance' to one on 'mission'* understood in the broad sense, so that mission becomes an active constituent of parish ministry.[255] There will still be need for formal agencies, but their presence *needs to be adequately balanced by commitment to action at the local level.* The Catholic worldview as understood theologically needs practical translation

---

255 This theme was well developed by Robert Rivers *From Maintenance to Mission: Evangelization and the Revitalization of the Parish* (New York: Paulist Press, 2005). It also has a central place in the *Lineamenta* for the 2012 general synod.

at the local level if it is to be taken seriously as a resource in making sense of the world. Catholic have been desensitised to mission as a consequence of its being institutionalised and reversing this trend will be a significant feat requiring major educational efforts.

The analysis given in the *Lineamenta* document for the 2012 general synod suggests that local churches in the West 'have grown weary' of proclaiming the Gospel. An alternative analysis might be *that Catholics in the West have been so reduced to a state of learned passivity by the 'business as usual' outlook of their local church leaders, that 'the energy of the Gospel'*, of which Paul VI speaks so forcefully in *Evangelii Nuntiandi, has been largely dissipated.*

This has been caused by a convergence of issues one of which is the formation of Church leaders where mission theology has been, and remains, peripheral in theological education.[256] This leaves parish leaders often ill-equipped to meet the mission challenges that now need to be addressed. Put another way, too few Church leaders can actually 'do theology', yet a truly missionary Church requires of all Catholics that they be able to theologise. This is a skill that can be learned.

'Doing theology' as a complement to 'learning theology'

That theology is a field of study with its own methods of enquiry comes as a surprise to many people. While they know about scientific method, the idea that there could be a *theological method* seems strange at first. The concept of theology as *something you do* is also novel. 'Doing mission theology' is a method of theological enquiry that can be learned and which needs to be mastered if the hopes outlined above are to be more than a pipe-dream. 'Doing mission theology' is a process with identifiable component parts that addresses the challenges and problems of life in a particular context. It brings together the insights of human experience, faith and culture in an endeavour to address the pastoral problems that lie at the core of mission in a local context. It is a form of *contextual theology* that often goes under the rubric of 'practical theology'.

When teaching Catholic educators to 'do theology' we find the following method to be helpful. It involves following six phases or steps:[257]

---

256 Many of today's clergy have been formed in a regime which made a clear distinction between pastoral theology and mission theology the latter being the province of those going into 'mission fields'. These fields now exist in every local church context – one result of globalisation with its consequent pluralism.
257 Those familiar with the field will recognise this model as a composite of models developed by Richard Osmer in *Practical Theology: An Introduction* (Grand Rapids, Michigan: William B Erdmans Publishing Company, 2008) and Patricia O'Connell-Killen and John de Beer *The Art of Theological Reflection* (New York: Crossroads, 2004). A third source we have found helpful, one which has a more European flavour, is by Clemens Sedmak and rather grandly titled *Doing Local Theology: A Guide for Artisans of a New Humanity* (Maryknoll, New York: Orbis Books 2002).

1. The Descriptive Phase
   Looking at a situation and discerning what its key features are. This involves describing the situation in non-judgemental terms (which is quite hard to do).
2. The Interpretive Phase
   Exploring the competing interpretations of the situation; cultural interpretations need to be viewed in the light of faith interpretations and vice versa.
3. The Evaluative Phase
   Determining the criteria, including those of the Gospel, that need to be employed in assessing the situation.
4. The Focusing Phase
   Judging what is the heart of the matter.
5. The Response Phase
   Formulating a response to 'the heart of the matter'.
6. The Review Phase
   Implementing the response and reviewing the outcome.

This model will be familiar to teachers involved in 'reflective practice'. Its aim is to take action that changes the original situation and moves it *in a Kingdom direction*. Reviewing the outcomes of this action then leads to further analysis of the situation and so on – the hermeneutical circle is joined.

A key aspect of the model is to use the early phases in order to get to *the heart of the matter* that is to address *causes rather than symptoms* –to formulate a response based on asking the right questions. The process seeks *to bring the sources of culture and faith together both*

- *in understanding an issue*
- *in determining the criteria required to frame an adequate response.*

This is important, since culture often plays the major role in determining whether or not a given response will be received, and so whether it can be implemented. Practical theology introduces people to a number of methods in 'doing theology'.[258]

'Doing theology' provides *a method of theological enquiry* that needs to sit *alongside the other methods of enquiry that students learn in a Catholic school*. Without access to appropriate methods of theological reflection, the hopes to which the 'new evangelisation' speaks will be frustrated. Given their narrative, Catholics will generally need tools, as well as good leadership, to engage effectively in local mission.

---

258 . This theme is developed extensively in our book on mission theology for Catholic educators *Explorers, Guides and Meaning Makers*.

Catholic schools and the mission of the Church

Catholic schooling has a major role to play in the new evangelisation if there is to be any large-scale re-orientation of Catholic parishes in the West away from their present focus on survival (maintenance) to a more missionary stance. 'Missionary parishes' require schools imbued with a vision of *what the Church can be*, not schools whose leaders are bogged down and distracted by where the vision and skills of the local church are currently. There is a global game afoot!

When we say, then, that a Catholic curriculum is about *passing on the faith and wisdom of the community to young people in a way that makes sense to them*, we are setting a demanding goal!

PRINCIPLE 21: THE PLAUSIBILITY PRINCIPLE

A Catholic curriculum promotes a particular understanding of:
- the school as a faith community,
- the mission of this community,
- the place of the faith community in the life-world of young people.

COMMENT

For most of its students, the Catholic school now provides what sociologists call the 'plausibility structure' for faith. It is here that they encounter *the significant others in faith,* and experience some level of identification with people for whom faith is a reality. It is also here that they learn about the worldview of faith as a public structure of meaning which can take a number of forms and, in particular, has a Catholic form. This means that the total life of the school is important in how young people come to understand 'a faith community in action'. This has important implications for the school curriculum particularly *how the life of the community is structured and how it is presented*. Of particular importance is the linkage between the stated mission of the school and what happens on a day-to-day basis. Students need to take away from the school the concept that, *within any community of faith life is mission-oriented*. They also need to take away the message that immediate relationships define how we have some experience of what 'living consistently in right relationships with others' is actually like. These forms of *Kingdom experience* provide a base line for the development of faith, and for many students the school provides the only plausibility structure within which this type of experience will be achieved in their formative years. Students are entitled to these Kingdom moments. A Catholic curriculum will be attuned to this need.

CONTINUING THE CONVERSATION

21.1 How does the school interpret its role as the principal plausibility structure for faith in the life of the majority of its students?

21.2 How is this interpretation reflected in formulating the mission of the school?

21.3 In what ways does the school seek to make links with other Catholic faith communities so that the Church–student link can be maintained beyond the school experience? How is this matter addressed within the curriculum of the school?

21.4 How does an understanding of the school as a primary plausibility structure for faith translate into the development of the curriculum and pedagogical practices in the teaching of religious education? Is the faith development and social justice initiatives pursued within the curriculum?

PRINCIPLE 22: THE INTEGRATING PRINCIPLE

A Catholic curriculum introduces students and their teachers to the knowledge and skills needed to 'do grassroots theology' as a means of bringing together life, faith and culture.

COMMENT

'Doing theology' is shorthand for being able to engage in 'theological reflection'. This is an interdisciplinary form of reflective practice that has great pastoral utility because of its use of multiple sources of knowledge to explore problems and formulate solutions that include a faith perspective. It is a very practical way of bringing faith and culture together to deal with the problems of everyday life, often enabling them to be seen in a new perspective in the process. There are a number of models that can be used, including the one in the text which we have found teachers master easily with some practice. Tom Groome's praxis model is known to many teachers. This is more oriented to work with a group than for use by individuals trying to make sense of situations and developing a way of addressing them meaningfully.

CONTINUING THE CONVERSATION

22.1 What strategies does the curriculum incorporate to bring the various disciplines together to explore the complex issues that characterise contemporary life? How adequately are these strategies used? How well do students understand their purpose?

22.2 In employing these strategies, what issues of concern are dealt with and how are these determined? What role is theology given in such interdisciplinary study?

22.3 Is theology given the status of a discipline in the curriculum and if so how? How are 'studies of religion' and theology related in the present curriculum?

22.4 What model of theological reflection ('doing grassroots theology') is promoted within the school in resolving pastoral problems? How effectively have staff been inducted into this model and how familiar are they with its use?

22.5 What efforts are made to introduce students to an age-appropriate model of theological reflection within the school community, and to using this model in addressing important issues with school leaders?

Part F
TOWARDS A CATHOLIC CURRICULUM

At the outset of this book we set out a 'working definition' of a Catholic curriculum which read:

> A Catholic curriculum assists young people to engage constructively with the wisdom and faith of the community in a way that is meaningful to them, living as they do in a particular cultural and historical setting, with the life-chances this setting has to offer, and the constraints that it imposes in the process of establishing their identity as individuals and as members of the community.

In the chapters which followed we have endeavoured to expand on the meaning this understanding conveys. While it embraces a number of elements, the major issues we have pursued have centred on the phrases 'engaging constructively with the wisdom and faith of the community' and 'meaningful to them living as they do in a particular historical and cultural context'.

The focus on meaning making as the aim of a Catholic curriculum brings to attention of teachers the simple fact that we live in changing times and teachers have a responsibility to understand the nature of the changes underfoot and the implications this has for the mission of a Catholic school and for the design of its curriculum. The school curriculum seeks to respond to the learning needs of students. However, good education requires a certain amount of guess work on the part of the school about how these needs are defined. School prepares young people to live in their life-world as it is now, but also seeks to prepare them for what it will be like in ten to twelve years' time. At the present rate of change that is hard to predict. The ability to make sense of life means acquiring a generic set of skills and understandings that transcend the particularities of culture and history. We have sought to reframe the conversation about a Catholic curriculum by putting meaning making at its core.

We repeat a caveat with which we began this exploration. There are a number of ways in which a school's curriculum can be considered 'Catholic'. This becomes evident when you consider the 22 principles we have argued to in the text. Each of these will have different levels of salience in different schools, primary and secondary, rural and city, boys' and girls', etc.

In Chapter 16 we set out two important themes in developing a Catholic curriculum that seem to transcend the particularities of individual school settings. The argument here is that a Catholic curriculum represents 'a mission to the heart of young people' and a 'mission to truth'.

There are three appendices attached to the text. The first sets out the twenty-two principles we have enunciated as we have proceeded. The second groups these into an instrument that could be used to profile the school's curriculum, or could be used by studies co-ordinators to look at the curriculum of particular key learning areas. The *Profile Instrument* is a self-assessment instrument and in any self-assessment there is need to make judgement *against standards*. The third appendix cumulates the discussion questions posed at the end of each chapter. The *Mapping Tool* does this using the five categories in the *Profiling Instrument*. There are a number of possible ways in which a school could use these instruments to arrive at a judgement about:
- the way in which the school's curriculum, or the curriculum of particular faculties, or levels, is Catholic
- whether or not this represents a satisfactory state of affairs
- where development needs to take place.

16
CATHOLIC CURRICULUM: A MISSION TO THE HEART OF YOUNG PEOPLE

In this book we set out to reframe the conversation about what a Catholic curriculum is and what features might characterise it. In the course of this exploration we have identified a number of principles that flow from discussion of context, the nature of meaning making, and consideration of the public worldviews that stand behind the traditions of meaning to which people most commonly refer. As well, we have identified principles covering content and process. These principles, when taken together, provide a structure within which a comprehensive theory of Catholic curriculum could be developed. Our objective has been to advance this possibility which we see as a next stage.

A CATHOLIC CURRICULUM AND ITS MISSION TO THE HEART OF YOUNG PEOPLE

In this final chapter we wish to draw together important themes that emerged along our journey of enquiry. Our approach has placed a good deal of emphasis on the notion of worldview. Empirical research on this topic is still in its infancy which creates its own dilemmas![259] We have pursued the concept as developed in cultural anthropology, missiology and psychology, drawing particularly on the work of widely acknowledged seminal thinkers.

The use of the term 'worldview' in these fields is somewhat more expansive than its use in philosophy, which provides the understanding of the term found in official Catholic documents on the Catholic school. Various synonyms for 'worldview' feature prominently in these documents. There we find that the Catholic school seeks to develop in the minds

---

259 Mark E. Koltko-Rivera summarises the available data in a meta-study 'The Psychology of Worldviews', *Review of General Psychology* (Vol. 8, No. 1, 2004), 3–58.

of students 'a specific concept of the world, of man, and of history',[260], 'a Christian vision of reality',[261] 'a clear idea of the meaning of life'.[262] One could multiply similar quotes. As used in these documents, 'worldview' clearly refers to a vision that can be expressed as 'a coherent set of ideas' and equates worldview with its cognitive dimension. In tracing the history of the worldview concept, David Naugle[263] suggests that the more expansive understanding approximates closely to the biblical understanding of 'heart'. He is our authoritative guide in what follows.

Worldview and the biblical 'heart'

Of all the terms used in biblical anthropology none is more important than that of 'heart'. According to Naugle, 'heart' is used over 850 times in the Old Testament, and 150 times by the New Testament writers, to refer to the centre of human consciousness from which thought, judgement, affection and action ultimately spring. As experienced subjectively, 'heart' is the wellspring of life. Since the heart holds the key to life, its contents must be examined, for in the biblical account it is into the heart that God looks.

In the New Testament, Jesus develops this theme teaching that 'where your treasure is, there your heart will be also' (Matt 6:21). Since we choose 'our treasure', we also choose where our heart will reside. This choice then is determinative of our lives. Switching metaphors, Jesus expands on this teaching – 'No good tree bears bad fruit, nor again does a bad tree bear good fruit; …The good person out of the good treasure of the heart produces good… (Luke 6:43–45).[264] For Jesus then, the foundations of human life are to be found in the heart. What we have called 'developing a personal worldview' can be understood by reference to the biblical understanding of the 'heart'. As Naugle succinctly puts it, 'the heart of the matter of worldview is that worldview is a matter of the heart'.[265] In particular, a personal worldview maps the 'orientation of the heart'.

Similarly, the collective worldview of a culture maps the 'treasure' held by a community as the core of its identity. In like vein, shared aspirations sit at the core of the worldview of a particular age as a 'prized possession' common across many cultures.

In equating the postmodern understanding of worldview with the biblical notion of heart, Naugle makes two important observations that have particular relevance for teaching and for a Catholic curriculum.

---

260 Sacred Congregation for Catholic Education *The Catholic School* 1977, #8.
261 ibid. #36.
262 Congregation for Catholic Education *Lay Teachers in Schools: Witnesses to Faith*, 1982, #17.
263 This section has its source in David K. Naugle's reflection in *Worldview: The History of a Concept* (Grand Rapids Michigan: William B Eerdmans 2002), 267–274.
264 Comparable passages are found in Matt 7:17–20 and Mark 7:21–23.
265 Naugle, 269.

Into the heart go the issues of life

The heart receives life from without and the work of teachers is important in sharing this gift of life so that it enters into the heart of the student who receives it. The heart is formed by nurture as well as by nature in a process in which things *have to be internalised before they can be externalised*. While the exact process by which this happens is not well understood,[266] nevertheless through it people adopt a religious posture, patterns of thought, the ability to judge, a sensibility in feeling and a capacity for action that enables them to interact with the external world and establish the relationships that come to define who they are. What can be said about this process is that:

> *As an individual passes through the various stages of human development, the heart obtains a vision of reality, even though it cannot explain exactly how. Over time this outlook is probably discovered, followed, confirmed, challenged, put in crisis, reaffirmed or replaced, and solidified as the individual clings to a first, second or even more 'naiveties' until death. There are periods of stability as well as tumult and change as new input makes its way into the heart, where it is filtered, accepted or rejected. Worldviews (personal) ... are always works in progress. Throughout life, therefore, the heart not only gives but receives, and what flows into the heart from the external world eventually determines what flows out of it in the course of life.*[267]

Here is a truth that teachers know from their own biographies. Students stand on the brink of an unfolding biography and have to take much on trust in what they welcome into the heart. This is what makes teaching such an important profession, why the relational environment of schools is crucial to learning, and why considering what a 'Catholic curriculum' really entails is so important.

Out of the heart come the issues of life

The heart of young people is a contested territory in contemporary life. The battle here cannot be won without some understanding of what the life-world of young people looks like *from the inside* from the young person's perspective. People will never know this perspective if opportunities and space are not created for it to be authentically articulated.

At some stage in their education, and it is hard to locate exactly when, the heart of the young person takes on board *the presuppositions that form the basis of life* providing the heart with its depth dimension – the foundational axioms on which all other thinking depends. Beyond this, the foundations are changed only with great difficulty. We know, of course, that in the order of grace, a fundamental metanoia of the human heart is possible. We also know that such grace is often mediated by another person.

---

266 This becomes very clear in Koltko-Rivera's summary of the way the worldview concept is employed in the various fields of psychology.
267 Naugle, 271. Word in brackets not in the original.

Once these foundations are set, young people argue from them, never to them. Naugle observes:

> Though mostly hidden, and often ignored, these most basic intuitions guide and direct most, if not all, of life. They are compass-like in effect... These baseline beliefs are so humanly significant, they are like the nest to a bird or the web to a spider.[268]

Because these intuitions are so fundamental, they are psychically well-guarded and can be approached only with caution and with respect. Naugle recognised the particular insight of Jung in this matter, articulated as far back as 1942, well before postmodernity's adoption of this more comprehensive approach to worldview.

> For Jung, one's worldview includes positions on reality that are typically addressed by doctrines of the various religions of the world...However, these are not dry intellectual positions, nor do they make one's worldview a merely intellectual construction. Worldviews like religious doctrines 'are emotional experiences...Logical arguments simply bounce off the facts felt and experienced'...Thus in Jung's thought, worldviews are an integral part of each individual's psychological makeup and greatly influence volition, affect, cognition and behaviour. Worldviews act outside of consciousness and are part of the warp and woof of personality, rather than being deliberate intellectual constructions.[269]

Jung differed fundamentally from Freud in that, in adopting scientism, he decried the existence of worldviews, even while doing so from within his own worldview of naturalism!

The foundational axioms adopted by students constitute a major challenge for educators in dealing with young people. On the one hand, they know the heart abhors a vacuum, and so a failure to consider issues is itself an issue, while on the other hand they are aware that to push too hard is to invite resistance. Additionally, they know that the human heart can easily fall prey to human sinfulness which distorts all understanding.

Students need to be made aware that all people believe in something, even the so-called non-believers, the question is what, on what basis and how strongly? Just as there is no culture-free zone in human life, and no history-free zone, there is no 'belief-free' zone either. Sooner or later we choose to believe in something, generally because we come to believe in someone. This is why heroes and heroines have the role in human affairs

---

268 Naugle, 272.
269 Koltko-Rivera, 9.

that they do. Personal belief is tied to narrative more often than it is tied to philosophy or theology! For this reason, the importance of being grounded in the Christian/Catholic narrative through a continual, and creative, re-telling of it, both in the formal Religious Education program and whenever opportunity presents, cannot be over-estimated. If we do not form our fundamental beliefs consciously this does not mean we will have none; rather it means they will be formed subconsciously and by default. Then we run the risk of not knowing what they actually are.

The 'orientation of the heart' the contours of our personal worldview emerges from its hiding place, and reveals itself, to some extent when we put questions to 'what comes out of the heart' and particularly to the impact that 'what comes out of the heart' has on the relationships that define our life-world. Thus, while one development of a Catholic curriculum is concerned with what goes into the heart, this needs to be balanced by a complementary development that helps young people reflect on their actions on 'what comes out of the heart' particularly on the motivations and commitments that underpin these, in order to discern what this tells them about the 'state of the heart' and 'the habits of the heart'.

Having a process to follow here is important, as it gives young people a way to find solid ground in the often shifting sands that constitute the human heart. In an older Catholic tradition, 'examining one's conscience' was a way of examining the heart. As traditionally conceived in Christian spirituality, this practice became discredited when it fell victim to a narrow Christian moralism. What we are suggesting is the need to retrieve a form of such reflection more closely matched to the original intention of the practice. It needs to include reflection on the whole of the life-world and the relationships that define it, together with the young person's growing understanding of what living in right relationships means in that life-world.

In biblical terms, 'living in right relationship with God' equates to treating people and the natural world justly. This is the hallmark of authenticity, because it demands the capacity to transcend self-interest, to define your 'treasure' as something other than yourself! The process we have in mind confirms or challenges the choices young people make to locate their heart in a particular place, and so pursue particular moral ideals in human living. This is an important element in the 'mission to the heart of young people'. It is a goal that a Catholic curriculum hopes to achieve. The biblical/cultural anthropological understanding of worldview, which equates 'worldview' with 'orientation of the heart', is a particularly rich way of bringing faith and culture together in the service of this mission.

CATHOLIC CURRICULUM AND ITS MISSION TO TRUTH

In a Catholic curriculum all subjects contribute to the student's ability to make sense of life. This is why academic disciplines have value within our culture and are included in the curriculum. They are central to education because they preserve and extend the methods of enquiry and the bodies of knowledge that result from the ongoing quest for intellectual excellence that has always characterised Western cultures. Meaning making is not just an outcome of education in the present situation. It needs to be a central outcome, and one to which all teachers contribute.

Bringing the disciplines together in the search for truth

Each discipline maps a certain section of the field of knowledge which is constantly expanding. Within their section of the field of knowledge the disciplines themselves tend to fragment as they expand, and as sub-specialities develop. This means that, in practice, the range of problems addressed by any one discipline becomes more and more diffuse and specialised over time. The result is, as the case of medicine illustrates most graphically, the discipline has to develop generalist experts the equivalent of physicians – whose role is to tell 'outsiders' which speciality in the discipline can address the real world problems that they need to have solved.

Schools do not deal with knowledge at this level; rather they seek to assist students to develop the general knowledge needed to orient themselves in a discipline and so see its relevance in solving the problems of life. If students do not see this relevance, then they do not choose to study the associated subjects. This has an important bearing on how the public curriculum in construed. Interest and content exist as theme and counter-theme in curriculum construction.

Figure 16.1 attempts to portray how the disciplines come together in the school curriculum to reinforce the unity of knowledge. The arrows indicate that knowledge construction goes on unabated. In the diagram, meaning making sits at the centre of the curriculum as the common goal that unites the disciplines and enables scholars to work together collaboratively in solving real life problems. No one discipline contains all the wisdom of the community. Depending on the problem, all have a contribution to make.

In this context, it is important that students have some introduction to multi-disciplinary problem-solving and investigation.[270] This can be done either by looking at particular problems or addressing across-the-curriculum

---

270 The ACARA brief makes ample space for this to happen within the Australian National curriculum, without being specific about how it can happen.

themes. Here it is possible to ask questions such as – what does science (and other disciplines) say to the problem? what are its ethical dimensions? what are its moral dimensions? etc., so that students see how knowledge converges to produce a solution. It is then possible to put questions to the proposed solution. These might take the form of asking – whose interests does the solution serve? who is likely to be marginalised by the solution etc.?, so that the social justice dimension of the proposed solution may be explored. What students learn in Religious Education thus becomes part of the investigation. This type of exercise forms part of the mission to truth pursued by a Catholic curriculum. It is a way of bringing faith and culture together in a practical way that has relevance to students and is an elementary form of what we have called 'grassroots theology'.

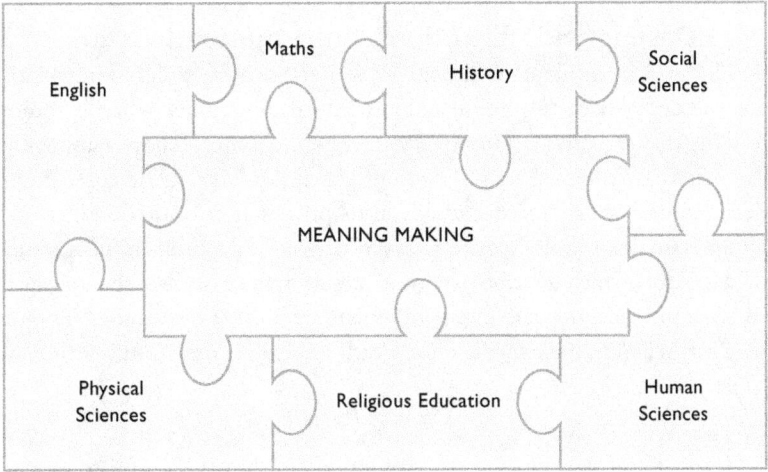

FIGURE 16.1 Meaning making as centrepiece in the jigsaw of knowledge construction

Seeing God in all things: The need for the discernment of culture[271]

In his mission theology, John Paul II puts this task into perspective in acknowledging that, while the worldview of a culture is influenced by human sinfulness, it is also shaped by God's action in the world.[272] Careful and critical discernment is therefore required to determine where God is at work. This cannot happen without critical engagement with culture since God is at work in the formation of all cultures. This is what creates the need for 'grassroots theology' by which we mean the process of bringing the resources of faith and culture to bear in making sense of the events and

---

271 The challenge of finding God in all things is associated closely with the teaching and spirituality of St Ignatius of Loyola founder of the Society of Jesus (Jesuits).
272 See John Paul II *Redemptoris Missio*, 1990, #29.

relationships that define us. As we have shown, this is not an easy task, living as we do in an age in which all cultures are evolving under the influence of two competing worldviews the modern and the 'postmodern'.

Skilling people to engage in this form of reflection is now a requirement in a Catholic curriculum. It is essential if students, parents and teachers are to develop the personal frame of reference needed to re-orient themselves in a cultural matrix characterised by shifting patterns of thought, shifting appreciation of values, and substantial loss of contact with the cultural narratives that underpin its identity. In such a context, a 'business as normal' approach to Catholic schooling is simply untenable. It runs the risk of leaving young people without the resources or skills needed to make sense of either their lives or their faith. This is an essential part of a Catholic curriculum's mission to truth.

Dealing with distortions in the mission to truth

The academic disciplines define the Western construction of knowledge and substantively underpin the 'wisdom of the community' when it comes to using that knowledge. However, the Western tradition is now haunted by distortions, or what we are calling here 'ghosts', and a Catholic curriculum needs to deal with these distortions in its presentation of that tradition.[273] Sometimes these are distortions of the original, and brilliant, insights of their creators which develop over time but claim the mantle of their creator. In other instances they are implicit in the limitations of the original insights themselves and in their formulations, and simply take time to break free.

Shades of Plato

The first 'ghost', as Sacks so clearly points out, is that of Plato. Plato's ghost contends that there is such a thing as 'universal man' and a 'universal truth' which humans can reach. As a distortion it makes its appearance when people begin to think that 'their truth' is the 'universal truth', and that if they are right, everyone who does not share their truth is wrong. From here they slide easily into the belief that they are superior to, even ontologically different from, others who do not share their 'truth'. As Sacks puts it, those who do not hold my 'truth', do not share my humanity, and so are classed as 'less-than-human' and can be ignored or treated with impunity. Human history, including Church history, shows that the consequences of this distorted view usually end in tears and human degradation.

A mission to truth is more modest. It holds that we can know things truly, but our knowledge is always qualified and provisional. It is qualified by language, and is provisional because, as human experience expands, we gain

---

273 The theme here owes its inspiration to Jonathan Sacks and his brilliant essay 'Exorcising Plato's Ghost' in *The Dignity of Difference: How to Avoid the Clash of Civilizations* Revised edition (London: Continuum, 2002), 45–66.

new insight into what we know, thus demonstrating that our access to truth is always incomplete. If the cosmologists are in any way accurate about the possible lifespan of the earth and that of the humans on it, we are still in the very early days of human history with much still to learn.

One important consequence of living in the 'postmodern world' is that we are learning to revalue the particular and to live with difference. As Jonathan Sacks cogently puts the matter:

> *What is real and the proper object of our wonder is not the Platonic form of a leaf but the 250,000 different kinds there actually are; not the quintessential bird but the 9000 species that exist today; not the metalanguage that embraces all others, but the 6000 languages still spoken throughout the world. Thanks to our new-found knowledge of DNA we now know that all life in its astonishing complexity had a single origin.*[274]

For Sacks, speaking from within the Hebrew tradition, the 'unity of heaven' is reflected in 'diversity on earth'.

Shades of Aristotle

The 'ghost' of Aristotle has long had a home in the Christian tradition. It appears in the construction of the human person as a combination only of intellect and will. This is not a view Aristotle or his principal Christian commentator Aquinas would support. However, it is a popular interpretation of his position. As a distortion of Aristotle it suggests that 'to know the good is to do the good; it is all a matter of will-power'. As a distortion, this ghost suggests that the function of will is to control feeling by directing feeling, which begs the question as to whether this is ever fully possible. It presents as a major hurdle for young people growing up in the postmodern world with its competing conceptions of what is 'good' in the relationships that define their life-world. The competing conceptions, beamed nightly into their homes, pose a serious question for young people – how do I judge which portrayal of the 'good' is trustworthy and authentic to who I am?

Infected by this ghost, young people tend to view institutional prescriptions of the 'good' with some suspicion because they do not to see institutions as being either totally trustworthy or particularly interested in their concerns. This being the case, young people are more likely to put their trust in people than in institutions. This is recognised in the rise of youth ministry, with its emphasis on a peer-to-peer approach, as a valuable resource in evangelisation. The importance of the witness of teachers as an element in a Catholic curriculum is also particularly underscored. To

---

[274] ibid. 53.

re-phrase Paul VI's much-quoted dictum in a new register – 'Postmodern young people listen more willingly to witnesses than to teachers, and if they do listen to teachers, it is because these are witnesses'.[275] This is now a foundational axiom in Catholic pedagogy.

The emerging understanding of 'postmodernity' as a 'sensibility' is also something of a counter to Aristotle's ghost, implying as it does, that the affective dimension of human life is integral to life, not peripheral to it. People feel when they hope that they can effect things. They also hope because they feel that they can effect things. There is a reciprocal relationship here that lies at the heart of all good teaching. To ignore the affective dimension of life is to ignore the role hope plays in human life.

Teaching is a profession built on hope. Human hope in Christian theology is also the realm in which God's Spirit works. Mobilising hope is therefore a critical element in a mission to the truth. This means tapping into human feeling and this is most readily done through culture, and the hopes embedded in the depth dimensions of all living cultures. In education it equates with using the resources of faith and culture to create a compelling vision of what the school can achieve. This is an important step in 'evangelising culture', beginning with the culture of the school. A Catholic curriculum has to be both part of this vision, and a vehicle for its implementation. Evangelising culture through the agency of curriculum is therefore central in any mission to truth.

Shades of Descartes

The third distortion in this mission to truth lies in the legacy of Descartes. This ghost haunts the imagination with the notion that human beings can somehow attain a God-like view of the world from which they can understand how it works, and so control it to suit their interests. In Charles Taylor's colourful description, Descartes' 'ghost' reduces humans to 'minds on legs'[276] and ignores what makes us truly human – our capacity to feel, and to work together, inspired by a common vision which mobilises feeling in the interests of goodness and truth.

Descartes' ghost hides out in intellectualised presentations of faith that ignore the fact that to be truly human, people of faith have to find a place for feeling. Faith without feeling is like soup without salt.[277] In traditional Catholicism, the feeling dimension of faith was often expressed through various devotions, feast-day celebrations, and so on. There may occasionally have been an element of superstition and folk-religion involved in such practices, and many fell out of favour in the post-Vatican II era. This has left a

---

275 Paul VI *Evangelii Nuntiandi* (1975), #41.
276 c.f. Taylors's lecture series *The Malaise of Modernity* delivered in April 2011 for CBC. Available in podcast.
277 Adrian Pittarello *Soup Without Salt* (Surry Hills, NSW: Centre for Migration Studies, 1980).

hole at the heart of Catholicism that now demands a creative response. Young people have a right to traditional, longstanding spiritual expressions of their faith, but the reclamation needs to be imaginative, bearing in mind that young people may now have little or no connection to the narratives that gave these devotions their meaning in the first place. The need for creativity therefore remains part of the mission to truth. Many schools use the expressive arts at assemblies and paraliturgies to tap into this missing dimension of Catholic life, and this is now an important element in a Catholic curriculum. The matter is also taken up in social justice initiatives which seek to promote empathy and solidarity with the marginalised and evoke a passion for social justice action. All of these strategies provide ways of exorcising a distorted view of what it means to be human implicitly introduced by Descartes.

Shades of Nietzsche

A final distortion in Western thinking to be dealt with is that introduced by Nietzsche. Nietzsche conveys this in his image of the lone and dishevelled madman holding his lantern aloft searching for God in the city square at midday. While a smug and bemused crowd looks on as he shouts at them – 'You have killed God. Do you realise what you have done?' With this he introduces the idea that modern man has 'killed' God and so now has to think through and live with the consequences of doing that.

Teachers in Catholic schools would recoil at the thought that they are part of the crowd in the square, but this is exactly what they are if they introduce students to the disciplines as though God were dead because they fail to put questions to the worldviews standing behind the disciplines which are the vehicles for their teaching. In such circumstances, Nietzsche's ghost freely wanders the corridors of the Catholic school.

When teachers comment that 'there is no such thing as Catholic Science' they are speaking only a partial truth. The imputation often is that 'there is such a thing as value-free science'. When science (or any other discipline for that matter) is approached as if it were value-free, then Nietzsche's ghost is alive and well, because the taken-for-granted value system of many scientific disciplines is that God is dead (which students encounter more overtly when they transfer to tertiary institutions). Science, and the other disciplines are not value-free. They have a value system built on the axiom that the world is a closed system and it is this unnecessary distortion that a Catholic curriculum seeks to address.

Nietzsche's ghost also appears in various approaches to 'tolerance' promoted by schools in responding to the multi-faith, multi-cultural nature of our society in a way that shies away from the notion that there are objective standards of truth and morality, and that these standards can be defended in the court of reason. Exorcising Nietzsche's 'ghost' is part of the wider mission that a Catholic curriculum provides in the service of truth!

Meaning making goes on in all classes

We believe the postmodern constructions of 'worldview' and of 'culture' provide useful integrating ideas in pursuing this mission to truth. In earlier chapters we have argued that the task of education is to help young people acquire the knowledge and skills necessary to critically engage the traditions of meaning in which they are immersed by virtue of living in a community and attending a Catholic school. This task cannot be confined to the Religious Education class.

Meaning making goes on in all classes as young people construct knowledge, acquire literacy in its various forms, and develop thinking skills. The problem peculiar to Catholic schools is that the framework for meaning making promoted in some subjects can, and unless recognised will, run counter to that used in other subjects, precisely because teachers are unaware of the worldview that lies behind their subject. They themselves have to learn the skills of critical discernment in their own discipline, if they are to help their students orient themselves in the academic world.

A return to the beginning

At the outset of this book we posed the question: How do we pass on the faith and wisdom of the community to our students in a way that is meaningful to them? In attempting to answer this question we set out a working definition of a Catholic curriculum which ran as follows:

> A *Catholic curriculum assists young people to engage constructively with the wisdom and faith of the community in a way that is meaningful to them, living as they do in a particular cultural and historical setting with the life chances this setting has to offer and the constraints that it imposes in the process of establishing their identity as individuals and as members of the community.*

In earlier chapters, we have explored the contours of this definition and, in the course of so doing, developed a number of 'principles' that flesh it out and show what is at stake. Our contention is that in the West, the wisdom and faith of the community are difficult to disentangle because they share a common narrative with developments in one leading to developments in the other.[278] Each lives in creative tension with the other and this tension rises and falls as history unfolds. The relationship took a decisive turn in modernity which the Church has since sought to redress. The Catholic school has an important role to play here.

---

278 Pope John Paul II deals with this theme insightfully in *Faith and Reason* (1998) (See Chapters 2 and 3).

We have chosen to situate discussion of a Catholic curriculum within this broader dynamic which is very much alive within the Western intellectual tradition at the present time, rather than to take a narrower, confessional view of the matter. In this sense we set the aim of our project as 're-framing a conversation'. We are aware that the conversation is already underway, and carried out in an intellectual world struggling to understand the 'postmodern turn' and to discern what lies beyond it. This is territory the reader has now explored at some length. It is in this context that we claim that a Catholic educator's 'mission to the heart of young people' is also 'a mission to truth'. This mission needs to be grounded in mission theology and we have suggested that the Church's teaching on mission as formulated by Paul VI and John Paul II is very helpful here, particularly the links made between faith and culture.

When one looks at the practices of schools, 'Catholic curriculum' has been pursued mainly though projects and with mixed results, as we know from first-hand involvement in some of them. These projects are generally of two types. The first has adopted the strategies of values integration. In this approach, a range of 'Catholic values' or 'Gospel values' have been identified and integrated in the content of the public curriculum through value-adding to normal lesson planning. In some cases quite sophisticated banks of resources have been developed to support teachers. The second proceeds by pursuing themes throughout the curriculum, for example, care for the earth or reconciliation with Aboriginal people. This second approach is also accompanied by some excellent resource material. These efforts, important though they are, represent only two ways of integrating 'faith and culture'. In this book we have taken a different approach, which is to identify what is at stake in a Catholic curriculum by outlining the principles at work in determining what constitutes a Catholic curriculum, thus opening up the way for a greater range of creative responses than has been the case to date. It is an approach which can and, we would argue, needs to underpin any particular project that a school or system undertakes. We see our efforts more in terms of creating a new starting point rather than a finishing point. Neither do we put the principles forward as a definitive list. Because our aim has been to reframe a conversation, we hope they open up new possibilities. The conversation needs to continue. In the appendices, we have provided some resources that may allow this to happen at both school and system levels.

We conclude by making two points. Whilst there are many ways in which a school can have a curriculum which is Catholic, the issue will always be problematic if it is not consciously pursued because the pressure to default to the public curriculum is always high. Setting out the issues that are at stake in developing a Catholic curriculum in our postmodern situation is to emphasise what a noble profession teaching in a Catholic school actually is. Our hope is that teachers will draw hope from this book, a hope that they can then deploy in continuing the conversation about the nature of their calling. This is necessary because to share in a mission to the heart of young people, and a mission to truth, is no small undertaking. It requires the involvement and the gifts of many.

EPILOGUE

At the heart of a Catholic curriculum lies a creative tension that needs to be acknowledged if it is to be employed as a source of energy in advancing the mission of the Catholic school. This tension arises from the way in which the traditions of meaning that stand behind our efforts to make sense of our life-world draw on different sources faith, local culture, and Western culture in its present configuration. These stand in a complex relationship to each other shaped by the experience of Western history and the aspirations which flow from the West's restless search for answers to the questions of life. We live in a transition age which introduces many new and challenging ambiguities that erode older 'certainties'.

Our students have the task of understanding the relationships that define their life-world and which also define them. Trying to understand what is 'right' in these relationships is no easy task in a world in which almost every construct of 'right' is questioned. A challenge facing teachers in delivering a Catholic curriculum is to bring some order to what otherwise can appear as a chaotic situation.

The tension referred to above plays out in the background of Western education as a contest between 'narratives'. The first is the narrative of a 'post-secular' society. In this narrative the Western construction of 'secular' is challenged as unworkable in a multi-faith society. The second narrative is that of a 'post-religious' society which sees 'religion' as a phase of human development that people in the West have now passed through. Students have to make a choice between these two narratives in determining the 'orientation of the heart' that shapes their personal worldviews. How these are presented in the school curriculum, both explicitly and implicitly, plays no small part in achieving the 'orientation of the heart' and the 'mission to truth' which a Catholic curriculum seeks to achieve.

The many conversations about Catholic curriculum to date have tended to focus on values in the curriculum, and have led to a first generation of Catholic curriculum projects employing values integration as a strategy.

What we have suggested in this book is the necessity to now reframe these conversations in terms of meaning making, and with this comes the need for a second generation of projects. In the course of making the case for meaning, we have identified a number of 'principles' that such projects need to respect and incorporate. A new conversation will test the validity of these principles, as will new projects.

We have endeavoured to set out this new challenge recognising that the mission of a Catholic school is carried out within the context both of the Church's mission and the broader context of God's mission to the whole of creation. Jesus summed up the latter by using the powerful symbol of 'the Kingdom of God' or 'the reign of God'. Relationship with Jesus, and commitment to His project of the Kingdom, remain the touchstone in any authentic articulation of a 'Catholic curriculum'.

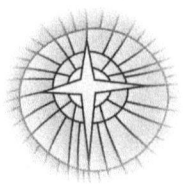

APPENDIX 1
PRINCIPLES OF A CATHOLIC CURRICULUM

PRINCIPLE 1: THE PIVOT PRINCIPLE

A Catholic curriculum places Jesus, his message, his mission, his community and his ethos at the centre of all learning, whether dealing with public meaning (teaching about worldviews) or personal meaning (helping students develop a personal worldview).

PRINCIPLE 2: THE PUBLIC CURRICULUM PRINCIPLE

A Catholic curriculum endorses the public curriculum and understands its function, but in doing so adopts a critical stance towards it.

PRINCIPLE 3: THE MISSION PRINCIPLE

While Catholic educators acknowledge that the curriculum can legitimately serve a number of purposes, the essential contribution of a Catholic curriculum to the mission of the school is meaning making.

PRINCIPLE 4: THE CONTEXTUAL PRINCIPLE

A Catholic curriculum is formulated in response to an explicit understanding of:
- the historical and cultural contexts in which it is implemented
- the dynamics shaping these contexts.

A Catholic curriculum attempts to respond to the needs which arise as these dynamics are played out in local contexts.

PRINCIPLE 5: THE LIFE-WORLD OF YOUNG PEOPLE PRINCIPLE

A Catholic curriculum is formulated in response to:
- the ways in which young people understand the major sets of relationships that define their life-world
- the progressive way in which this occurs
- their ongoing struggle to determine what is 'right' in these relationships.

PRINCIPLE 6: THE UNDERSTANDING LIVING CULTURES PRINCIPLE

A Catholic curriculum seeks to incorporate a coherent view of culture into the curriculum so that students can understand, and critically engage with, the strengths and limits of their own culture as a meaning system, and so discover the way in which it shapes how they see the world and make sense of it.

PRINCIPLE 7: THE EXPRESSIVE PRINCIPLE

In a Catholic curriculum, faith and culture work together to provide expressive outlets for students so that they learn to manage the emotional depth of their experiences in constructive ways.

PRINCIPLE 8: THE FAITH AND CULTURE PRINCIPLE

A Catholic curriculum draws on multiple knowledge bases and methods of enquiry to explore the changing relationship between faith and culture as this has unfolded in the development of the Western intellectual tradition, showing both the light and shade in the narrative of its development.

PRINCIPLE 9: THE PUBLIC MEANING PRINCIPLE

A Catholic curriculum ensures that young people understand the major worldviews that act as sources of public meaning. It seeks to show the inter-related nature of these sources, their limits, and their importance in meaning making.

PRINCIPLE 10: THE PERSONAL MEANING PRINCIPLE

A Catholic curriculum assists students to understand, articulate and critique what they learn, and in the process establish the key elements in a coherent and personally appropriated worldview.

PRINCIPLE 11: THE HERMENEUTICAL PRINCIPLE

A Catholic curriculum is informed by an explicit theory of meaning making.

PRINCIPLE 12: THE WORKING MODEL PRINCIPLE

A Catholic curriculum consistently promotes, across all disciplines, an understanding of the world as an open system.

PRINCIPLE 13: THE DECONSTRUCTION PRINCIPLE

A Catholic curriculum acknowledges the value and autonomy of the academic disciplines that stand behind the public curriculum, but takes a critical stance towards the worldview they often implicitly contain.

PRINCIPLE 14: THE PROPHETIC PRINCIPLE

A Catholic curriculum defends the existence of objective standards of truth and moral values as important constructs in the Western intellectual tradition. In doing so it highlights the gap that exists between what ideological relativism promises and what it delivers.

PRINCIPLE 15: THE PUBLIC SQUARE PRINCIPLE

A Catholic curriculum helps students understand the tensions that exist in their society in its presentation of 'the public square' and its recognition of the important place the public square holds in a democratic society.

PRINCIPLE 16: THE NATURE OF LEARNING PRINCIPLE

A Catholic curriculum respects knowledge developed through science with its subject–object form of knowing. As well, it respects knowledge developed inter-subjectively, holding that most of what is learned in schools happens in this mode.

PRINCIPLE 17: THE DIGNITY OF DIFFERENCE PRINCIPLE

A Catholic curriculum promotes a particular understanding of the human person as both a 'self' and as a 'person-in-community'.

PRINCIPLE 18: THE AUTHENTICITY PRINCIPLE

The school curriculum is the principal means by which most students encounter the worldview of faith as a worldview. Hence within a Catholic curriculum its presentation needs to be authentic to the Catholic faith, but also authentic in its acknowledgement of the life-world in which young people live.

PRINCIPLE 19: THE SACRAMENTAL PRINCIPLE

The Catholic community is distinctive in being an intensely sacramental people. A Catholic curriculum, therefore, introduces students to the central role language, the symbolic, and ritual play in the cultural and religious dimensions of life.

PRINCIPLE 20: THE KINGDOM PRINCIPLE

A Catholic curriculum is open to the worldview of faith in all its variety. Conscious of its own identity and mission, the Catholic community seeks to engage people of goodwill in building the Kingdom of God.

PRINCIPLE 21: THE PLAUSIBILITY PRINCIPLE

A Catholic curriculum promotes a particular understanding of:
- the school as a faith community
- the mission of this community
- the place of the faith community in the life-world of young people.

PRINCIPLE 22: THE INTEGRATING PRINCIPLE

A Catholic curriculum introduces students and their teachers to the knowledge and skills needed to do 'grassroots theology' as a means of bringing together life, faith and culture.

APPENDIX 2
PROFILING TOOL FOR A CATHOLIC CURRICULUM

MAP 1   Understanding the Context

NO	GUIDING PRINCIPLES	STRONG	MODEST	WEAK
4	A Catholic curriculum is formulated in response to an explicit understanding of: • the historical and cultural contexts in which it is implemented • the dynamics shaping these contexts A Catholic curriculum attempts to respond to the needs which arise as these dynamics are played out in local contexts.			
5	A Catholic curriculum is formulated in response to: • the ways in which young people understand the major sets of relationships that define their life-world, • the progressive way in which this occurs, • their ongoing struggle to determine what is 'right' in these relationships.			
21	A Catholic curriculum promotes a particular understanding of: • the school as a faith community, • the mission of this community, • the place of the faith community in the life-world of young people.			

Appendix 2 Profiling tool for a Catholic curriculum

MAP 2   The Structures of Meaning

NO	GUIDING PRINCIPLES	STRONG	MODEST	WEAK
1	A Catholic curriculum places Jesus, his message, his mission, his community and his ethos at the centre of all learning, whether dealing with public meaning (teaching about worldviews) or personal meaning (helping students develop a personal worldview).			
3	While Catholic educators acknowledge that the curriculum can legitimately serve a number of purposes, the essential contribution of a Catholic curriculum to the mission of the school is meaning making.			
10	A Catholic curriculum assists students to understand, articulate and critique what they learn, and in the process establish the key elements in a coherent and personally appropriated worldview.			
14	A Catholic curriculum defends the existence of objective standards of truth and moral values as important constructs in the Western intellectual tradition. In doing so it highlights the gap that exists between what ideological relativism promises and what it delivers.			
20	A Catholic curriculum is open to the worldview of faith in all its variety. Conscious of its own identity and mission, the Catholic school seeks to engage people of goodwill in building the Kingdom of God.			

MAP 3 Introduction to the Sources of Public Meaning

NO	GUIDING PRINCIPLES	STRONG	MODEST	WEAK
9	A Catholic curriculum ensures that young people understand the major worldviews that act as sources of public meaning. It seeks to show the inter-related nature of these sources, their limits, and their importance in meaning making.			
13	A Catholic curriculum acknowledges the value and autonomy of the academic disciplines that stand behind the public curriculum while also taking a critical stance to them.			
15	A Catholic curriculum helps students understand the tensions that exist in their society in its presentation of 'the public square' and its acknowledgment of the important place the public square holds in a democratic society.			
18	The school curriculum is the principal means by which most students encounter the worldview of faith *as a worldview*. Hence within a Catholic curriculum its presentation needs to be authentic to Catholic faith, but also authentic in its acknowledgement of the life-world in which young people live.			

MAP 4 Curriculum Content

NO	GUIDING PRINCIPLES	STRONG	MODEST	WEAK
2	A Catholic curriculum endorses the public curriculum and understands its function, but in doing so takes a critical stance towards it.			
6	A Catholic curriculum seeks to incorporate a coherent view of culture into the curriculum so that students can understand, and critically engage with, the strengths and limits of their own culture as a meaning system, and so discover the way in which it shapes how they see the world and make sense of it.			

Appendix 2 Profiling tool for a Catholic curriculum

7	In a Catholic curriculum faith and culture work together to provide expressive outlets for students so that they learn to manage the emotional depth of their experiences in constructive ways.			
8	A Catholic curriculum draws on multiple knowledge bases and methods of enquiry to explore the changing relationship between faith and culture as this has unfolded in the development of the Western intellectual tradition, showing both the light and shade in the narrative of its development.			
12	The Catholic curriculum consistently promotes, across all disciplines, an understanding of the world as an open system.			
17	A Catholic curriculum promotes a particular understanding of the human person as both a 'self' and as a 'person-in-community'.			
19	The Catholic community is distinctive in being an intensely sacramental people. A Catholic curriculum, therefore, introduces students to the central role language, the symbolic and ritual play, in the cultural and religious dimensions of life.			

MAP 5 Curriculum Processes

NO	GUIDING PRINCIPLES	STRONG	MODEST	WEAK
11	A Catholic curriculum is informed by an explicit theory of meaning making.			
16	A Catholic curriculum respects knowledge developed through science with its subject–object form of knowing. As well, it respects knowledge developed inter-subjectively, holding that most of what is learned in schools happens in this mode.			
22	A Catholic curriculum introduces students and their teachers to the knowledge and skills needed to 'do grassroots theology' as a means of bringing together life, faith and culture.			

APPENDIX 3
MAPPING TOOL

MAP 1   Understanding the context

PRINCIPLE 4: THE CONTEXTUAL PRINCIPLE
A Catholic curriculum is formulated in response to an explicit understanding of:
- the historical and cultural contexts in which it is implemented
- the dynamics shaping these contexts.

A Catholic curriculum attempts to respond to the needs which arise as these dynamics are played out in local contexts.

4.1 What are the most evident manifestations of globalisation in the lives of your students?
4.2 How are the needs, which these manifestations generate, addressed within the curriculum at present?
4.3 How does secularisation impact on the work of your school? How does the school seek to offset the influence of its more extreme form – secularism?
4.4 What are the faces of pluralism that most impact on the teaching-learning process in your school?
4.5 How are these addressed within the curriculum at present? How adequate is this treatment?

PRINCIPLE 5: THE LIFE-WORLD OF YOUNG PEOPLE PRINCIPLE
A Catholic curriculum is formulated in response to:
- the ways in which young people understand the major sets of relationships that define their life-world
- the progressive way in which this occurs
- their ongoing struggle to determine what is 'right' in these relationships.

5.1 As teachers we look at the life-world of young people from the outside; they live it from the inside. How is this difference in perspective best understood? What are the curriculum implications of such an understanding?

5.2 What level of importance do the four sets of relationships that define the life-world of young people (with the social world, the natural world, family and friends, the faith community) have in the curriculum? Which relationships receive most emphasis? Is the treatment balanced?

5.3 What concept of 'living in right relationship' is promoted across the curriculum? Is this theme handled developmentally? If so how?

PRINCIPLE 21: THE PLAUSIBILITY PRINCIPLE

A Catholic curriculum promotes a particular understanding of:
- the school as a faith community
- the mission of this community
- the place of the faith community in the life-world of young people.

21.1 How does the school interpret its role as the principal plausibility structure for faith in the life of the majority of its students?

21.2 How is this interpretation reflected in formulating the mission of the school?

21.3 In what ways does the school seek to make links with other Catholic faith communities so that the Church-student link can be maintained beyond the school experience? How is this matter addressed within the curriculum of the school?

21.4 How does an understanding of the school as a primary plausibility structure for faith translate into the development of the curriculum and pedagogical practices in the teaching of religious education, and in the faith development and social justice initiatives pursued within the curriculum?

MAP 2   Structures of meaning

PRINCIPLE 1: THE PIVOT PRINCIPLE

A Catholic curriculum places Jesus, his message, his mission, his community and his ethos at the centre of all learning, whether dealing with public meaning (teaching about worldviews) or personal meaning (helping students develop a personal worldview).

1.1 What opportunities does the school provide so that students learn how to pray? How are these structured into the life of the school?

1.2 What are the school's essential messages about Jesus and how are these secured within school life?

1.3 What is the connection between the Gospel values witnessed to in school life and the mission directions pursued by the school in its strategic planning? What are the curriculum implications of such a connection?

1.4 In what ways does the school use its symbol system and narrative to identify with, articulate and celebrate those Gospel values alive in the ongoing life of the school? Which particular values have currency as the charism of the school and how does the school make this determination?

1.5 If the charism of the school is located within the great spiritual traditions of Catholicism which have their source in religious orders, how is it translated into language and symbols that have meaning for lay people whose connection with the narrative of these traditions is indirect? How well is the translation process accomplished in your school? How does it influence the school's curriculum and pedagogical practices?

PRINCIPLE 3: THE MISSION PRINCIPLE

While Catholic educators acknowledge that the curriculum can legitimately serve a number of purposes, the essential contribution of a Catholic curriculum to the mission of the school is meaning making.

3.1 Does the school's curriculum include a coherent theory of meaning making? If so, how is this articulated and by whom? If not, what steps need to be taken to develop a better understanding of this process and its pedagogical implications?

3.2 How do you think students construct meaning? What are the sources they depend on?

3.3 What are the recurring biases in their thinking which they seem to draw most frequently from 'the common stock of knowledge'? How does the curriculum seek to address these?

PRINCIPLE 10: THE PERSONAL MEANING PRINCIPLE

A Catholic curriculum assists students to understand, articulate and critique what they learn and in the process establish the key elements in a coherent and personally appropriated worldview.

10.1 How does the school promote thinking skills within the curriculum?

10.2 What strategies and processes are used to assist students recognise and adapt biases within their thinking?

10.3 How does the school encourage students to articulate what it is that they really believe? Is this confined to particular areas, and if so why?

10.4 How does the curriculum encourage self-reflection or reflection-on-action among students? In what areas is this most likely to happen? What scope exists to make this an across-the-curriculum issue? What goal should such a curriculum policy seek to achieve?

PRINCIPLE 14: THE PROPHETIC PRINCIPLE

A Catholic curriculum defends the existence of objective standards of truth and moral values as important constructs in the Western intellectual tradition. In doing so it highlights the gap that exists between what ideological relativism promises and what it delivers.

14.1 How does the curriculum address the difference in perspective that people bring to the consideration of issues because of their different cultural backgrounds and the different histories that determine these backgrounds?

14.2 How does it address the legitimate differences that arise, even within the one culture, because of differences in class and gender?

14.3 How does it account for difference in religious outlook and the way in which this influences what people hold to be true:
- within Catholicism?
- across Christian denominations?
- between faiths?

14.4 Given the legitimately different ways of viewing the world, what concept of truth and moral values does the curriculum convey to students? Is the portrayal cohesive? Do students understand it as cohesive?

14.5 What understanding of 'tolerance' is developed within the curriculum? Is this consistent with the affirmation of truth as objectively determinable?

PRINCIPLE 20: THE KINGDOM PRINCIPLE

A Catholic curriculum is open to the worldview of faith in all its variety. Conscious of its own identity and mission, the Catholic school seeks to engage people of goodwill in building the Kingdom of God.

20.1 What sources do staff draw on in determining their aspirations for students and what the school can achieve for them? What process is involved in articulating these aspirations and what level of consensus exists about what they are? How are these aspirations currently articulated?

20.2 Is there a 'Kingdom of God' theme implicit or explicit in these aspirations? If so, what is it and how is it translated into curriculum and pedagogical practices?

20.3 Do students understand the meaning that teachers are trying to convey in their witness to the coming of God's Kingdom in the way school life functions, or do they see school life more in functional/transactional terms?

20.4 How can school life best be reframed in transformative terms and what are the curriculum implications of school renewal framed in these terms?

20.5 In what ways does the school seek to assist parents become more effective agents in the faith development of their children, particularly in multi-denominational and multi-faith homes?

MAP 3   Introduction to the sources of public meaning

PRINCIPLE 9: THE PUBLIC MEANING PRINCIPLE
A Catholic curriculum ensures that young people understand the major worldviews that act as sources of public meaning. It seeks to show the inter-related nature of these sources, their limits and their importance in meaning making.

9.1   How is the 'worldview of culture' and its status as a public source of meaning addressed within the curriculum?

9.2   How are the variety of cultural worldviews alive in the narratives of the families that make up the school community acknowledged and celebrated?

9.3   How does the school curriculum seek to show the connections between the Australian narrative and the Western narrative, and acknowledge the Australian contribution to this narrative?

9.4   How does the curriculum link the Australian narrative with the narrative of the Australian Catholic Church and so acknowledge the contribution the Church has made, and continues to make, to civic life in this country?

9.5   What understanding do staff have of the transition from a modern to a postmodern sensibility occurring in our society? How aware are they of the impact this has on debate in the public square or its translation into school curricula? Does this issue need to be addressed? If so, how?

PRINCIPLE 13: THE DECONSTRUCTION PRINCIPLE
A Catholic curriculum acknowledges the value and autonomy of the academic disciplines that stand behind the public curriculum, but takes a critical stance towards the worldview they often implicitly contain.

13.1   Is the structure of the academic disciplines and their strengths and limits as sources of meaning, addressed as an issue within the curriculum? If so, where and how?

13.2   How is the autonomy of academic enquiry addressed? Are teachers aware of the Church's teaching on this matter?

13.3   What approach does the curriculum presently take to interdisciplinary enquiry? Is this adequate to a Catholic curriculum?

13.4   How is the 'structure of knowledge' presented as a topic within the curriculum? Is the treatment consistent across the curriculum. If not, why not?

PRINCIPLE 15: THE PUBLIC SQUARE PRINCIPLE
A Catholic curriculum helps students understand the tensions that exist in their society in its presentation of 'the public square' and its acknowledgment of the important place the public square holds in a democratic society.

15.1   Does the school have its own equivalent of the 'public square' in

which issues of importance in school life for students can be raised, debated and resolved? If not, why not?
15.2 What level of self-governance by students is encouraged within school life?
15.3 How does the curriculum develop its understanding of the 'public square' and the place in civic life this has in a democratic society?
15.4 In what ways does the curriculum identify, and then develop, the skills and attitudes students need to participate effectively in the 'public square'?
15.5 Does the curriculum address the issues that stand behind contemporary debate about a 'post-secular' public square?

PRINCIPLE 18: THE AUTHENTICITY PRINCIPLE
The school curriculum is the principal means by which most students encounter the worldview of faith as a worldview. Hence within a Catholic curriculum its presentation needs to be authentic to Catholic faith, but also authentic in its acknowledgement of the life-world in which young people live.
18.1 How adequately is the worldview of Catholic faith presented as a source of public meaning within the curriculum?
18.2 How well are the cognitive, evaluative, and affective dimensions of the Catholic worldview presented?
18.3 How is the question – 'What does it feel like to be Catholic today?' raised, explored and addressed with teachers and students? What are the curriculum implications of raising this question?
18.4 How is the narrative structure of the Catholic worldview presented? How are the heroes and heroines given emphasis in this presentation? On what basis are they chosen and how are the commitments that characterised their lives related to their understanding of the worldview of faith? How is a balance effected between living witnesses and historical characters?
18.5 How is the mission dimension of the Catholic worldview addressed as an across-the-curriculum theme with relevance to the four sets of relationships that define the life-world of young people? What implication does the understanding of mission have for 'living in right relationships' in these four areas of life?
18.6 How are the connections between the worldview of Catholic faith and the worldview of Australian culture drawn together within the curriculum?

MAP 4 Curriculum content

PRINCIPLE 2: THE PUBLIC CURRICULUM PRINCIPLE
A Catholic curriculum endorses the public curriculum and understands its function, but in doing so adopts a critical stance to it.

2.1 Is the public curriculum simply taken at face value at your school or is it adapted in some way?

2.2 If it is adapted, on what basis does this occur? Who does it?

2.3 What is your reading of the dominant curriculum theory behind the design of the public curriculum? On what assumptions is this theory built? Whose interests does the public curriculum serve? What does this mean for the school's clientele? Who benefits and who loses out?

2.4 What implications do the above questions have for how your school implements the public curriculum? How well are these thought through? How well are they addressed?

PRINCIPLE 6: THE UNDERSTANDING LIVING CULTURES PRINCIPLE

A Catholic curriculum seeks to incorporate a coherent view of culture into the curriculum so that students can understand, and critically engage with, the strengths and limits of their own culture as a meaning system, and so discover the way in which it shapes how they see the world and make sense of it.

6.1 Is a cohesive understanding of 'culture' operative in the curriculum? If not, how can this be addressed?

6.2 How well is Australian culture, as a 'living culture', developed as a theme within the curriculum? Is the treatment largely at the surface levels?

6.3 How are the depth dimensions of Australian culture explored? How are the cultural narratives that define Australian culture addressed?

6.4 What attempt is made to situate students within these narratives?

6.5 Is there any explicit attempt to relate the dynamic values of Australian culture to those of the Gospel? If not, why not?

PRINCIPLE 7: THE EXPRESSIVE PRINCIPLE

In a Catholic curriculum faith and culture work together to provide expressive outlets for students so that they learn to manage the emotional depth of their experiences in constructive ways.

7.1 What are the major expressive opportunities provided within the curriculum?

7.2 Are these developed to achieve intentional goals? If so what are they and who decides what they are? What message is given to students about these goals?

7.3 How well do you think students understand this message? Why is this?

7.4 What level of home–school co-operation exists in this area? What are the major issues that need to be addressed in improving liaison on this matter?

PRINCIPLE 8: THE FAITH AND CULTURE PRINCIPLE

A Catholic curriculum draws on multiple knowledge bases and methods of enquiry to explore the changing relationship between faith and culture as this has unfolded in the development of the Western intellectual tradition, showing both the light and shade in the narrative of its development.

8.1 In what specific ways does the curriculum seek to situate students within the Western tradition and the interplay of the ideas that characterises this tradition?

8.2 How is the faith/culture theme dealt with as an across-the-curriculum issue? How does the school negotiate this theme in developing the curriculum?

8.3 How are major themes and narratives of Western culture addressed within the Religious Education curriculum?

8.4 Who are the major heroes and heroines presented within the curriculum? What do they stand for? And how are they chosen? Are there any guidelines that apply here?

8.5 How is the 'narrative structure of all knowledge' dealt with as a theme in the development of the curriculum?

PRINCIPLE 12: THE WORKING MODEL PRINCIPLE

A Catholic curriculum consistently promotes, across all disciplines, an understanding of the world as an open system.

12.1 How aware are teachers of the worldview that sits behind the disciplines they teach?

12.2 How do they deal with this in class?

12.3 How aware are teachers that open and closed worldviews constitute working models and that these permit choices that can be made without compromising the autonomy of the disciplines? If not, how can this issue best be addressed?

12.4 How is this principle suitably dealt with as an across-the-curriculum issue?

PRINCIPLE 17: THE DIGNITY OF DIFFERENCE PRINCIPLE

A Catholic curriculum promotes a particular understanding of the human person as both a 'self' and as a 'person-in-community'.

17.1 How does the school set about promoting a healthy self-esteem among students? What are the curriculum implications in pursuing this goal? How are these addressed across the curriculum?

17.2 What is the school's central message to students about developing their talents? Is this presented in ethical/moral terms? When the overall curriculum design is taken into account, how well do 'message' and 'practice' align?

17.3 Who are the 'marginalised' in the school? How is this determined? What provisions are made to overcome the 'gap' between what the school promises all students and what it delivers to these students? Where is this prophetic voice located within the school community and how well is it listened to?

PRINCIPLE 19: THE SACRAMENTAL PRINCIPLE

The Catholic community is distinctive in being an intensely sacramental people. A Catholic curriculum, therefore, introduces students to the central role language, the symbolic, and ritual play, in the cultural and religious dimension of life for people living in Western societies.

19.1 What are the major rituals of school life and how are these used to establish meaning? What meanings are these rituals meant to convey? How effective are they in achieving their goal?

19.2 How well does the school utilise the array of talent at its disposal to convey meaning intentionally through the use of the expressive and performing arts?

19.3 How effective are school liturgies in building a sense of community among students? What meaning do students draw from their liturgical experiences? Are these productive or counter-productive?

19.4 How well-developed is the symbol system of the school? How rich are its symbols and how dynamically are they developed? In what ways is the symbol system tied to the school's narrative system in conveying meaning by highlighting the students' immersion in a shared story?

MAP 5   Curriculum processes

PRINCIPLE 11: THE HERMENEUTICAL PRINCIPLE

A Catholic curriculum is informed by an explicit theory of meaning making.

11.1 In what specific ways does the curriculum place a premium on the skills of meaning making?

11.2 Does the curriculum, in fact, include a coherent understanding of meaning making? If so, how is it articulated?

11.3 What strategies do teachers customarily use so that students see the whole in terms of the parts and vice versa? Is the hermeneutical circle used as a pedagogical principle in the development of the curriculum?

11.4 What light does the model of moderate hermeneutics throw on the use of these strategies? What changes/alternatives does it suggest?

11.5 Is it possible, or even desirable, for the school to promote a cohesive approach to meaning making? What are the pros and cons associated with such an approach? What impact would such an approach have on the pedagogical practice in the school?

PRINCIPLE 16: THE NATURE OF LEARNING PRINCIPLE

A Catholic curriculum respects knowledge developed through science with its subject–object form of knowing. It also respects knowledge developed inter-subjectively, holding that most of what is learned in schools happens in this mode.

16.1 How does the curriculum address the pedagogical challenges that arise when learning is defined in inter-subjective terms?

16.2 In what specific ways does the pedagogy of the school seek to balance the hermeneutics of trust with the hermeneutics of suspicion? Or is this simply left to chance?

16.3 When the relational environment of the school is examined, in what ways are student treated as objects? As subjects? Is there a balance point here, and if so how is it determined?

16.4 How does the analysis implied in the above questions influence the learning environment of the school and the curriculum theory of the school as these operate in practice?

16.5 Is this influence consistent with, or counter-productive of, the school's stated mission?

PRINCIPLE 22: THE INTEGRATING PRINCIPLE

A Catholic curriculum introduces students and their teachers to the knowledge and skills needed to 'do grassroots theology' as a means of bringing together life, faith and culture.

22.1 What strategies does the curriculum incorporate to bring the various disciplines together to explore the complex issues that characterise contemporary life? How adequately are these strategies used? How well do students understand their purpose?

22.2 In employing these strategies what issues of concern are dealt with and how are these determined? What role is theology given in such interdisciplinary study?

22.3 Is theology given the status of a discipline in the curriculum and if so how? How are 'studies of religion' and theology related in the present curriculum?

22.4 What model of theological reflection ('doing grassroots theology') is promoted within the school in resolving pastoral problems? How effectively have staff been inducted into this model and how familiar are they with its use?

22.5 What efforts are made to introduce students to an age-appropriate model of theological reflection within the school community, and to use this model of thinking in addressing important issues with school leaders?

A

academic discipline paradigm 27
Adelaide Declaration (1999) 15
affirmation of ordinary life 178
the age, worldview of 4, 20–1, 62, 104, 116–17, 118, 129, 189
agnostic perspective 26
analogical models of culture 81–4
Anderson, Bernhard 192
anthropological worldview 105
anthropology 79, 81, 168, 172
ANZAC Day 82–3
Apostel, Leo 124–6
Aquinas, Thomas 134, 135, 245
Aristotelian philosophy 134, 135, 139, 245–6
Arthur, James 13n
Asian perspectives 18
astronomy 135
Augustine 133–4
Australia
 belief in 'a fair go' 61–2
 as multi-cultural society 53
 national policy on education 15–18
 nature of school curriculum 14–15
Australian Curriculum, Assessment and Reporting Authority (ACARA) 15
 curriculum premised on modern worldview 18, 20
 discipline-based learning 18–19, 30
 multi-disciplinary problem-solving and investigation 242–3
 The Shape of the Australian Curriculum (policy paper) 17
authenticity
 and personal identity 177
 as a powerful moral ideal 175–6
 and self-fulfilment 176–7
authenticity principle (Principle 18) 202–3, 254, 258, 265

B

'being Catholic'
 as a way of being human 187
 what it means in practice 35
beliefs 108n, 110, 115, 124, 240–1,
 see also worldview(s)
 and values, associated with culture 82–3
Benedict XVI, Pope 34, 170
Bevans, Stephen 211–12
Bible 142, 143
biblical critique of Western construction of knowledge 198–201
biblical 'heart', and worldview (Naugle) 238
 into the heart go the issues of life 239
 out of the heart come the issues of life 239–41
Brueggemann, Walter 193, 195–6, 197

C

Caputo, John 162
Catholic Church
 concerns about the mission of 223
 ethos 210–11
 mission and identity 224–7
Catholic curriculum 249–51
 assists young people to engage constructively 37–8
 as 'Catholic' 32–5
 and Catholic worldview 216
 context 1–2
 core concepts 19–22
 creative tension in 250
 current perspectives 25–6
 as curriculum 26–30
 empirical perspective 32
 failings within The Catholic School 100–1
 as mission to the heart of young people 2, 31, 32, 237–41, 249

Index

as mission to truth 242–7, 249
practices in schools 9–10, 249–50
principles 23, 36, 59, 71–2, 87, 101–2, 113–14, 127–8, 146, 165–6, 181–3, 201–3, 218–21, 232–4, 248, 252–5
profiling tool 256–9
scope of the conversation 24–35
theological dimension 34–5
and traditions of meaning 126
United Kingdom 13, 14
working definition 3, 37–45, 235, 248
and young people's worldview 71
Catholic education see Catholic schooling
Catholic educators
challenge to deliver a Catholic curriculum 250
'doing theology' 230–1
erosion of trust in institutional authority 54
importance of national curriculum for 17, 22
'living wisely' 45
promotion of holistic education 18–19, 20
and the worldview dilemma 112
Catholic mission theology
and Catholic education 41, 89
Declaration on Christian Education (Gravissimum Educationis) 92–3
Ecclesiam Suam 89, 90
faith and culture in 88, 90–9
Gaudium et Spes 91
of John Paul II 97–9, 223, 243
of Pope Paul VI 93–5, 185
source documents 89–90
The Catholic School 41, 89, 99
failings in construct for devising a Catholic curriculum 100–1
integration of faith and culture 99–101
Catholic schooling
and Declaration on Christian Education 90–1

faith and culture in documents on 99–101
Vatican documents on 33, 41, 89
Catholic schools
aims 33, 39, 73, 76
and Catholic curriculum 9–10, 249–50
Church's deficiency in understanding 41
and Church's mission 232
defining 13
guided by received wisdom 33–4
meaning making in all classes 248
mission 6, 33
mix of students in 53
place of public curriculum in 11–12
theological locus 35
worldview 237–8
Catholic worldview 187, 188, 204, 211–17
articulation challenges 212–17
Bevans and Schroeder's Constants in Context 211–12
Church mission and Church identity 224–7
distinguishing features (Rohr and Martos) 214–15
'evangelisation' and 'new evangelisation' 223–4
from maintenance to mission 229–322
God's Kingdom as the central focus of mission 227–9
mission defines the Church 222–4
pastoral orientation 214–16
postmodern developments 222–32
Rohr and Martos' views 213–16
variables influencing articulation 212–13
Walker's views 216–17
Catholic young people, Hoge's study 67–8
change see deep change
Christian churches 210–11
Christian worldview 204–11, see also Catholic worldview

challenges inherent in 204
community 208–9
constituent elements 205–6
ethos 210–11
genesis 180–1
Jesus in 204–11
Me–Jesus relationship 206
message 207–8
mission 209–10
Church
   control of knowledge systems 134–5
   as institution 228
   social role beyond the parish 228–9
Church agencies 228–9
Church renewal 93
Church's identity 227, 228
Church's mission 93, see also mission
   and Catholic schools 232
   church – missionary by its very nature 224–5
   and Church's identity 228
   confusion about 223–4
   from maintenance to mission 229–32
   God's Kingdom as central focus of 227–9
   horizon beyond the parish 228–9
   modes and forms 226–7
   need for 'new evangelisation' 224
   reclaiming the mission orientation of the local parish 229
   social role in the community 228–9
civil society 167, 228–9
'civilised' society, culture as the characteristic of 78–9
classicist understanding of culture 77–9
closed system
   as ideology 144
   Nature as 139, 142–3
   as working model 144
   world as 144
colonial perspective 26
commitment, and worldviews 107, 109, 110
commodification of knowledge 157–8
communicative knowledge 169

communicative reason/communicative action 170
communism 119
community(ies)
   of Israel 195, 196, 197
   Jesus' 208–9, 226
   mediating traditions 115, 118
Constants in Context (Bevans and Schroeder) 211–12
constructed self 175
construction of knowledge 42
   by young people 69–71
contextual principle (Principle 4) 59, 252, 256, 260
contextual theology 230
Copernicus 135
core knowledge 70
critical theory 28–30
cross-curriculum perspectives 18
cultural anthropology 79, 81
cultural dimension of pluralism 53
cultural identity 83, 86
cultural 'myths' 83
cultural pluralism, educating in the context of 85–6, 100
cultural wisdom 38
culture 76–84
   analogical models 81–4
   at work, case study 82–3
   as battle between themes and counter-themes 85
   beliefs and values 82–3
   as the characteristic of 'civilised' society 78–9
   classicist understanding 77–9
   core of 83–4
   as defining characteristic of society 79
   and faith 33, 73, 76, 88–101
   internal structure 81–2
   modern understanding 79–81
   narratives of 83
   onion model 81–2
   as personal refinement 77
   pervasive influences 76–7
   postmodern concept of 84–7

re-contextualising 86–7
working definition 81
worldview of 4, 21, 61–2, 83–4, 104, 116, 118
curriculum, see also national curriculum
in the Australian context 14–19
Catholic curriculum as 26–30
empirical perspective 31–2
in the perspective of critical theory 28–30
theories 26–8
and worldviews 30–2
curriculum content (Map 4) 258–9, 265–8
curriculum development, history, Australia 29–30
curriculum leadership dilemma 2–3
curriculum process (Map 5) 259, 268–9
cyber bullying 51

D
Declaration on Christian Education (Gravissimum Educationis), faith and culture in 92–3
deconstruction principle (Principle 13) 165–6, 253, 258, 264
deconstruction prophets see prophets of deconstruction
deep change
and globalisation 50–2
growing up in an era of 60–71
main drivers of 50–8
making meaning in a changing world 58–9
and modern pluralism 53–5
and secularisation 55–8
teachers experience of 49
democratic society, theory of (Habermas) 170
Derrida, Jacques 158
deconstruction can move in two directions 161
interpretations can be true or false 160–1
issues in interpreting texts 158–9

life as 'reading' and interpretation 159–60
'reading' as interpreting an 'event' 160
reading and meaning 158, 159
'there is nothing outside the text' 160
Descartes, Rene
critique of his theory of knowledge 172–4
philosophy 137–8, 168, 246–7
philosophy of science 139–40
dialectic 133–4
dialogue, and mission 98–9
dialogue theology 197
different kind of knowledge 70
dignity of difference principle (Principle 17) 201–2, 254, 259, 267
discipline-based learning 29, 30
discipline-based national curriculum 18–19
doing theology 230–1
phases 231

E
Ecclesiam Suam (Paul VI) 89, 93, 98
policy Ecclesiam Suam (Paul VI)
goals of the Church 90
reflections on see Gaudium et Spes
educating
in an era of deep change 48–58
in the context of advanced cultural pluralism 85–6
education policy, Australia 15–19
empirical approach to curriculum 31–2
'engaging with a tradition' 37–8
environmental perspectives 18
ethos, Jesus' 210–11
Evangelii Nuntiandi 41, 89, 93
'evangelisation'
as embracing forms of mission 227
versus 'new evangelisation' 223–4
evangelising culture 246
exclusive humanism 131, 143
Exodus 193, 194

expressive principle (Principle 7) 101–2, 253, 259, 266

F
faith
   and culture see below faith and culture
   definition 38–9
   heroes and heroines of 39
   and life, integration 33, 73, 76
   and truth 21–2
   and wisdom, association with community 38–9
   worldview of 4, 21–2, 34–5, 54, 104, 117, 118, 130
faith and culture 33, 73, 76, 88–101
   in Catholic mission theology 88, 90–9
   in Declaration on Christian Education 92–3
   in the documents on Catholic schooling 99–101
   in Gaudium et Spes 91
   historical origins 88–90
   in the mission theology of Pope Paul VI 92–5, 185
   relationship between, source documents 89–90
   in the theology of Pope John Paul II 95–9
faith and culture principle (Principle 8) 253, 259, 266–7
Foucault, Michel 161–2, 168
   historical case studies of modern institutions 162–3
   masked power–knowledge relationships 163
   'power is knowledge' 162
   suspicion of modern institutions 163–4
fragmentation of meaning, and reconstruction of personal worldviews 124–6
freedom from religion 58
freedom for religion 58
Freire, Paulo 29

G
Galileo 135, 138, 139
Gallagher, Michael 95–6
   'ten commandments' of postmodern worldview 148–50, 175
   tensions in Catholic theology 197–8
Gallagher, Shaun 119–21
Gaudium et Spes, faith and culture in 91
Generation Y Study 64–5
   reports from 65–7, 69
Genesis, narrative of 199
global warming 41–2
globalisation 50
   impact on the migrant experience 52
   and the knowledge economy 51
   living in a globalised world 52
God
   of the Bible 143
   of Deism 143
   in the Hebrew Bible 195–7, 199–200
   in Israel's worldview 191–4
God's Kingdom see Kingdom of God
God's 'prophets' 196
God's Spirit
   in development of Kingdom of God 99
   role in the mission 97–8
God's two books 142
Gospels
   and the community 208–9
   explanation of the significance of Jesus' life 207
   and the message 207–8
   and the mission 209–10
Gravissimum Educationis 92–3
Greeks, methods of enquiry 133
Grundy, Shirley 28, 29

H
Habermas, Jürgen 28, 167, 168–9, 173
   communicative knowledge 169
   communicative reason/ communicative action 170
   knowing inter-subjectively 168–71
   modes of knowing

subject to object 169
subject to subject 169–70
　reconstructing modernity 171
　theory of democratic society 170
hard secularism 58
Hay, David 67, 123
heart see biblical 'heart'
Hebrew Bible 190, 194
　essential message of 199
　God in 195–7, 199–200
Hebrew tradition
　and community 195, 196
　dynamic by which the tradition is sustained 195–9
　dynamic by which the tradition was created 194–5
　sustaining identity 197
　Torah voice 196, 197
　voice of the prophet 196, 197
　Wisdom voice 196–7
Hebrew worldview 190–4
　significance of 198, 199–200
　themes 191
　tradition of hope within history 191–4
hermeneutical circle 121
hermeneutical principle (Principle 11) 128, 253, 259, 268
hermeneutics 73, 119–20
　of suspicion 69
　of trust 69
heroes and heroines 38, 39
Hiebert, Paul 61, 84, 108
'high culture' 95–6
History curriculum, criticism of 18
Hoge, Dean 67–8
holistic education 18–19, 20, 32, 51
Hughes, Philip 65, 66, 67, 69–70
human knowledge interests (Habermas) 28–9
human mind, structure of the 140–1
human person, as object to be studied by science 143
human refinement 77
human sensibility 77, 97, 132

I
identity
　establishing, as individual or member of a community 43–4
　personal, and authenticity 177
　transcendent dimension of 177–8
ideological pluralism 53–4
ideologies
　closed systems as 144
　worldviews as 119
Indigenous perspectives 18
Indigenous students 16
individual identity, establishing 43–4
inequity 51
institutional role of the Church 228
instrumentalism 142
integrating principle (Principle 22) 169, 233–4, 255, 259, 269
intellectual cohesion, development 54
intellectual enquiry 132–40
internet 51, 52
interpreting experience 119–21
interpretive map, development 4–6
Israel 190–1
　community of 195, 196, 197
　sustaining identity 197
Israel's worldview 191, see also Hebrew Bible; Hebrew tradition
　Israel worships the God who liberates 192–3
　Israel's God as the God of history 192
　Israel's God is a God who does justice 194
　Israel's place among the nations 191–2

J
Jesus
　in the Christian worldview 204, 205–11
　community 208–9, 226
　ethos 210–11
　as hero par excellence 39
　Jesus' life, explained by authors of the Gospels 207

knowing Jesus 207
   meaningful relationship with 2
   message 207–8, 211, 225–6
   mission 93, 209–10, 211
   teaching about Kingdom of God 34, 93, 117
   vision of the Kingdom of God 34–5
   worldview 191
Jewish religion 195
John Paul I, Pope 95
John Paul II, Pope 90, 95–9
   constants in mission: dialogue 98–9
   inter-religious dialogue 187
   Kingdom of God revisited 99
   and 'living cultures' 96–7
   as 'man of culture' 95
   mission theology 97–9, 243
   'new evangelisation' 223
   role of the Spirit in God's mission 97–8
   theology of faith and high culture 95–6
Jung, Carl 107, 240

K

Kant, Immanuel, structure of the human mind 140–1
Kingdom of God
   as central focus of mission 227–9
   and Church renewal 93
   development under action of God's Spirit 99
   dimension, in Catholic curriculum 34–5
   embracing Jesus' teaching 34, 93, 117
   and Jesus' message 207–8, 225–6
   Jesus' vision of, pursued in local contexts 34–5
   and mission 211
   and proclamation of the Gospel 94
   reach beyond the Church 226
   and worldview of faith 117
kingdom principle (Principle 20) 219–20, 254, 257, 263
knowing Jesus 207

knowledge
   acquisition (Habermas) 168–71
   commodification of 157–8
   construction of 42, 69–71
   created through constructive reasoning 141–2
   as human interpretation of reality 140–1
   narrative 156, 157
   progress in 145
   scientific 157
   secularisation of 55–6
   theory of 137–8, 139, 141, 172–4
   types of 70, 156–7
   utility of 142
   Western construction, Biblical critique 198–201
knowledge economy, and globalisation 51
knowledge systems 106
   Church control of 134–5
Koltko-Rivera, Mark 107, 108n, 237n, 239n

L

language role, and traditions of meaning 123–4
late Middle Ages, intellectual enquiry 133–4
learner-centred approach 27
liberal theology and deism 143
liberation theology 197
life and faith, integration 33, 73, 76
life-chances
   offers and constraints 41–2
   through globalisation 51
life-world of young people principle (Principle 5) 71–2, 252, 256, 260–1
Lineamenta (2012) 224, 230
lived experience of teachers 48–9
living in a cultural and historical context 40–1
'living cultures' 96–7
living in a globalised world 52
living in right relationships 241
low socioeconomic background

students 16
Luzbetak, Louis 81
Lyotard, Jean-Francois 154–5
   'be suspicious of meta-narratives' 155
   commodification of knowledge 157–8
   and incredulity to meta-narratives 154–8
   The Postmodern Condition 150, 151
   problem of legitimation 155–6
   types of knowledge 156–7

M
MacKillop, Mary 39
making sense of everyday life, model 121–3
making sense of the world 119–21
Mandela, Nelson 38
mapping tools 260–9
maps of reality, and traditions of meaning 118–19
Martos, Joseph 213–16
Mason, Michael 65–6, 67
matrix model 66, 204
Me–Jesus relationship 206
meaning making 39–40, 73, 129, see also traditions of meaning
   in all classes 248
   implications for Catholic curriculum 126
   self-reflection role 124
meaning making process 121–2
Medieval Europe, intellectual life 133–4
Melbourne Declaration (2008) 15–16, see also Australian Curriculum, Assessment and Reporting Authority (ACARA)
   collective responsibilities 16
   education that is holistic 18–19
   intended educational outcomes for young Australians 16–17
member of a community (identity) 43–4
message, Jesus' 207–8, 211, 225–6

Middle Ages, intellectual enquiry 133–5
migrant experience, globalisation impact on 52
mission, see also Church's mission
   concerns about the mission of the Catholic Church 223
   defining the Church 222–4
   and dialogue 98–9
   of the faith community 209–10, 211
   God's Kingdom as central focus of 227–9
   and problem of 'evangelisation' versus 'new evangelisation' 223–4
   and proclamation 94, 227
mission principle (Principle 3) 36, 252, 257, 262
mission theology see Christian mission theology
mission to the heart of young people 241, 249
   Catholic curriculum as 2, 31, 32, 237–41
mission to truth, and Catholic curriculum 242–7, 249
   bringing disciplines together in search for truth 242–4
   dealing with distortions in 243–6
   shades of Aristotle 245–6
   shades of Descartes 246–7
   shades of Nietzsche 247
   shades of Plato 244–5
modern pluralism 53–5
modern understanding of culture 79–81
modern worldview 18, 20, 62, 104–5, 130, 131
modernity 167
   addition story 167
   beyond 144–5
   Derrida's contribution 158–61
   Descartes' contribution 137–40, 168
   Foucault's contribution 161–4, 168
   Habermans' contribution 168–71
   and instrumentalism 142
   Kant's contribution 140–1
   Lyotard's contribution 150, 154–8

naturalism as ideology of 142–3
Nietzsche's contribution 151–4
and positivism 141–2
prime movers in creation of modern ideology 136
reconstructing 171, 178, 180
subtraction story 167
Taylor's contribution 167, 172–4
Thornhill's contribution 179–80
within Western intellectual tradition 132–7
worldview of 131–45
moral ideals
and authenticity 175–6
definition 175
moral–spiritual development of students see spiritual–moral development of students
multi-disciplinary problem-solving and investigation 242–3
multiculturalism in Australia 53

N
narrative knowledge 156, 157
national curriculum 1, 11, 13, 15, 27
ACARA policy paper 17
discipline-based 18–19
importance for Catholic educators 17, 22
key competencies 18
National Study of Youth and Religion (NSYR Project) 64
popular religious beliefs of young people 68–9
reports from 64
natural sciences, entangled with theology 135
naturalism 106, 139–40
becomes the ideology of modernity 142–3
Nature
book of 142
as a closed system 139, 142–3
human person within 143
nature of learning principle (Principle 16) 168–9, 183, 254, 259, 268–9

Naugle, David 238–41
nazism, and Nietzsche 153–4
'new evangelisation'
interpretation 224
need for 224
versus 'evangelisation' 223–4
Newton, Isaac 136
Nietzsche, Frederick 151, 247
decline 154
image of the madman 152
life story 152–3
and nazism 153–4
ramifications of 'killing God' 151–2, 153
Thus Spake Zarathustra 153
nihilism 106

O
onion model of culture 81–2
open systems, and postmodernity 164–5, 167
orientation characteristic of worldview 107, 108, 109
orientation of the heart 238, 241, 250
Our Vision Our Values (Walker) 216

P
pastoral orientation (Catholic worldview) 214–16
Paul VI, Pope 41, 89, 90, 246
Church renewal 93
constants in mission: proclamation 94
Ecclesiam Suam 89, 90, 93, 98
evangelisation of cultures 94–5, 185
faith and culture in mission theology of 93–5
Jesus' mission and the Church's mission 93
Peace Builders initiative 29
personal autonomy 143
personal identity, and authenticity 177
personal interpretive map 4–5
personal meaning principle (Principle 10) 127, 253, 257, 262
personal refinement, culture as 77
personal worldview 61, 63, 103, 238,

241, 250
  acquiring 63–4
  in the construction of modernity 63
  influences at work in forming 62, 63
  reconstruction, and fragmentation of meaning 124–6
Phan, Peter 222, 227, 229
phenomenology of the human person 42–4
philosophic enquiry 133
philosophical worldview 105, 106
philosophy
  Aristotle 134, 135, 139, 245–6
  Derrida 158–61
  Descartes 137–8, 168, 246–7
  Kant 140–1
  Lyotard 150, 154–8
  Nietsche 151–4, 247
  Plato 132, 134, 198, 199, 244–5
philosophy of science 137, 139–40
pivot principle (Principle 1) 23, 220–1, 252, 257
Plato 132, 134, 198, 199, 244–5
plausibility principle (Principle 21) 232–3, 255, 256, 261
pluralism 53
  cultural dimension 53
  ideological dimension 53–4
  and search for social cohesion 54–5
politics, secularisation of 57–8
Pontifical Council for Culture 95
Pontifical Council for Inter-religious Dialogue 90
popular religious beliefs of young people 68–9
pornography 51
positivism 141–2
postmodern
  as an era in history 148
  meanings of 148–50
  as a sensibility 148–50, 246
postmodern concept of culture 84–7
postmodern condition 111, 150, 168, 171, 198
The Postmodern Condition (Lyotard) 150, 155

postmodern critique 20, 30–1, 42
  prophets of deconstruction 151–64
  prophets of reconstruction 167–80
  of worldviews as 'packages' 111
postmodern equation 167
postmodern sensibility 148, 150, 175, 246
postmodern thinkers 150–1
  Derrida 158–61
  Foucault 161–4, 168
  Habermas 28, 167, 168–71, 173
  Lyotard 150, 154–8
  Nietzsche 151–4, 247
  and prophets of deconstruction 151–64
  and prophets of reconstruction 167–81
  Taylor 167, 168, 171–8
  Thornhill 132, 133, 135, 136–7, 151, 157, 179, 179–80
postmodern worldview 62, 106–8, 148
  definition 107, 108–9
  'ten commandments' (Gallagher) 148–50, 175
postmodernity 147
  understanding the world as an open system 164–5, 167
practical theology 230–1
pressures on teachers 48
principles of a Catholic curriculum 248, 252–5, see also specific principles, e.g. public curriculum principle (Principle 2)
  mapping tools 260–9
  profiling tools 256–9
proclamation
  of the Gospel 94
  and mission 94, 227
profiling tool for a Catholic curriculum 256–9
prophetic principle (Principle 14) 181, 254, 257, 262–3
prophetic voice 196, 197
prophets of deconstruction 151–64
  Derrida's views 158–61
  Foucault's views 161–4, 168

Lyotard's views 150, 154–8
Nietzsche views 151–4, 247
prophets of reconstruction 167–80
   Habermas' views 167
   Taylor's views 167, 171–8
   Thornhill's views 179–80
prophets of renewal 151
Provincial Council (1862) 14
psychological worldviews 107
Ptolemy 135
public curriculum, place in Catholic schools 11–12
public curriculum principle (Principle 2) 23, 252, 258, 265–6
public discourse 19
public knowledge 19
public meaning principle (Principle 9) 113–14, 253, 258, 264
public policy on education 29, 58
public square 167, 168
public square principle (Principle 15) 182, 254, 258, 264–5
Putting Life Together: The Findings from Australian Youth Spirituality Research (Hughes) 65, 66
   model 66–7

R
rabbinical tradition 194–5
Radical Math movement 29
received wisdom, utilising 32–4
reconstruction prophets see prophets of reconstruction
re-contextualising cultures 86–7
Redemptoris Missio 90, 99
reflective practice 231
Reformation 135–6, 137, 173–4, 210
religion(s)
   as different kind of knowledge 70
   worldview 62
religious beliefs of young people 68–9
Religious Education
   colonisation of other school disciplines 26
   as intellectual discipline 25
   as part of multi-disciplinary

   problem-solving and investigation 243
   time allocation to 13–14
revelation theology 197
Rohr, Richard 213–16
Romantic movement 174
Rousseau, Jean-Jacques 175

S
Sacks, Jonathan 167, 198–200, 244
sacramental principle (Principle 19) 218, 254, 259, 268
scepticism 137–8
Schiro, Michael 26–8, 29
scholar academic perspective 27
scholasticism 133–4
Schroeder, Roger 211–12
science, dethroning of 42
scientific knowledge 157
scientific methodology 136
scientism 119
secularisation 55, 167, 168
   definition 55
   distinction from secularism 58
   of knowledge 55–6
   limits to 57–8
   as a political phenomenon 57–8
   of social institutions 56–7
secularism 58
self relativism 178
self-determining freedom 175–6
self-fulfilment, and authenticity 176–7
self-reflection, role in meaning making 124
sensory layer of culture 81
sexual abuse 54
Singleton, Andrew 65–6, 67
Sire, James 105, 106, 108, 110, 111
Smith, Christian 68–9
Smith, James 160, 161, 162
social cohesion, development in pluralist society schools 54–5
social efficiency perspective 27, 29
social institutions, secularisation 56–7
social reconstruction approach 28, 29
social role of the Church 228–9

society, culture as defining characteristic of 79
Socrates 133
soft secularism 58
Soul Searching: The Religious and Spiritual Lives of American Teenagers 64, 67
Souls in Transition: The Religious and Spiritual Lives of Emerging Adults 64
sources of public meaning (Map 3) 258, 264–5
Spirit see God's Spirit
The Spirit of Generation Y report (Mason, Singleton and Webber) 65–6, 67
'spiritual', young people's limited ability to describe 54
spiritual–moral development of students and the curricula 18–19
   through teachable moment approach 25–6
spirituality
   Hughes' frame of reference 67
   as relational consciousness (Hay) 67
structure of the human mind (Kant) 140–1
structures of meaning (Map 2) 257, 261–3
suspicion, hermeneutics of 69
sustainability 18

T

Tanner, Kathryn 79–80, 85
Tarnas, Richard 133, 157
Taylor, Charles 131, 167, 168, 170, 171–2
   authenticity and personal identity 177
   authenticity as a powerful moral ideal 175–6
   authenticity and self-fulfilment 176–7
   critique of Descartes' theory of knowledge 171–4
   reconstructing modernity 178
   the self and the search for authenticity in a secular age 171–8
   transcendent dimension of identity 177–8
   understanding of the human person 172–3
   understanding knowledge 173
   understanding society 173–4
teachable moment approach 25–6
teachers, see also Catholic educators
   difficulties in presenting a worldview 112
   experience of deep change 49
   factors shaping their contemporary experiences 48–9
   making meaning in a changing world 58–9
   pressures on 48
   responsibilities 6
teaching, as profession built on hope 246
technological change 41–2
   and globalisation 51
theological dimension of Catholic curriculum 34–5
theological enquiry 134, 135, 230, 231
theological method 230
theological reflection 231, 244
theory of knowledge 137–8, 139, 141
   critique of Descartes' view 172–4
Thornhill, John 132, 133, 135, 136–7, 151, 157, 179
   modernity: from movement to ideology 179
   modernity's quest for autonomy 179
   re-launching modernity as movement 179–80
   reconstructing modernity 180
Torah voice 196, 197
traditional worldviews, comparing 110–11
tradition(s)
   engaging constructively with 37–8
   genesis of 132–3
   Hebrew 194–8

Western intellectual, and modernity 132–7
and worldviews 4, 105
traditions of meaning 129, see also fragmentation of meaning; meaning making
   implications for a Catholic curriculum 126
   as interpretive maps 118–19
   and making sense of everyday life 121–3
   mediated by communities 115, 118
   and role of language 123–4
   role of self-reflection 124
   and worldview of the age 116–17, 118
   and worldview of culture 116, 118
   and worldview of faith 117, 118, 188–90
   and worldviews 115–19
trust, hermeneutics of 69
truth
   and faith 21–2
   notion of, status and defence of 42

U
unbelief as normative 143
understanding living cultures principle (Principle 6) 87, 253, 258, 266
understanding the context (Map 1) 256, 260
United Kingdom, Catholic curriculum 13, 14
United Nations Declaration on Human Rights 92

V
values 53–4, 82–3, 110
values–integration approach 25
Vatican Congregation for Catholic Education 11, 13
Vatican II 33, 41, 88–9, 90, 224, 227

W
Walker, Bishop David 216–17
Webber, Ruth 65–6, 67
Western construction of knowledge, Biblical critique 198–201
Western culture 78
Western education, creative tension in 250
Western intellectual tradition
   Church control of knowledge systems 134–5
   Descartes contribution 137–40, 168
   genesis 132–3
   late Middle Ages 133–4
   and modernity 132–7
   rise of modern academy 135–6
   sustaining a 'shared and accountable enquiry' 136–7
wisdom
   definition 38
   and faith of the community 38–9
Wisdom voice 196–7
working model principle (Principle 12) 146, 253, 259, 267
world, as closed-system 144
worldview of the age 4, 20–1, 62, 104, 129, 189
   and traditions of meaning 116–17, 118
worldview concept 103–13
   student engagement with 104
worldview of culture 4, 21, 61–2, 83–4, 104, 189
   and traditions of meaning 116, 118
worldview of faith 4, 21–2, 34–5, 54, 104, 130, 187–201, see also Catholic worldview; Christian worldview; Hebrew worldview
   conceptual model 205, 206
   contemporary tensions 188–9
   integrating with worldview of culture and the age 189–90
   as source of meaning 187
   as a tradition of meaning 117, 118, 188–90
worldview of young people 60–2, 71
   common themes 68–9
   major studies 64–8
worldview(s) 20

as an interpretive framework 118
anthropological perspective 105
articulating 108–9
and the biblical 'heart' 238–41
by religions 62
Catholic 187, 188, 204, 211–17
Catholic schools 237–8
Christian 190–1, 204–17
and commitment 107, 109, 110
and curriculum 30–2
and the dilemma for Catholic educators 112
Hebrew 190–4, 198, 199–200
as ideologies 119
Israels' 191–4
Jesus' 191
and knowledge systems 106
making meaning of convergence of 103–8
mediated by communities 118
modern understanding 18, 20, 62, 104–5, 130, 131
of modernity 18–19, 131–45
orientation characteristic 107, 108, 109
personal 61, 63, 103, 108, 124–5, 238, 241, 250
philosophical perspective 105, 206
postmodern critique 111
postmodern definition 107, 108–9
postmodern understanding 62, 106–8
psychological perspective 107
as sources of meaning 4–5
as subjective and cognitive constructs 61
traditional 110–11
and traditions of meaning 115–17, 118

Y
Young Adult Catholics: Religion in the Culture of Choice (Hoge) 67–8
young people
acquiring a personal worldview 63–4
Catholic curriculum as mission to heart of 2, 31, 32, 237–41, 249
construction of knowledge 69–71
development with the wisdom and faith of the community 38–9
engaging constructively 37–8
establishing identity 43–5
growing up in an era of deep change 60–71
life-chances offers and constraints 41–3
limited ability to use traditional religious language to understand 'spiritual' 64
living in a cultural and historical context 40–1
living in a globalised world 52
making meaningful sense of their lives 39–40
orientation to life 67
popular religious beliefs 68–9
putting life together 66–7
spirituality 67
web of relationships 66
worldview of 60–2, 64–9, 71

www.ingramcontent.com/pod-product-compliance
Lightning Source LLC
Chambersburg PA
CBHW061345300426
44116CB00011B/1998